ALSO BY ROBERT HOLDEN, Ph.D.

BOOKS
Be Happy*
Success Intelligence*
Shift Happens!*
Balancing Work & Life (with Ben Renshaw)
Every Day is a Gift (with Marika Borg)

CD PROGRAMMES
Be Happy*
Success Intelligence*
Shift Happens!*
Happiness NOW!*

FLIP CALENDARS
Success NOW!*
Happiness NOW!*

❖ ❖ ❖

*Available from Hay House

Please visit Hay House UK: **www.hayhouse.co.uk**
Hay House USA: **www.hayhouse.com**®
Hay House Australia: **www.hayhouse.com.au**
Hay House South Africa: **www.hayhouse.co.za**
Hay House India: **www.hayhouse.co.in**

HAPPINESS NOW!

TIMELESS WISDOM FOR FEELING GOOD FAST

ROBERT HOLDEN PhD

HAY HOUSE

Australia • Canada • Hong Kong • India
South Africa • United Kingdom • United States

First published and distributed in the United Kingdom by:
Hay House UK Ltd, 292B Kensal Rd, London W10 5BE. Tel.: (44) 20 8962 1230; Fax:
(44) 20 8962 1239. www.hayhouse.co.uk

Published and distributed in the United States of America by:
Hay House, Inc., PO Box 5100, Carlsbad, CA 92018-5100. Tel.: (1) 760 431 7695 or
(800) 654 5126; Fax: (1) 760 431 6948 or (800) 650 5115. www.hayhouse.com

Published and distributed in Australia by:
Hay House Australia Ltd, 18/36 Ralph St, Alexandria NSW 2015. Tel.: (61) 2 9669 4299;
Fax: (61) 2 9669 4144. www.hayhouse.com.au

Published and distributed in the Republic of South Africa by:
Hay House SA (Pty), Ltd, PO Box 990, Witkoppen 2068. Tel./Fax: (27) 11 467 8904.
www.hayhouse.co.za

Published and distributed in India by:
Hay House Publishers India, Muskaan Complex, Plot No.3, B-2, Vasant Kunj, New
Delhi – 110 070. Tel.: (91) 11 4176 1620; Fax: (91) 11 4176 1630. www.hayhouse.co.in

Distributed in Canada by:
Raincoast, 9050 Shaughnessy St, Vancouver, BC V6P 6E5. Tel.: (1) 604 323 7100; Fax:
(1) 604 323 2600

Cover design: Steve Williams with Lizzie Prior

A catalogue record for this book is available from the British Library.

ISBN 978-1-8485-0170-6

Printed and bound in Great Britain by TJ International, Padstow, Cornwall.

Dedicated to those
who dare to sprinkle kindness,
radiate love, and scatter joy.

'No one who comes here but
must still have hope, some lingering
illusion, or some dream that there is something
outside of himself that will bring happiness and peace
to him. If everything is in him this cannot be so. And
therefore by his coming, he denies the truth about himself,
and seeks for something more than everything, as if a part
of it were separated off and found where all the rest of it
is not. This is the purpose he bestows upon the body; that
it seek for what he lacks, and give him what would make
himself complete. And thus he wanders aimlessly
about, in search of something that he cannot
find, believing that he is what he is not.'

– *A Course in Miracles*

Contents

CHAPTER ONE

Happy Already!

Picture the following scene:

I am at my friend Jane's house. It is mid-afternoon, and we are having tea. Jane and I are engaged in a deep and meaningful conversation when her two boys run into the room. They're young, full of energy, lively and noisy. Tom is four years old, and Ben is three. Ben follows Tom everywhere.

Jane and I continue to talk, but soon we can't hear each other speak because the boys are in a dispute.

'What's the problem?' Jane asks.

Tom throws Ben off him, takes a deep breath, and says, 'It's *my* turn to play on *my* bike, but Ben won't leave me alone, and he's already ridden *my* bike once today.' A few more things are said, but no agreement is reached.

'Go outside and sort this out. Robert and I are talking,' says Jane. The boys are dismissed.

After only a minute or two, the boys run into the room again . . . with the bike! Before Jane can chastise the boys for bringing it into the house, Tom says, 'We've worked it all out.'

'Good,' we both say.

Tom continues, 'Today the bike belongs to me all day, and tomorrow the bike belongs to Ben all day.' Both boys nod their heads with great enthusiasm.

'Are you both agreed?' asks Jane, sounding quite surprised.

'Yes,' they both say.

'Good, now go along and play,' says Jane.

The boys turn around to leave, and just before they do so, Ben pipes up at the top of his voice, 'I know – let's pretend it's tomorrow!'

Tom and Ben's story illustrates perfectly how children use possibility thinking to enjoy happiness *now!* I believe that, contrary to popular opinion, a baby's favourite toy is not a thing, it's a moment – a moment called *now.* Children are born only with an awareness of *now* – past and future are meaningless at first. In the beginning, *now* is the whole world to children, their entire playground. This fascination and reverence for *now is* entirely natural; it is neither learned nor fabricated.

Kids like Tom and Ben are completely unimpressed by the idea of 'future happiness' – above all, they want happiness *now!* Those who are yet to be indoctrinated or conditioned fully by meaningless 'laws of time' don't know how to wait for happiness. Why wait for heaven when the possibility for heaven exists right here and now?

I believe that as a young child, you too were alive to the infinite possibilities of the present moment. Like other children, you were full of wonder, imagination, awe, and appreciation for the precious present. *You got so much from 'now' because you gave so much to 'now'* – and for the entire time you were engaged with the present, you were happy to leave the past and future exactly where they were. *Now* was your treasure island, and you believed wholeheartedly that happiness was here and now, waiting to be seen. The more you believed this, the more you would look; and the more you looked, the more happiness you found. Here is an important key to happiness.

Milking the 'Sacred Now'

The world has changed greatly in recent times in an effort to accommodate our desire for happiness *now*. Everything has sped up. We live life fast – faster than ever. Fast technology, fast travel, fast careers, fast relationships, and fast results are all the rage in our 'I want it *now*' world. Indeed, the world is fast becoming a vast convenience store where you can get everything in an instant – instant coffee, microwave foods, minute-meals, half-hour film developing, 24-hour banking, drive-thru funerals, quickie divorces, television shopping, home delivery of everything and, of course, instant credit. We're sold on signs that read 'No queues', 'No need to wait', 'One stop', 'Open all hours', and 'Buy now – pay later'.[1]

One way of looking at our 'I want it now' world is to see it as a highly egotistical and selfish pursuit of happiness that is fuelled by impatience, violence and greed, doomed from the very start to 'end in tears'. Indeed, many people are voicing their concerns at 'the way the world is going', believing that traditional values and morals are fast being corroded and obliterated by the chase for happiness now.

Another way of seeing our 'I want it now' world is that this clamour for happiness *now* reflects an instinctive wisdom and a great spiritual truth, which states that . . .

> **everything – absolutely everything –**
> **is available to you 'now'.**

There's a famous story from the Zen tradition that tells of an encounter between a young, eager student and a well-respected Zen master, noted especially for his perpetual grace and happiness:

'Master, I dream of everlasting happiness. What is the highest wisdom you can teach me?' asked the student.

The master smiled. He took his brush and wrote, as if for the first time: 'Attention.'

'Wonderful,' said the student, 'and what comes next after attention?'

The master smiled. He took his brush and wrote, as if for the first time: 'Attention. Attention.'

'Yes,' nodded the student, utterly perplexed. 'Anything more?'

The master smiled. He took his brush and wrote, as if for the first time: 'Attention. Attention. Attention.'

'Okay, so what does "attention" mean?' asked the student, unable to see.

The master spoke: 'Attention means attention.'

'Is that all?' asked the student, obviously dispirited.

'Attention is all,' said the master. 'Without attention, happiness is nowhere; *with* attention, happiness is now here. Attention is freedom from all. Attention offers all.'

Every authentic school of wisdom and spirituality teaches you that *now* is the most abundant moment of your life. The bibles of the world, be it the Old Testament or the New, the Koran or the Bhagavad Gita, the Dhammapada or the Tao Te Ching – indeed, any true spiritual text – all agree that *now* is an eternal treasure chest dripping with beautiful, everlasting gifts of peace, happiness, love and joy freely available to all on a 24-hour 'Don't pay now – don't pay later' basis.[2]

Now is sacred! This is what the Zen master is trying to tell the eager young student in the story above. Indeed, talk to any spiritual teacher or guru worth their mantra, so to speak, and this person will tell you that *now* is always sacred. But why and how is *now* always sacred, you may ask? What if you've just been stood up on a date or you've just opened a bill or you've just chipped a tooth or your football team has lost again – how sacred is that?!

One approach to milking the *sacred now* is to place your attention on what is happening around you right at this minute and aim to appreciate, respect, and value it as much as you believe possible. You can do this right now. Before you read on, look around you and appreciate fully for a moment what your senses pick up. When you do so, you'll experience first hand how pleasurable appreciation can be. Events sometimes seem to make this exercise hard, but willingness can overcome this.

In my workshops for The Happiness Project, I often show a slide that reads:

HAPPINESSISNOWHERE.

When I ask people to call out what they can see, I always get two distinct answers, one being *happiness is nowhere*, the other being *happiness is now here*. Often, then . . .

> **the difference between 'happiness is nowhere'**
> **and 'happiness is now here' has something to do**
> **with the event, and everything to do with how**
> **you *see* the event. Your perception is key.**

The real secret to milking the *sacred now is* to place your attention not out in the world about you, but within yourself – your inner, unconditioned *Self*. In truth, the *sacred now* is an inner potential. It is eternal and abundant; and its geography is spiritual, not physical. In other words, the *sacred now* represents a permanent potential within you to experience love, freedom and joy regardless of time, place, or circumstance.

The gift of happiness is wrapped in your heart, not the world. Thus, your happiness will never be posted to you! And it can never get lost in the mail! In truth, your happiness has already been delivered, sitting in your inner mailbox – your heart – waiting to be opened. This is what the *sacred now is* really all about. In essence, then, you *are the key to happiness*. More than what happens to you, it is your perceptions, your thoughts, your beliefs and your overall response that are essential; your Self, your original Self, is the real key.

The real reason *now* is so naturally abundant is because when you allow yourself to be unrestrained by fear and uninhibited by worry, it is *you* who is so naturally, originally abundant. In truth, then . . .

Now *has enough wisdom to last you forever,*
because within you, right now, there is all
the wisdom you listen for in others.

Now *has enough love to last you a lifetime,*
because within you, right now, there is the
love you continually cry out for.

Now *has enough peace to last you an eternity,*
because within you, right now, peace of mind
is one thought away at most.

And now *has enough joy to outlast the world,*
because within you, right now, the joy you
chase is not in things – it is in you.

The problem with our 'I want it *now'* society isn't that we want happiness *now,* but that we've lost sight of how to experience it now. In particular, we say, 'I want it *now',* but we doubt and don't really believe that 'it is here *now'.* We've lost faith in *now* and have placed all of our faith in some imagined future. Similarly, we've lost faith in our *Self* and have placed all our attention on the world outside. Now it is the world, it seems, that must 'make us happy' – *and herein lies the source of all our misery.*

As long as you believe that it's the world that must make you happy, you leave yourself open to great disappointment and much sadness. Why? Because as long as you refuse to see your inner potential for happiness *now,* you will not see it in the world. *How can a mirror change the way you look?* Think about that, for the world is only a mirror. You will only see in the world what you're prepared to see in yourself – nothing more and nothing less.

Know, therefore, that the journey to true happiness and to happiness *now is* not a journey of physical distance or time; it is one of personal 'self-recovery', where we remember and reconnect consciously to an inner potential for joy – a paradise lost – waiting to be found. One moment we look within and we see *happiness nowhere;* the next moment we look within and this time we see *happiness now here.* This is a revelation. This is enlightenment. This is joy!

The faster we chase the world and the future, the quicker we appear to overlook the possibility that happiness is here already. Every morning as we wake up, the alarm clock sings *'now'*, and from that moment on we do not give *now* another thought as we desperately chase our future. But are you so sure that happiness isn't already here with you *now?* Have you really looked? I mean, *really* looked?

Milking the *sacred now* is excavation work. It's about rediscovering an inner potential for original joy – a potential that already exists but has been buried beneath a pile of fears, doubts, guilt, conditioning and history. Think of this potential for original joy not as something to arrive at, but as something you bring with you wherever you go. Recultivating this potential is our task, and the task begins with the realisation that . . .

joy waits on welcome, not on time.[3]

Diving for Treasures of the Soul

Psychology school taught me a lot about our potential – in particular, our potential for unlimited amounts of misery, pain, weakness and despair! We studied every affliction, every neurosis, and every mental dis-ease available at the time. In a nutshell, my psychology training consisted of: *Year 1,* an introduction to basic suffering; *Year 2,* the study of advanced suffering; and *Year 3,* a qualification in inspired suffering.

The focus was entirely on our inner potential to mess life up. My curriculum was the A–Z of suffering, from anger to zoophilia – including stress, depression, anxiety, neurosis, psycho-sis, neurotic-psychosis and psychotic-neurosis, hysteria, schizo-phrenia, obsessive-compulsive disorders, phobias, inferiority complexes, kleptomania, suicide, insanity and delusion. At no time did we consider our potential for joy, love, or peace of mind. In effect, I was studying for a Ph.D. in misery!

Studying suffering full-time had a big impact on my way of thinking. I once read that history has no evidence that there ever lived a happy psychologist. I can see why now. After a while, I was able to work out just how low I was going to feel on any given day by looking at my lecture timetable. For instance, when we studied depression for a week, I remember that the entire class eventually felt totally depressed by the end. The same was true for any and all of the complexes, afflictions, disorders and fixations. Getting an unexpectedly low mark for my paranoia essay didn't help at all!

Do you remember when in nursery or primary school you were given a lecture on the importance of bodily hygiene and the dangers of head lice? And do you remember how, after 20 minutes of listening to this woman who showed you great big blown-up slides of head lice with six-inch teeth, you became absolutely convinced you had a nest of these things in your hair? Well, that's what it was like in my psychology lectures. Doctors-in-training will tell you that their experience was also the same.

I learned a very important lesson about perception and focus during those years, which is . . .

be careful what you look for because you *will* find it.

I immersed myself thoroughly in the study of misery. I received distinctions for the most part in every study I undertook. As I increased my focus, I soon realised that there was not *one* type of depression, but 100. Furthermore, there was not *one* sort of schizophrenia, but 30, 40, or more. Whatever you focus on, expands. Each day I hoped we might dive for pearls, but instead we merely collected crabs!

After a full six years of study, I still hadn't been given a sin-gle lecture on our potential for joy, peace, unity, wholeness and success. Psychology, originally defined as *the study of the soul,* had been reduced to a study of illness and neurotic behaviour. Freud and Behaviourism, in particular, reduced human beings to no more than a pitiful bag of blood and bones housing a mind full of neurotic defences and endless psychotic potential for aggression and psychosexual hang-ups. Never was there any mention of the soul, of spirit, of divinity, of God, of love.

My training in psychology, with its almost exclusive focus on pain, is a very common story. It also reflects a tendency in our society to focus on negatives. Doctors, for instance, study illness, not health. Business leaders analyse failure, not success. Economists study cost, not value. Philosophers mostly debate original sin, not original blessing. Christians talk endlessly about crucifixion, not resurrection. Mental-health organisations publish books on 'Understanding Depression', 'Understanding Stress', and 'Understanding Bereavement', but not on 'Understanding Joy' and 'Understanding Love'. The media is full of journalists suffering from an addictive, antisocial, obsessive-compulsive need to communicate and make up bad news. Literature and art is full of depressed poets and painters – can you name three joyful poets?

What you focus on most often becomes familiar, and what is familiar feels real to you. In our society, we focus on pain before joy, tears before laughter, and fear before love, so we gradually grow blind to our inner, ever-present potential for happiness. I remember well how my lecturers frowned on happiness. What they taught me essentially was: 'If you find that you're experiencing happiness – don't worry – you're just in denial and the pain will soon return!'

Happiness appeared to have no value, other than that it offered a temporary respite between periods of pain and trauma. It was defined simplistically as the absence of pain. Other messages I received included, 'Happiness is superficial, pain is deep', 'Laughter is a common symptom of manic depression', 'Smiling a lot means you're suppressing a hidden pain', 'Optimism is often unrealistic and delusional', and 'Talking to God is the first sign of a nervous breakdown'.

Of greater concern to me, though, is the large body of thought within the psychology profession that suggests that happiness is in some way a dysfunctional behaviour in light of all the suffering in the world. The idea is: 'If you have normal blood pressure living in our troubled world, you're not taking it seriously enough.' There have been several recent studies that have tried to suggest that happiness is only an avoidance of real issues, a selfish coping strategy, or a superficial form of escape. This thinking doesn't take into account that your happiness is an inspiration, a gift to others and a way out of suffering.[4]

When I asked my lecturers why we didn't study happiness, they usually challenged me to look at my resistance to embracing my pain more fully! The most common explanation given, however, for why happiness, love, peace and God aren't studied by psychologists is that they cannot be measured as easily as fear and pain. In other words, they are inner potentials that don't show up on laboratory apparatus designed to measure externals.[5]

Just because psychologists choose not to focus on joy, however, doesn't mean to say that joy doesn't exist. We can refuse to look at the sun, for example, but that won't make it go away. One problem, though, with not focusing directly on happiness is that what has emerged in place of the truth is a myth of happiness where happiness has become *a potential time forgot,* clouded in misperception, superstition, doubt and cynicism.

The Oasis in the Desert

It was while studying communications that I met a man in my class who was to change my life forever. His name was Avanti Kumar. Avanti was an Asian gentleman, a mature student of about 24 years old, and the spitting image of the actor Danny DeVito – short build, stocky, no hair directly on top of his head but wild curly bushes of growth either side, big bronzed cheeks, a great smile, and a beautiful and radiant light in his eyes.

Avanti always sat at the back of the class, and in the early weeks he was always last in and first out. 'Who is he?' we all wondered. All we knew about him was that he was quiet and he was always smiling. In fact, he was never *not* smiling. It was as if he had a private joke running in his head all the time.

I was deeply intrigued by Avanti from the very first moment I laid eyes on him. It was as if I somehow knew him already. There was a familiarity I felt but couldn't explain. I remember wanting to talk to him but feeling, unusually for me, too nervous to approach.

I'll never forget our first conversation. I asked him why he'd chosen this course to study. His answer was, 'To meet you, of course.' His smile really was infectious.

After that, I made sure we drank coffee together most days. I asked questions, and he gave me cryptic clues. I remember asking him one day, 'What are you?'

'A yogi,' he replied.

'A what?' I asked.

'A student of yoga,' he said.

'Oh! You mean like Jane Fonda!' Fortunately, we enjoyed each other's humour. Soon, another student, Phil, joined our coffee sessions. We became inseparable. We were one.

It was as if Avanti were fresh out of some Himalayan cave or esoteric monastery, where, I imagined, he'd been sitting for centuries in blissful meditation. He was my first direct experience of someone consciously connected to, and aware of, the inner potential for joy – anywhere, anytime. Over the next few months, he carefully and lovingly reacquainted Phil and me with this inner awareness as we talked about yoga, metaphysics, spiritual wisdom, and the more enlightened schools of psychology.

'So far all you've learned about is a psychology of the ego, or lower self,' Avanti explained, 'which is immersed in separation, fear and suffering. If you'd like, I will teach you about another psychology, a psychology of wholeness and of the Higher Self, which teaches you how to allow your inner joy to shine on the world once more.'

It was with Avanti, then, that I first began to focus directly on happiness. It was Avanti who first taught me that happiness is not just the absence of pain, but that . . .

**true happiness is an inner power –
natural, healing, abundant, and always available.**

Like all great teachers, Avanti loved to tell stories. One day he introduced me to the story of two birds, first written in an ancient Hindu text called the *Mundaya Upanishad.*[6] It reads:

Two birds
*   inseparable companions*
*   perched on the same tree.*
One eats fruit,
*   the other looks on.*

The first bird is our individual self,
*   feeding on the pleasures and*
*   pains of this world;*
The other is the universal Self,
*   silently witnessing all.*

'Think of the two birds as two thoughts flying about in the sky of your mind,' said Avanti. 'The first bird, *the individual self,* is your ego. It "desires" happiness, and it tells you that you must search the world to find it. The second bird, *the universal Self, is* your spirit. It "knows" happiness, and it tells you that you are happy already, that you were created happy, that all the happiness you have ever dreamed of rests in the centre of your real *Self* right now.

'Like an oasis in the desert, the *universal Self* is wholly joyous, wholly abundant, and wholly peaceful,' said Avanti. 'It is home to the *sacred now,* your inner potential for immediate peace and joy anywhere, anytime.'

With Avanti's guidance, I immersed myself in Eastern and Western literature in an effort to understand further the concept of the *individual self* and the *universal Self.* There are many names for these two selves, some of which I've listed in Table A.

conditioned self	Unconditioned Self
learned self	original Self
false self	real Self
fearful self	loving Self
critical self	creative Self
lower self	higher Self
dissociated self	unified Self
ego	holy spirit
split self	whole Self
body/mind	spirit/soul
persona	atman
flesh	christos
nothing	'I am'
sin	source
hell	heaven
fallen self	divine Self

Table A

Today, many years later, I now think of the universal Self as your unconditioned Self – the Self that exists behind the mask of your personal history, your conditioning, your learned limitations, the roles you play, your persona, your defences, your doubts and your fears. This unconditioned Self is the original you, untouched by the world, completely safe and whole. It is who you really are, and not who you have been taught you are by parents, teachers, friends, lovers, anybody else, and most of all, yourself.

Your unconditioned Self is the presence of peace. Three words, in particular, describe the unconditioned Self, and they are: (1) *wholeness;* (2) *love;* and (3) *joy.* The oriental mystics called the unconditioned Self the 'uncarved block'. Other names for it include the Zen term 'the original face', the Buddhist phrase 'the sacred happiness', the North American name 'free spirit', the Taoists' 'inner smile', and the Christian mystics' 'inner Eden'.

E.G.O. – Everything Good is Outside

The following story helps to describe the plight of the ego, or conditioned self:

> Each morning at 4 A.M., Brother Daniel would be the first to rise in the monastery. He got up early by choice, and he was proud to do so. While his teacher and all of his brothers slept peacefully, Brother Daniel busily exerted great effort in his prayer, study, and meditation practices. Enlightenment was his goal.
>
> Every day, Brother Daniel would pray longer and louder for enlightenment. He worked hard at improving his physical posture for meditation, and, above all, he would labour to memorise all of the ancient spiritual texts at the monastery. Rarely, if ever, did Brother Daniel rest, eat, or sleep, for he wanted to get to enlightenment and he wanted to get there fast. Brother Daniel liked to meditate and pray, but most of all, he immersed himself in scriptures. He liked to be quiet and still, but he rarely had time, for he found that there was always so much to do. He liked the silence, but he would rather hear his teacher talk of the silence.
>
> Brother Daniel's teacher, a gentle, peaceful man who was always smiling, would encourage Brother Daniel to slow down, enjoy the sun and watch the grass grow. But he was too keen and in too much of a hurry to heed the advice.
>
> 'Why do you rush, speed, and hurry so?' his teacher asked.
>
> 'I am after enlightenment,' said Brother Daniel.
>
> His teacher smiled. 'When will you get there?'
>
> 'Oh, one more prayer perhaps, my next meditation hopefully, or an act of service maybe,' replied Brother Daniel.
>
> 'Why are you so sure enlightenment is running on ahead of you?' asked his teacher. 'Perhaps if you stood still

awhile, you would find that enlightenment is here now – but you are too busy running away from it!'

In this story, the monastery is a symbol for your mind; the teacher is a symbol for your unconditioned Self, or spirit, which is always smiling; and Brother Daniel is a symbol of your conditioned self, or ego. The unconditioned Self experiences wholeness, while the conditioned self searches for wholeness.

Much has been written about the ego, or conditioned self. The term *the ego* can be misleading, for when we say it, it sounds as if we're talking about a person, a child, or something real. Essentially put, the ego is a 'small idea' about your individual self. And the idea *is:* Everything Good is Outside. So conditioned and convinced are we by this frightening thought that we chase the world, just like Brother Daniel, searching for success, happiness, love and peace of mind. And we dare not look within ourselves, for what if all we find is nothing, or, worse still, something rotten?

I remember once reading, although I'm not sure where now, that the word *ego* also stands for Edging God Out. This is a similar idea to Everything Good is Outside. Your conditioned self is acting on information that something is missing inside you, and that you have to search outside of yourself to find it. This thought of lack, of *not being enough,* is very frightening; and it leaves us needy, disoriented, and chasing shadows.

The ego is fear. It is also the denial of inner happiness. The ego's prayer, therefore, is always *Look out!*

'Look out, look out!' cries the ego, but the ego is blind because it doesn't believe. It looks but never finds; it asks but doesn't receive. In effect . . .

the ego is like a thirsty fish – it is confused!

Imagine a thirsty fish – a fish dying of thirst that is born in water, made of water, and surrounded by water! Just because the fish refuses to drink doesn't mean there *isn't* any water. Another analogy is to think of the ego as a bird flying high, trying to reach the sky, while all the time being *in* the sky. And a final analogy would be to think of the ego as a sparkle in a diamond while insisting there *is* no diamond.

The ego is a doubt that you are whole – that is, your conditioned self doubts that there even *is* an unconditioned Self. The unconditioned Self declares: 'I am whole', but the conditioned self asks, 'Am I whole?' as I've shown in Figure 1. This doubt in your essential goodness, your essential beauty, and essential wholeness is where all your pain and suffering stems from.

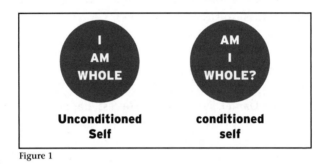

Figure 1

Our unconditioned Self is forgotten but not entirely lost as we roam the world. Every now and then we catch its fragrance, its melody, its taste. In childhood we're told stories, the significance of which hits us much later on.[7] For instance, Hans Christian Andersen's tale of 'The Ugly Duckling' is a wonderful description of the ego (the duckling) and the spirit (the swan). What is the ego other than a mistaken identity?

> **Just like the ugly duckling, we're afraid we're
> not good enough, wrong, bad, and nothing; and
> just like the ugly duckling, we'll eventually
> learn that this isn't true.**

'Sleeping Beauty' is a tale that encourages us to wake up to our inner beauty – that is, our unconditioned Self. 'Beauty and the Beast' shows us how love (beauty) can help us transform our ego-thinking (beast). 'Peter Pan' beckons us to remember, to imagine, and to fly free again. Pick any children's tale – 'Aladdin', 'The Lion

King,' and 'Pinocchio', for instance; and we're told of a sp..
journey that moves from ego to Self, fear to love, pain to joy.

One final thought about our conditioning: *It's all made up!* It
has been made up, and it isn't true. What you think about yourself
and what other people have told you about you is just an opinion,
not a fact. It is helpful, therefore, to remember that the ego is just
a thought, a thought of limitation, *that is not true*. The final verdict
of the ego is that it's a mistake. It offers a small, poor, dull, limited
likeness – a bad snapshot that doesn't capture the real you. In
other words, *the ego is not real.*

Michelangelo, God, and Miracles

When the renowned Italian artist Michelangelo was asked by
a great admirer, 'How do you create your beautiful sculptures?' he
gave a reply that became famous and is still told around the world
to this day. He said, 'The beauty is already there, my friend. I do
not create beauty; God creates beauty. I merely chip away the surrounding marble so as to reveal the beauty. The beauty is already
within. It is already perfectly in place.'

The surrounding marble Michelangelo refers to is like our conditioning; and the beauty already within the marble is like our
true, unconditioned Self.

My friend Avanti encouraged me to read poetry whenever I
could, particularly the metaphysical poets such as William Wordsworth, William Blake, and Robert Browning; and also the Indian
poet Rabindranath Tagore and the Sufi bard Rumi, to name just a
few.[8] In one of Robert Browning's works, he refers to our 'imprisoned splendour' in much the same way that Michelangelo talks of
the beauty already within the marble. He writes:

> *Truth is within ourselves, it takes no rise*
> *From outward things, whatever you may believe.*
> *There is an inner centre in us all*
> *Where truth abides in fullness; and around*
> *Wall upon wall the gross flesh hems it in*

That perfect, clear perception which is Truth.
A baffling and perverting carnal mesh
Binds all and makes all error, but to know
Rather consists in finding out a way
For the imprisoned splendour to escape
Than in achieving entry for a light
Supposed to be without.[9]

Alongside Avanti's tutoring, I also began to investigate schools of psychology and psychotherapy that aren't so well covered in university syllabi. My research showed me that since the end of World War II, in particular, many new schools have emerged that go way beyond Freud and Behaviourism in their definition of what it means to be human. Freud, particularly, maintained that humans have two basic drives, *sex* and *aggression,* and that our goal in life is to be as sexy and as aggressive as politely possible. There was no higher Self, according to Freud.

The idea of a higher, spiritual, unconditioned Self is now re-emerging. More and more schools of psychology now see that healing is about outgrowing your limited self-concept of the ego to embrace your true Self, one that is not conditioned or altered in any way by the world (see Table B). The terminology varies from school to school, but the basic principles and understanding are very similar.

Psychologist	School	Ego	
Alfred Adler	Individual Psychology	Guiding Fiction	
Carl Jung	Analytical Psychology	Persona	
Fritz Perls	Gestalt Therapy	Self-image	Self
Roberto Assagioli	Psychosynthesis	Sub-personalities	I
R. D. Laing	Primal Integration Therapy	False Self	Real Self
Arthur Janov	Primal Integration Therapy	Unreal Self	Real Self
Eric Berne	Transactional Analysis	Adapted Child	Free Child
Dr. J. L. Moreno	Psychodrama	Conserved Roles	Spontaneity

Table B

An increasing number of psychologists are changing their minds about the limited models and concepts that have so governed human understanding. It is of interest to note that even Sigmund Freud changed his mind about many of his ideas towards the end of his life. In one of my books, *Stress Busters,* I quote from Freud, who just before he died wrote: 'In the final analysis, we must love in order not to fall ill.'[10] Psychology is finding its soul once more. And now all that remains, it seems, is for us to change our minds about ourselves.

I also became absorbed in Eastern philosophy, with its rich, vibrant, and poetic vision. Although many of these authors describe the unconditioned Self using mystical images and deeply spiritual metaphors, they are at pains to point out that an experience of this whole Self is a natural, normal, commonplace, everyday possibility. The Buddhist term *satori,* for instance, refers to instant enlightenment, *available for all and to all.*

I found the works of Sri Ramakrishna, a 19th-century mystic, to be particularly fascinating. Every word seemed strangely familiar to me. He wrote extensively about the unconditioned Self, which he referred to as the Divine Self. In one passage, he explains:

Know thyself, and thou shalt then know the non-self and the Lord of All. What is my ego? Is it my hand, or foot, or flesh, or blood, or muscle, or tendon? Ponder deep, and thou shalt know that there is no such thing as I. As by continually peeling off the skin of the onion, so by analysing the ego it will be found that there is not any real entity corresponding to the ego. The ultimate result of all such analysis is God. When egoism drops away, Divinity manifests Itself.[11]

Over and over during my search for greater understanding, I felt I was being pulled along by a golden thread of teaching that made a connection between the unconditioned Self and God within: 'Search not in distant skies; in man's own heart God lies', said one Japanese text. In the Sikh bible, The Granth, it is written: 'God is in thy heart, yet thou searchest for him in the wilderness.' In the Psalms, it is written: 'You too are gods, sons of the most High, all of you.' Jesus tells us in the Bible: 'Ye are Gods.' Islam purports: 'Those who know themselves know their God.' And in Buddhism, it is written: 'Look within, you are the Buddha.'[12]

The god I first learned about as a child was like a huge inflated ego, living in the sky. He was very jealous, sported a long beard, was middle-aged, had an anger problem, and was very aloof. This god blessed bombs, fixed football games, found you parking spaces and helped you win the lottery. It was a special god that loved and hated some people more than others.

This ego-sized god apparently needs and enjoys sacrifices of live animals and young babies; and has a penchant for tobacco, drugs and beer. It is obviously a god of fear; and therefore, a god of punishment, attack, vengeance and judgment. Clearly . . .

**great unhappiness is caused by our
misperceptions of our Self and God.**

Slowly but surely, with the help of Avanti and many other teachers and mentors I met along my spiritual path, I began to heal my misperceptions of my Self and of God.[13] Layer by layer I let go of my conditioning. It's enough to say here that I now relate

to God as pure, unconditional love; and tha
ence between unconditional love and the t'

It was approximately nine years after *r*
down together with my first wife, Miran
A Course in Miracles, which changed my life to...
able work that offers spiritual psychology training as i.
our fearful thoughts into loving thoughts, and in giving up
ego for our real unconditional Self.[14]

I didn't really appreciate this book at first. It was so big – bigger than *War and Peace* – more than 1,200 pages long, and full of religious metaphor. If truth be known, Miranda and I had both bought this book long before we met each other, and it had sat on both our shelves idle for five years! Every time I'd tried to read it, my eyes would glaze over and I'd soon be asleep, no matter what the time of day.

Other than being a great remedy for insomnia, I discovered that the *Course* had other uses, too. It made an excellent doorstop, for instance, a great paperweight, and, most important, it looked very impressive on the bookshelf. Finally, one day, Miranda and I returned to the *Course,* opened a page at random, and began to read.

The words we read were: 'The self you made [the ego] is not the Son of God [your unconditioned Self].' This message is repeated many, many times throughout the entire book. Later, there is a meditation that reads:

> *My true Identity is so secure, so lofty, sinless, glorious*
> *and great, wholly beneficent and free from guilt,*
> *that Heaven looks to It to give it light. It lights*
> *the world as well. It is the gift my Father gave to me;*
> *the one as well I give the world. There is no gift*
> *but This that can be either given or received. This*
> *is reality, and only This. This is illusion's end. It is*
> *the truth.*
> *My Name, O Father, still is known to You. I have*
> *forgotten it, and do not know where I am going, who*
> *I am, or what it is I do. Remind me, Father, now,*
> *for I am weary of the world I see. Reveal what You*
> *would have me see instead.*

Course in Miracles is a constant affirmation that you are cre-
by an unconditional thought of love that appears to have lost
self in a world of fear. Freedom, joy, and peace of mind are yours
again when you remember and reconnect to your unconditioned
Self. As the book says: 'Salvation requires the acceptance of but
one thought; you are as God created you, not what you made of
yourself.'

Choosing to Remember or to Forget

You are, in any given moment, either remembering or forgetting about your unconditioned Self, your true spiritual identity. Nothing else is really happening. When you remember that
you're free, you feel happy, hopeful, trusting, generous, loving
and, above all, safe. When you doubt, however, and you forget
the truth about yourself, you become afraid, isolated, and desperate; you go it alone; you protect and defend; you strive and you
attack.

Perhaps you know this famous passage by William Wordsworth:

Our birth is but a sleep and a forgetting:
The soul that rises with us, our life's Star,
Hath had elsewhere its setting,
And cometh from afar:
Not in entire forgetfulness,
And not in utter nakedness,
But trailing clouds of glory do we come
From God, who is our home:
Heaven lies about us in our infancy!
Shades of the prison-house begin to close
Upon the growing Boy,
But He beholds the light, and whence it flows,
He sees it in his joy;
The Youth, who daily farther from the east
Must travel, still is Nature's Priest

and by the vision splendid
Is on his way attended;
At length the Man perceives it die away,
And fade into the light of common day.[15]

Unhappiness is a symptom of forgetfulness, as much as joy is a symptom of remembering. When we're unhappy, balance gives way, perspective collapses, faith falters, communication often breaks down, doubt doubles, panic ensues and a thousand different symptoms spill all around us. The disharmony we feel is ultimately a disharmony with our self. We've stepped out of our centre; and we 'lose heart', 'lose spirit', and lose our Self.

Healing is remembering. It is what author Marianne Williamson calls 'a return to love.'[16] Much of my therapeutic work with clients is, therefore, about helping people to rediscover the *trailing clouds of glory* within. We talk, we meditate, we laugh, we cry, we pray, we sing, we dance . . . we do whatever is necessary to help us remember the truth and let go of the pain.

At my seminars hosted by The Happiness Project, I occasionally share a poem of mine that helps me remember what my own healing and my own work is all about. It reads:

There once was a moment,
a mad, forgetful moment, that slipped
past eternity into time.
And in that moment, mad and
forgetful as it was, out of nowhere
an entire world, separate from God,
was dreamed up.
And although it was only a moment,
it felt like forever.
And although it was only a dream,
it felt so real.
In this mad, forgetful world, the
Ocean prayed to God,
'Give me water. I want water.'
The Sun, brilliant and bright, would

pray, 'Dear God, fill me with light.'
And the mighty, powerful, roaming Wind
would plea, 'Set me free, set me free.'
One time, all of sudden, and I don't quite
know why, the Silence began to speak,
'God grant me peace, grant me peace.'
Then, Peace Itself, fell to its knees,
'Dear God, please, what can I do to be
more peaceful?'
Now, looking quite perplexed, prayed,
'Dear God, what next?'
Even Eternity began to pray,
'I want to last forever and ever and ever.'
Infinity felt small,
'Dear God, help me to grow.'
And Life itself, began to cry,
'I don't ever want to die!'
And You and I, who are the essence of Love,
we cried out for love,
'God please love me,' we prayed.
'God, fill me with love,' we prayed.
'God, grant me love.'
Mad and forgetful as it was, that moment
in time soon slipped, tripped, and fell
away back into eternity.
It's all over now, save the memory –
a mad, forgetful memory, it too ready
for eternity.

In the Buddhist scripture, The Dhammapada, there is the famous 'Eight Fold Path', which refers to eight spiritual freedoms, one of which is *right remembrance,* or right mindfulness.[17] Disciples of Buddhism are called upon to 'Arise! Watch. Remember and forget not.' In a similar way, Jesus asked us to 'watch and pray'.

To be happy, it's good to make a point of knowing what it is in your life that helps you remember truth. What is it that helps you to love, to be real, to be free? What is it that helps you wake up from the slumber of your conditioning? As for myself, I love the sounds of laughter and friendship. I love to look at the stars, to walk in nature, to listen to the river's song, to smell the heavenly scent of stargazer lilies, to watch a roaring fire, to feel its warmth and see its light. I love to be still, to smile, to meditate and to pray. How about you?

It's important to remember what helps you to remember! For I guarantee that the next time you're ill or unhappy, you will move away from everything that supports you, strengthens you and inspires you. Indeed, you must have already moved away or you wouldn't be so unhappy. How curious it is that we abandon our greatest sources of strength when we're stressed or challenged in some way. We tell ourselves, 'First I must work my problems out', and only then will we ask for help.

Remembering to remember *now* is the key!

For four years I worked with the BBC as a counsellor and executive coach. There was a church opposite the main building that had a prominent sign outside that never changed in all the time I was there. The sign read: O GOD, SHOW ME WHAT IS WRONG WITH ME. This was, I imagine, a call to worship. It often struck me that this church needed a new marketing manager!

I was once introduced to a truly beautiful prayer, the exact opposite of this church sign, which I believe offers a perfect example of how to remember and reconnect to our true, unconditioned Self. It's a prayer by a woman named Macrina Wiederkehr, and it reads:

'O God, help me to believe the truth about myself,
no matter how beautiful it is.
Amen.'[18]

This is real prayer. Try it. Give yourself seven days. Say this prayer each day, first thing in the morning, and then sit and listen for guidance. This prayer offers a wonderful frame of mind for remembering and reconnecting to your unconditioned Self. As you take hope into your silence, you will surely draw hope from that silence. Try this prayer for a week and you'll see what I mean.

Seeing the Light!

> **First, you believe, and then you see the Light.**
> **Next, you go towards the Light. Soon, you**
> **are *in* the Light. Now you *are* the Light.**

Paul was a self-made multimillionaire. He told me so the first time we met. He talked and I listened. He told me about his wife, his life, his work, and, most of all, his children. 'I have three children I love more than anything,' he said. 'I want to give them everything I didn't have when I grew up. I tell them constantly that they can be what they want. I encourage them to strive, to work hard, to give everything every effort, to be the best they can. I always remind them they can do better, they can give more, they can be more – there are no limits.'

I listened to Paul talk about his children for almost 30 minutes. Eventually, I asked, 'Paul, what are you trying to tell me?'

He paused for a moment and bowed his head. His bullish confidence and upbeat mood vanished. I think I even saw a tear. 'The problem is,' he said, 'my children hate me. I've given them everything, and they hate me.'

'Have you ever told your children that they are wonderful, right now, just the way they are?' I asked him. He obviously had not. 'Paul, your children don't need to be told how great they're *going* to be; what they really need is to be told how loved and how wonderful they are *now*,' I said. I also suggested that by telling his children how wonderful he thinks they are *now* he was also investing wisely in their future.

Paul had only one hesitation: 'What if I tell them

they're complete and whole as you say and then they get complacent?!' We explored this common fear for a while.

'Would you have become complacent if your father had ever once told you he loved you?' I asked.

'Certainly not,' said Paul.

'Well, you have your answer then. See the Light in your children now, Paul. See the Light in them, for their sake and yours. Trust in their Light, for their sake and yours. *See* the Light,' I said.

As a psychologist, I had originally been trained to be a problem spotter. In fact, initially, I prided myself on how good I was at being able to spot people's weaknesses, neuroses, fears and hang-ups. You see, I wanted to be a really good psychologist; and, as you probably know, a really good psychologist is someone who can always find more wrong with you than an average psychologist can!

My original training, therefore, involved: (1) spotting the problem you had that you were going to tell me about; (2) spotting the problem you had that you were *not* going to tell me about; and (3) spotting the problem you had that you didn't even know about yet! That's how creative psychology can be – you come in with a few minor problems and you leave with some major ones!

Over time, I began to have a change of heart. I started to realise that the greatest psychotherapy of all is not in pointing out people's problems and failures, but rather, in pointing people toward their Light. You see, I really do believe now that . . .

a true healer helps you to remember and reconnect consciously with your inner Light.

By 'Light', I mean your innate unconditional potential to be happy, to be loving, to be free of fear and to be creative beyond your greatest imagination. You can never really lose your Light because your Light is *you* – your unconditioned Self – but you can forget about it. This Light feels so real when you're happy, and so unreal when you're unhappy. Hence, the pain, the fear, the loneliness, and the grief of unhappiness. When in darkness, we wonder if we will ever see the Light again.

I can remember the exact day when I first realised the absolute necessity of being able to see the Light of the unconditioned Self in healing. I was at my Stress Busters Clinic, a clinic I'd been running through the National Health Service in West Birmingham for a couple of years.[19] I looked out on a sea of people who'd gathered for another two-hour session. This time I didn't actually see people, though. All I saw was a group of alcoholics, depressives, heart-attack victims, cancer sufferers, drug addicts, AIDS victims, people suffering phobias, and one schizophrenic.

At first I felt a wave of absolute hopelessness. I remember thinking, *How can I help all these people – their problems are so huge and so completely different from one another?!* It occurred to me that what I really needed to do was set up an individual clinic for each illness – a clinic for depression, for anxiety, and so on. Before I could really panic, I instinctively said a quick prayer: *'Dear God, help me to see this differently.'* Then, in true British fashion, I had a sip of tea. As I opened my mouth to speak, I quickly shut it again before any words could spill out. My mind was on to something. A new idea was formulating, coming through like a fax or e-mail. I had another sip of tea while the downloading continued.

It dawned on me that although these people's illnesses certainly appeared very different, they were in fact all symptoms of one single illness. Essentially put, these people were ill because they were unhappy. Each of them had somehow become unhinged from the happiness of their *unconditioned Self.* I realised, therefore, that they had come to the clinic not just to de-stress, but to remember and reconnect to happiness. They had come to see the Light.

Years earlier I'd read the works of the Greek philosopher Pythagoras, who had said: 'There is no illness, only ignorance.'[20] Now, at last, I was beginning to see that maybe the ignorance he was referring to was the forgetting and separating from the Light of our unconditioned Self. I also began to see that my work at Stress Busters was probably, like the Tower of Pisa, slightly off-centre.

Until that time, the emphasis of my work had been, like my

psychology training, problem-oriented. I had spent days studying every illness, dis-ease, and stress-related problem I could find.
And, although I'd mentioned happiness many times, I had never
given a workshop specifically on that topic. The same was true for
love, for peace of mind, for success, and for joy. Now it occurred
to me that if these people could remember how to be happy again,
maybe they would experience less dis-ease, and they would also
handle their challenges in a much more healthy and wise way.

Sometime later, I wrote in my daily journal some words that I
still call upon to this day for inspiration. They read:

Know Love; no fear
Know Joy; no pain
Know Light; no darkness
Know Wholeness; no dis-ease
Know Now; no past
Know Truth; no lies
Know God; no separation
Know Self; no other

True healers take into account any type of darkness, but their
real task is to see the Light in their clients so as to help them
remember and consciously reconnect to their own inner Light. In
this way, both healer and client are healed together. Parenting is
the same. The ultimate gift of a parent to a child is to care for the
inner Light of children until they can care for it themselves. True
friends are those who believe in you through thick and thin. They
still see the Light in you even when your moods and behaviour
are dark and low. Mentors, managers, leaders, visionaries, peace-
makers, and everyone who truly serves . . . they all see the Light.

❖ ❖ ❖

CHAPTER TWO

Giving Up
the Search

One day at the beginning of another new session at the Stress Busters Clinic, I decided to try a completely new tactic. The room was full. Thirty people or so were chatting, drinking tea, and waiting for me to begin.

'Welcome, everybody, to Stress Busters. Have you had a good week since we met last?' I asked.

'Not bad,' said someone.

'Not too bad, thanks,' said another.

'Oh, can't complain,' came a voice from the back.

This opening was not my new tactic, by the way. That came next.

'What I'd like you to do is tell everybody about your good week,' I said. I then asked the entire group to stand up, and I explained to them that I wanted them to meet each other one-to-one and share a piece of good news, anything happy, that had happened to them over the last seven days. The only rule was that they had to come up with a different piece of good news for each person they met.

I noticed that as I was explaining the game to the group, most people had begun to stop breathing. The room was full of tension, nervous laughter, defensive postures, and on-the-spot prayers like, 'Oh, God!' 'Christ!' 'Good Lord', and 'Heaven help us!'

'What? You mean like twenty pieces of good news in the last week?' asked someone.

'Yes, twenty or more things that made you smile, lifted your spirits, helped you feel good, and that you were grateful for,' I explained.

'But what if we can't find anything?' asked someone.

'Let's start looking and then maybe we'll begin to see,' I said.

What I'd asked the group to do was very simple yet highly significant. Most previous sessions at the clinic had seemed to slip automatically into a round-up of bad news, setbacks, and new problems. No report was ever made of good news and personal breakthroughs. And yet I knew people were benefiting from our time together. Indeed, the Stress Busters Clinic had won national recognition over the previous couple of years for its effective support and care.

Looking back, I see now that it was as if we'd all agreed to follow an unspoken rule of 'problems only'. Just like in my own psychology and psychotherapy training, we had put happiness and love on the back burner for the moment, and we were now fully preoccupied – and I have to say, strangely comfortable – with our problems. Worse than this, I also noticed from time to time that certain people in the group were competing for who'd had the worst week.

In a sort of sad, macabre way, it was as if we were trying to prove our personal worth by how much suffering we were enduring. In our minds, an unofficial points system had developed along the way – that is, 5 points for headaches, 10 points for migraines, depression 15 points, anxiety only 7 points, but anxiety plus a phobia attack was worth 20 points! The more points, the more self-worth, plus more airtime in the group.

In fairness, I suppose we were only doing what we thought we were supposed to do, which is talk problems. That's what psychology is all about, isn't it? There was a strong overall reluctance to discuss happiness. The assumed rule in the Clinic was: *If you have a problem, speak up; if you're happy, be quiet.* Happiness didn't appear to have any value. No one had actually ever said that happiness was allowed.

Now, for the very first time, everyone was talking about good news. By the end of the good-news game, which I now call 'Blessings', the energy of the group had been transformed. Everyone looked like sunshine, radiating a spirit of warmth and joy that filled the room. One or two people had found the exercise close to impossible, but most were truly astonished to find how much good news there was in their lives.

Feedback from the 'Blessings' game was spontaneous. 'That was wonderful,' said someone.

'Thank you,' said another.

'Great!' said someone else.

One woman stood up and said, 'All of your good news helped me to remember all my good news that I'd forgotten or over-looked.'

Another woman said, 'I've had a far better week than I realised!'

There was a natural pause, and then an old man called Graham, known by all at the Clinic for his simple wisdom, said, 'It occurs to me that maybe we're all a lot happier and more blessed than we realise.'

Don't Give Up on Happiness

Happiness will always bring out the best in you. You were born to be happy. Happiness is natural. It suits you completely. You look good and you feel good when you let happiness ooze from within you. Your step is light, your mind is free, and your spirit soars when you let happiness *happen*. The whole world responds well to you.

When you're truly happy, you're radiant and you function fully. Above all, you are loving, for the essence of happiness is love. You're also naturally kind, generous, open, warm, and friendly. This is because where there's true happiness, there is no fear, no doubt and no anxiety. You're unrestrained and uninhibited. You are fully present, here and now, and not lost in some past or future.

When you're truly happy, you're on point and on purpose. You're also very real. It is, after all, impossible to be happy and play small, to be happy and hide, to be happy and inauthentic, to be happy and defensive. Indeed, the real reason why happiness feels so good is that when you're truly happy, *you are being your Self – your unconditioned, original Self.*

**Like a fragrance to a flower, true happiness
is an expression of your unconditioned Self – the real You.**

True happiness is also very attractive in that it literally attracts great things. Happiness, by its very nature, encourages trust, spontaneity, optimism and enthusiasm – all of which bring great gifts. In particular, when you dare to be happy, you find that people instinctively gravitate to you and like you, although they may not know why. Maybe it's something to do with your smile. Whatever it is, your happiness is an inspiration and a gift to everyone. *Everyone benefits from true happiness . . . everyone benefits from <u>your</u> happiness.*

Not surprisingly, then, happiness is very important to us. It is, along with love, *the* goal of life. Everybody wants to be happy. Can you think of anyone in your life who would genuinely refuse an offer of true happiness? No! The question is, then, if happiness is the common goal, why is happiness so uncommon in our world? Hands raised – who knows more than three genuinely happy people? When I ask this question in a room full of a thousand people, I see only about five or six hands go up.

No one talks about happiness; the topic is edited out of most conversations. In my workshops, I often ask participants to recall specific conversations on happiness that they've had with their parents. What follows is usually a profound silence. All parents want their children to be happy, but so few parents talk about it.

Also, judging from our day-to-day conversations with friends, family members and colleagues, no one is happy. Either that, or if they are, they're certainly not letting on.

'How are you?' we ask, when we greet one another.

The replies arrive thick and fast – 'Not bad', 'Not so bad', and 'Not too bad'. Some slightly more creative people say:

'Could be better.'
'Could be worse.'
'Holding up.'
'Oh, so-so.'
'Fair to middlin'.'
'Hangin' in there.'
'Surviving.'
'Can't complain.'
'Okay.'
'I'm still here.'
'Don't ask.'
'Getting by.'
'Keeping my head above water.'
'Hanging by a thread.'
'No news is good news.'
'Not dead yet.'

How about that! I call this type of inane conversation 'not-so-badder-itis'. It's like a 'near-life experience'. as opposed to a 'near-death experience', in that there's no happiness, no sadness, no commitment, no nothing. In our fast and furious world, where no one appears to have the time to engage in mindful conversations, 'Not so bad' has become a learned response, a type of social shorthand. It's quick, it's easy, and we have no idea what we're talking about.

The point is, though, even when we *do* have the time, and even when there has been some good news or we feel genuinely happy, we still respond with 'Not so bad'. We've given up talking about happiness. Furthermore, we've grown accustomed to hiding our happiness as if in fear. But what on earth are we so afraid of? What is there to fear about happiness?

I first became aware of the fear of happiness in my one-to-one psychotherapy private practice, where I experienced three repeating patterns with clients – patterns that my training had in no way prepared me for.

In the first pattern, I would help clients address a particular fear or problem to the point of letting it go. Then, when I was convinced they were now ready to let go of their pain and be happy, they would suddenly stop coming. Without notice, they'd disappear. All my telephone calls would go unreturned. Where I was able to follow up, my clients would most often say, 'I'm just too busy to come' or 'I don't have any money'. The offer of payment later was always declined. Sometimes my clients would simply say, 'I'm just not ready.'

The second pattern I called 'the familiar devil', derived from the common saying 'Better the devil you know'. In this pattern, a client would get to the point where he or she was ready to let go and move on past something painful and destructive, only to decide at the very last minute to stay put. One client, Jonathan, came to see me after having a heart attack while working in a highly demanding and very unrewarding job. He often spoke of looking for a more fulfilling career, something that suited him better, once he was healthy enough to work again. When he was well again, he went straight back to his old job. 'It's all I know,' he told me.

My client Susan's case perfectly illustrated the third repeating pattern. She was single, in her late 20s, living with a boyfriend who was consistently abusing her both emotionally and physically. 'I've come to see you to get the strength to leave my boyfriend,' she told me during our first meeting. Susan *did* eventually leave her boyfriend, despite great hurt and fear to herself. Happiness now beckoned. Her friends had hardly gotten the celebrations under way, however, before Susan moved in with a *new* boyfriend who also started to abuse her.

By witnessing these three patterns, I began to see that helping people resolve a problem isn't the same thing as helping them experience personal happiness. One obvious reason for this is that happiness is quite clearly much more than just the absence of pain or problems. More than that, though, I began to realise that until you develop a healthy, conscious, creative, and unconditional relationship to happiness, you'll always experience unhappiness and illness.

Facing Your 'Happychondria'

Happiness feels so natural and normal to us, yet we often relate to happiness as something special, odd, lucky, a bonus, or a win. Instead of greeting happiness with open arms, as we would a dear and intimate friend, we shy away from it . . . our thoughts full of suspicion, doubt, cynicism, and fear – 'waiting for the fall'.

Clearly, we *want* happiness, but we don't *trust* it. Certainly, we allow ourselves trickles of delight every now and then, but when the experience of happiness is more vivid, real, and long term, we're often racked with self-doubt and thrown about by our fears. We doubt happiness as much as we doubt ourselves.

In short, we're afraid of happiness.

The greatest irony is that we're actually afraid of everything we like. For instance, according to fear, success will corrupt you, money is the root of all evil, fame will ruin you, love makes you blind, happiness is selfish, and retirement will be the death of you. Strangely, *that which we most desire frightens us the most*.

'Happychondria' is the term I use to describe the fear of happiness, and, in particular, the utterly morbid superstitions we've gathered and placed before happiness. Happiness is so natural to our unconditioned Self, yet our conditioning has somehow taught us to cloud our experience of happiness with endless misperceptions, fearful beliefs, false prerequisites, and unnecessary dogma.

The next time you experience genuine happiness, watch your thoughts awhile and see how unconditional you can be in your acceptance of it. Notice, for instance, how your unconditioned Self greets this happiness so wholeheartedly, full of love and deep gratitude. Watch, also, though, how your conditioned self is tempted to question your happiness, to control it in some way, to hold it at arm's length, or to tighten the grip for fear the happiness might fly away.

Have you ever noticed that when you're happy, you think highly fearful conditioned thoughts such as 'Watch out for the fall', 'What did I do to deserve this?' and 'This is too good to be true'? Keep looking and you may also notice other fears such as 'What have I forgotten?' 'This can't last', 'What's the catch?' 'Maybe I've left the stove on', 'I'll have to pay for this', 'Unbelievable', 'Did I lock the back door?' 'All good things must come to an end', 'There will be tears before bedtime', and more. Take a moment, before reading on, and add to this list if you can. Awareness of these fearful, limiting thoughts (plus a big smile!) is an important step to undoing them and outgrowing them.

When happiness occurs, we experience a mix of great gratitude and nagging self-doubt. Fear's advice is: *When happy, hide it.* We're afraid to show our happiness for fear of being thought of as conceited, selfish, juvenile, or an irresponsible airhead, perhaps. We especially fear that too much happiness will endanger our professional status. Many people work in highly fearful, uncreative cultures, in which appearing to be happy twice in one week is definitely not good for the career.

We somehow have it wired up in our conditioned thinking that *happiness is blasphemy.* We fear that if we're too happy, then we'll somehow upset others, draw envy, and invite rejection. We've come to believe that the moment we step out of 'not-so badder-itis' territory, we'll be hated and persecuted for our happiness.

Not only have we learned to feel very afraid when we're happy, but we've also learned to feel very guilty. Too much happiness – far from being seen as a gift for all – is targeted as an enemy that will lead to hedonism, a lack of moral restraint, a collapse of values, an absence of order or control, and the death of the world. It's as if we've learned to believe that happiness reveals an innate 'badness' rather than our natural, unconditioned goodness. Furthermore, there's an implied fear that, if there's too little suffering, the world won't be able to work as it is!

We've also been taught to believe that while the gods will

tolerate occasional happiness, anything over half an hour or so will evoke high payment at least and terrible wrath at worst! Fate is also a real killjoy, it seems. Hence, when happy, we keep our fingers crossed, hold our breath, avoid walking under ladders and look out for black cats.

The fear of happiness has been passed down from generation to generation, each one carefully elaborating on the myths, superstitions, and trickery that went before. We too have played our part, so that now, according to 'happychondria', happiness no longer begets happiness; rather, it merely heralds the onset of further suffering. No wonder we've learned to be afraid of happiness.

Several years ago I had the pleasure of meeting and counselling a priest named Harold. He was about 65 years old at the time, of medium height and build, with slightly hunched shoulders, as if he were carrying a weight of some kind. Harold had big bushy eyebrows, a half-smile, and a face full of character lines. There was an air of sadness all around him.

'I've come to see you, Robert, because I'm unhappy and have been for a long time.' Harold had a wife, 15 years younger, whom he described as 'lovely, lively, and active'.

'We seem to be growing apart lately,' he told me. In truth, Harold had been cutting himself off from the world. He felt increasingly isolated, unable to make much sense of anything, and very sad.

'Talk to me about happiness, Harold,' I said one day.

It was too long ago for me to remember Harold's exact answer, but I do remember him saying, 'Happiness is something I fully expect to experience through the grace of our Lord in the hereafter.'

I asked him, 'What about before then? Is it acceptable for you to be happy before you die?'

Harold always looked down at the floor when we talked. I could tell he was puzzled. 'I don't know,' he murmured.

Because Harold was a Christian, I reminded him that the gospel of Jesus is one of joy. I encouraged Harold to read again how the New Testament speaks of the 'joy of thy Lord', and how it refers to joy as 'the fruit of the spirit' and heaven as 'a kingdom of joy.'

My challenge to Harold was that heaven isn't a place in the

sky, but rather a choice, a consciousness available to him now. 'You can have heaven *now* if you like, Harold, because heaven, like love and happiness, waits on welcome, not on time,' I said.

Harold and I met quite a few times, and he was a perfect gentleman. He would always express gratitude for our time together, and he would always nod profusely in agreement with everything I said. At least intellectually, he liked these 'new ideas', as he called them. I tried to convince him that my ideas weren't so new.

I remember Harold saying on one of our last visits together, 'I don't know, Robert. Maybe I'm just not worthy of happiness.' Here, I believe, was the crux of the matter.

I don't know how much I was able to help Harold. I often think of him, though. He taught me so much. At the very least, he taught me that unless we believe we're entirely worthy of happiness, we can't accept happiness fully, for we will always attempt to question it, control it, and ultimately push it away. In essence, happiness is perhaps the greatest challenge of all, then, in that . . .

happiness challenges us to make peace with ourselves.

Undoing the Confusion

We're certain we want happiness, but we're confused about what happiness is.

How many times have you bought what looked like a ticket to certain happiness, only to discover later that the ticket was invalid? How many times have you chased something – a career, a relationship, a possession – absolutely convinced that happiness must be there, only to find that it somehow got lost soon after you arrived? For a lifetime, *we work hard at happiness without ever really working out what happiness is.*

One very telling measure of how confused we've become about happiness is the language we use to convey our joy. Our language reveals our thinking, and our thinking is obviously very confused or we wouldn't *use the language of pain to describe our joy.* Look at the following phrases, for instance:

'I had a hell of a time.'
'It was awfully good.'
'Like a house on fire.'
'What a blast.'
'To die for.'
'It was crazy.'
'Bad!'
'Wild!'
'Really wicked.'
'I nearly died!'
'Drop-dead gorgeous.'
'It was damn good.'
'So good it's a sin.'
'Dying to see you.'
'Let's get wasted.'
'Unreal!'

Our confusion is compounded by our *dis-illusion.* Our present perception of happiness has become clouded and misted up with the unresolved pain and disappointment of our past. Thus, we still dream of happiness, but we've also become afraid and cynical. Confusion reigns. It knows no bounds. Comedian Woody Allen revealed the full extent of our learned neurosis when his character said this to a woman in the 1975 movie *Love and Death*:

> To love is to suffer. To avoid suffering one must not love, but then one suffers from not loving. Therefore, to love is to suffer, not to love is to suffer, to suffer is to suffer.
>
> To be happy is to love. To be happy, then, is to suffer. But suffering makes one unhappy. Therefore, to be unhappy, one must love or love to suffer. Or suffer from too much happiness.

Somehow we appear to have lost our mooring to the happiness that is our unconditioned Self. Much in the same way that humankind has so divorced itself from Mother Nature, we appear to have distanced ourselves from our own inner happiness to the point that we're no longer really certain what happiness is. In fact, we feel so distanced that we even question the existence of *inner happiness,* for it feels so foreign, unreal and untrue.

Our confusion is conditioned. It is learned. It is a forgetfulness. It is in no way inherent to our unconditioned Self. To the unconditioned mind, happiness is natural; to the ego, or conditioned mind, happiness is special. To the unconditioned mind, happiness is within; to the ego, everything good is outside. To the unconditioned mind, happiness is constant; to the ego, happiness never lasts. To the unconditioned mind, happiness is free; to the ego, happiness requires suffering, sacrifice and payment.

In a nutshell, then, our conditioning has confused us. The conditioned mind is a confused consciousness. Thus, your conditioned self is not only confused about happiness, it is confused about *everything,* including love, life, God, purpose and your true identity. This learned confusion essentially takes three routes, as shown in Figure 2.

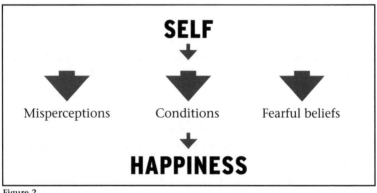

Figure 2

Route 1 is about our misperceptions of what happiness really is. What is happiness? Is it physical pleasure, a worldly pursuit, a cognitive choice, a spiritual joy, or something else? Route 2 is about the unnecessary conditions and prerequisites we've created that say happiness must first be 'earned', 'worked for', and 'deserved'. Route 3 is about the fearful beliefs we have about happiness – that is, our 'happychondria'.

All of your conditioning about happiness is both learned and unreal. In fact . . .

**nothing real stands between you and your
happiness, only illusion and your own confusion.**

I know that many times you've felt as if happiness is so very far away from you, somewhere on the other side of the world, perhaps, or even on another planet. I've experienced the same myself many times. Although these painful moments feel very real, it's important to realise that they're not the truth. This pain is illusory (that is, it's not the truth about you). Indeed, *all pain comes from holding on to illusions about your Self.*

After spending several years dedicated to the study of happiness, I now know that there is, in truth, no distance between us and our happiness. I believe, therefore, that the healing journey isn't a physical journey as such. Rather, it's a journey of consciousness, of truth emerging from illusion, of light dawning through darkness, of love replacing fear. This journey is an unfolding of that which is already within. To be happy, therefore, you must first be willing to undo and unlearn your misperceptions, false conditions, and fearful beliefs.

I have two friends, Eddie and Debbie Shapiro, both wonderfully enlightened healers, who describe this undoing process as 'Undoism'. I remember very well the first time I went to a gathering of theirs in the heart of the English countryside. From the front of the room, Eddie proclaimed, 'I have a new religion for you – "Undoism" – unlearning your fears of joy!'[1]

Still Getting There!

My client Michael was a perfect example of what psychologists sometimes call 'successful malcontents'. He was rich, famous, powerful, middle-aged, and deeply unhappy. All of his life he had 'gone for *it*' but had never in his opinion ever quite 'gotten *it*'. That was why he'd come to see me. We met maybe a dozen times and made quick progress.

It was during our last session together that I asked Michael, 'What is the most important lesson you've learned about happiness?'

Michael paused. He didn't speak for a full two minutes or so. Then he smiled and said, 'In my 20s, I worked so damned hard that I hoped I'd be happy in my 30s; in my 30s, I struggled every day so that I might be happy in my 40s; in my 40s, I sacrificed everything so as to be happy in my 50s. Now that I'm 50, I don't want to wait until my 60s! All my life I've been struggling and searching for happiness, instead of just being happy. I'm ready to give up the search and be happy *now*.'

**The search for happiness has brought
with it much unhappiness.**

Since the beginning of time, we've searched the world for our happiness. Over the centuries we've listened to countless stories of the Holy Grail, the Philosopher's Stone, Excalibur, the Golden Fleece, the Ark of the Covenant, secret manuscripts of truth, hidden sacred temples, universal elixirs, soul mates, alchemy and magic, pots of gold at the end of rainbows, yellow-brick roads, and more.

All of these stories testify to a belief in a happiness 'out there' and to a distinct absence of happiness within. This is where fear enters. Indeed, the source of all our fears is the erroneous belief that *happiness is somewhere else.*

So convinced are we that the world holds our happiness that we roam the earth hunting down anything that looks like happiness. We strive, we struggle, we suffer more than our neighbour, more than our parents, more than anyone we know in an effort to get ahead. The more we get ahead, the more we lose the heart of happiness in the process. In other words, *the more we pursue happiness, the more we forget how to be happy.*

With our almost exclusive focus on the world, Self-knowledge is eclipsed by the need for world acknowledgment; authentic Self-expression is tempered by a need for approval and popularity; Self-realisation is sacrificed as we attempt to make the world realise how deserving we are of happiness. Gladly we sell our soul to the world, for we believe the soul has nothing to offer and the world has everything.

So addicted do we become to the pursuit of happiness that we will justify any means to 'get there'. We will cheat, lie, steal, and even murder. Soon the pursuit of happiness becomes the goal rather than happiness itself. A further irony is that . . .

> **as we become even more strongly addicted to the pursuit of happiness, we are in no way prepared for happiness when it arrives.**

Look at the society and the lifestyles we've created. We're too busy to be happy *now*. We're in too much of a hurry to be happy *now*. We're too focused on our bright futures to be happy *now*. We haven't enough time to be happy *now*. Our schedules won't allow us to drop out of the race and be happy *now*. We're too busy 'getting there', yet the more we chase happiness, the more it flees.

The pursuit of happiness is our greatest mistake.[2] It is a fabrication, an illusion, a lie, and an invention of the ego or conditioned Self, which believes that everything good is outside. The world doesn't have your happiness; *you* have your happiness. Certainly, events, experiences and people can help you recover your happiness if you let them, but they can't give you what you're refusing to see in yourself.

The pursuit of happiness is essentially the denial of happiness. And, in effect . . .

> **the pursuit of happiness must always fail because it is based on a lie – happiness is *not* outside you.**

Until you change the belief that *happiness is somewhere else*, you'll only experience a life in which you're always 'getting there' but are never quite 'there'! You'll always be striving, but never arriving. You'll always be looking, but never seeing. You'll always be busy, and you'll never be at rest. How can you afford to rest if you insist on believing that peace isn't already within you?

One more thought: has it ever occurred to you that the pursuit of happiness stems, deep down, from a lack of Self-acceptance? In other words, *whatever it is you pursue – be it peace, happiness, love, or God – is what you currently cannot accept.* Thus, you pursue happiness because (1) you cannot accept it for your Self right now; and (2) you cannot accept that it may already be in your Self – your unconditioned Self.

It's ironic that the only joy you ever experience while pursuing happiness is when you very occasionally allow yourself to rest, relax, and stop pursuing happiness. Think of what joy you'd experience if you dared to stop pursuing happiness completely. Think how fearless you would be, how creative and at peace you would be, and how free you would be to enjoy the world more fully if you were to stop pursuing happiness and simply start accepting and allowing happiness to happen.

Just One More Thing!

Happiness is not in things; happiness is in *you*.

The most significant educational experience during my childhood had nothing to do with school. School was academic. It was my family who taught me the most valuable lessons of life . . . especially my grandparents.

The marriage of my mother and father shouldn't have happened, according to many. It was a marriage of 'wealth and poverty', not to be confused, by the way, with *War and Peace!* My mother was born into the English aristocracy, the landed gentry, a family of the British Empire. She was young and beautiful. My father wasn't what my mother's family had in mind for their daughter. For one thing, he worked for a living. His family was distinctly working class.

Everyone had a theory about my parents' marriage: it was ill advised, blessed, wrong, true love, doomed from the start, an act of rebellion by my mother, opportunism by my father, and so on. Upon marrying my father, my mother was instantly cut off from her financial heritage, as both punishment and caution, I suppose.

Lack of money was a recurring theme of my childhood. Three memories stand out in particular – one was a string of rented accommodations, including a miserable one-bed flat in a heavily vandalised block situated next to a busy railway line; another was being invited by Mum and Dad to attend an emergency family financial budget meeting on the eve of my 11th birthday; and another was the huge dirty, ripped, brown leather sofa we'd picked up from an auction for 50 pence (about a dollar in U.S. currency today). That sofa was our pride and joy.

Visiting both sets of grandparents was a bewildering experience. My father's parents lived on the south coast of England, in a town called Seaford, near Brighton. They lived in a rented flat over a fish-and-chip shop. I remember three smells in particular: (1) cigarettes – my grandparents smoked like chimneys; (2) Guinness – my grandpa loved it; and (3) the stale smell of old oil from the shop down below. We would spend many of our summer holidays with my father's parents.

My mother's parents lived in the heart of the English countryside in Twyford, near Winchester. We would visit much more regularly, almost every other weekend, as we lived only a few miles away. Granny and Grandpa lived in a huge mansion with acres of gardens, farmland all around, a beautiful river, and an exotic kitchen garden full of peaches, nectarines, strawberries, raspberries, gooseberries, and more. The gardens were so beautiful that they were often opened to the public. My mother had two elder sisters and one elder brother who lived in equally beautiful and stately homes, and we would visit them every now and then. The disparity between 'us' and 'them' was truly shocking and bewildering.

One side of my family appeared to have everything the world could offer, and the other side appeared to have very little indeed. And yet I swear, with hand on heart, *there was no more happiness in those huge mansions than there was in that little flat above the fish-and-chip shop.* On the contrary, the laughter I remember most bounced off the walls of the flat and not the mansion's.

Please note that I'm not suggesting as some people do that money makes you miserable. I carry no 'Money is the root of all evil' banners. On the contrary, I appreciate money greatly! What I *did* learn, however, from a very early age indeed, is that no amount of money can make you happy. More precisely, I would say, money can *encourage* you to be happy, but it cannot *make* you happy.[3]

This leads me to another very important principle of happiness that forms a central part of my teaching at The Happiness Project:

> **Nothing in the world can *make* you happy;**
> **everything in the world can *encourage* you to be happy.**

We live our lives in the hopes that *just one more thing* will complete our happiness. The ego's conditioned thought is that *something is missing.* And so we look for the missing piece to bring us salvation. And yet, no matter how many *things* we purchase, gather and collect, we still feel as if something's missing. Indeed, there is – the unconditional awareness that *nothing* is missing. We are, in truth, complete and whole already.

Nothing can make you happy if you won't accept for yourself that happiness rests within you. You see . . .

I know people with fancy dishwashers who aren't happy.

I've met people with elaborate stereo-sound TV sets, complete with remote control, who are absolutely miserable.

I know men who wear Armani and still feel inferior.

I know women who can afford to buy a dozen Gucci watches but still have no time for themselves.

I have friends who are married and happy, and I have friends who are married and unhappy.

I have friends who are famous and loved by millions, yet they cannot bear to love themselves. I have friends who can afford a house cleaner, but still, all their life is a chore.

I've counselled people with extreme wealth, yet they feel as if they have nothing.

I've worked with directors of vast international corporations who are still looking for their first really meaningful achievement.

I have friends who hoped parenthood would bring them happiness – to some it did and to some it didn't.

I know women who wear real diamonds but still have no real sparkle in their lives.

I know men who drive sports cars to nowhere in particular.

It is the conclusion of the most extensive psychological and sociological research into happiness, or 'subjective wellbeing', as it's termed, that *nothing can make you happy.* Just as it's true that the pursuit of happiness fails to make you happy, so too does materialism fail to make you happy. Social psychologist David Myers has written an excellent study called *The Pursuit of Happiness,* in which he collates much of the most recent research into the *how* of happiness. He concludes:

> . . . whether we base our conclusions on self-reported happiness, rates of depression, or teen problems, *our becoming better off over the last thirty years has not been*

accompanied by one iota of increased happiness and life sat-isfaction. It's shocking, because it contradicts our society's materialistic assumptions, but how can we ignore the hard truth: *once beyond poverty, further economic growth does not appreciably improve human morale.* Making more money – the aim of so many graduates and other American dream-ers of the 1980s – does not breed bliss.[4]

Perhaps you've heard the old joke 'Nothing makes me happy: I've tried poverty and wealth, and they've both failed!' Material-ism isn't bad or evil; it's simply not enough to replace the happi-ness within. The world isn't here to *meet* your needs; the world is here to show you that you *have* no needs.

When people are depressed, they often say, 'Nothing makes me happy.' This is the truth! Indeed, the first stage of depression is very often disillusion with the world. The world gives us the appearance of happiness, but not the source. It's like a hyped-up glossy holiday brochure that fails to deliver. The way out of depression is, therefore, to know that (1) the world cannot make you happy, and (2) your happiness exists within.

To sum up, nothing can actually *make* you happy, but every-thing can *encourage* you to choose happiness. Money can't *buy* you happiness, but it can certainly help you *choose* happiness. A sense of security is important, but again it's no real prerequisite or guar-antee of happiness. Health helps, but it cannot *make* you happy. Exercise can inspire wellbeing, and it's highly recommended.[5] So too is a good diet[6] and a healthy sleep pattern.[7] However, it's pos-sible to be physically fit, full of vitamin C, get eight hours of sleep, and still feel miserable. Nothing can *make you* choose happiness. Choosing happiness is your function.

There's also a reverse of the principle that *nothing in the world can make you happy; everything in the world can encourage you to be happy.* And that is . . .

**nothing in the world can *make* you sad;
everything in the world can *encourage* you to be sad.**

The world cannot take away your right to happiness or sadness. It may often appear to be trying very hard to take this choice away, but truly it cannot. Events in life can so conspire that you may lose sight of this choice, but never is the choice destroyed. In truth, the decision to be happy or sad always rests with you, whether you can see it or not. It's when you temporarily lose sight of this choice that you must ask for help.

Happiness Is a Decision Only You Can Make

Whenever I meet somebody new away from work – on a golf course, at a party, or on a holiday, perhaps – conversation usually gets around to the 'So what do you do?' question. I often hesitate to answer, but I usually end up saying, 'I study the psychology of happiness.' What tends to follow is a very long and profound silence, several nonplussed looks, some awkward body language, and, eventually, a comforting word of reply such as 'Oh' or 'Gosh!' or 'That's nice.' Often I'm also asked, 'But isn't happiness just happiness?'

Society parades three broad ideas about happiness: (1) happiness is luck, (2) happiness is circumstance, and (3) happiness is a decision.

The Oxford Dictionary of English defines happiness as 'fortunate; lucky; feeling or expression of satisfaction.' I've interviewed thousands of people about happiness over the years for various radio and television programs, and the most common answers to the question 'What is happiness?' are 'Winning the lottery,' or 'Winning on the horses', or 'Winning the football pools'. Happiness appears to be a bet, and luck is the answer.

The problem with the belief that *happiness is luck* is that there's no role left for you to play in your own life. With luck as your great hope, your life and your happiness is on hold while you wait for the dice to roll your number. Luck denies you any responsibility or influence on how your life may turn out. Your life is determined *for* you, not *by* you. Most often those people who gamble on luck see themselves as unlucky victims of the world.

The second view, that *happiness is a circumstance,* is very common. Certain circumstances, particularly those you judge to be 'good' and 'right', can be satisfying, but once again I would refer you to the principle that *nothing in the world can make you happy; everything in the world can encourage you to be happy.* In other words, there is no one circumstance that can completely guarantee happiness.

The belief that *happiness is a circumstance* also suggests, as with luck, that the attainment of happiness is ultimately out of your hands. In other words, your happiness is 'good' only as long as you judge that the circumstances in your life are 'good'. But what happens to your happiness when you spill red wine on your shirt, when your car breaks down, or when your child crams another ginger snap into the DVD player? How strong is your happiness?

I once made friends with a man named Christopher after spending a day training staff at a local hospice. Christopher was 108 years old, and he was the oldest and most lively patient on the ward. At his last birthday party, I asked him, 'What is the secret of life?'

I'll never forget his reply, both for its humour and its wisdom. He said, 'Well, Robert, I tell everyone that the first 100 years of life are definitely the most challenging – after that it gets easier! I also tell people that life is 10 per cent circumstance and 90 per cent your *response* to circumstance.'

The view that *happiness is a decision* is both radical and true. I was once given a quotation by a workshop participant that I like very much. The words belong to a gentleman named John Homer Miller:

> **'Circumstances and situations do colour life,
> but you have been given the mind to choose
> what the colour shall be.'**

Life is powerful, but your thoughts about life are even more powerful. In one of my books, *Living Wonderfully,* I wrote:

> There is a fantastic force in life that has a miracu-
> lous power to transform fatigue into energy, despair
> into delight, and anxiety into action. This force can

make 'bad' things 'good', and 'wrong' things 'right'. An 'upset' can become a 'set-up', a 'misfortune' can lead to 'fortune' and a 'failure' can become a prelude to 'success'. This miraculous force has the power to decide.

The great news is that you are perfectly entitled to use this fantastic force, if you so choose. If you do, you may well find that, quite miraculously, obstacles turn into opportunities, adversity into advantage, breakdowns into breakthroughs, and unhappy endings into bright new beginnings. This force, if you haven't already guessed, is the power of thought.[8]

The second half of the 20th century has seen a rapid rise in the number of cognitive schools of psychology, which very much support the idea that happiness is a decision.[9] In other words, *whatever the picture, it is your frame of mind that ultimately counts.* Circumstances can be helpful, attitude is crucial, for as Hugh Downs once wrote:

> **'A happy person is not a person**
> **in a certain set of circumstances, but rather**
> **a person with a certain set of attitudes.'**

The perception that *happiness is a decision* affirms that attitude is first, circumstance is second. It teaches you that whatever is happening, you always carry the deciding vote when it comes to happiness, success, love and peace of mind. Sometimes this is easy to remember; other times it's not so easy. Once again, it's when you forget that you must ask for help.

Happiness is a decision feels good and empowering, but even this philosophy offers a limited perception of true happiness. For example, have you ever thought about what happens to happiness when you're low and your attitude is suffering? Does happiness disappear like a pathetic wisp of smoke? Can happiness be pulled around so easily by the world? Is happiness really that weak?

Contrary to popular belief, true happiness is not a fickle little something, a dizzy little airhead that finds it hard to keep a commitment, always coming and going, appearing and then disappearing, waving 'Hello!' one minute and then shouting 'Goodbye' the next. True happiness is faithful – it does not and cannot leave you.

True happiness is constant, not transient; it is strong, not weak. Try not to think of happiness as something external that travels to you or away from you, but think of it as a potential you carry within you always – a potential you are, in any given moment, either opening to or withdrawing from. In truth . . .

**happiness doesn't come and go; what comes
and goes is your *attunement* to happiness.**

Above all, my work has taught me that, no matter how much pain you're in . . . no matter how low, how hurt, how hopeless, how consumed by anger, how bitter, how fearful, or how awful you feel, the potential to experience peace and happiness never goes away. Just as clouds in the sky can eclipse the sun but not destroy it, so too can fear and pain eclipse your happiness but not destroy it. The potential for happiness is with you permanently. Happiness is just a thought away.

The reason for this is that happiness is the very nature of your unconditioned Self. Happiness is the makeup of existence itself. Thus, happiness is not a peak experience; it is central. It's not the top of the mountain; it's the heart of the mountain. As you throw off your conditioning, you reveal a joy that exists independent of the world. I think the writer J. Donald Walters described this joy beautifully when he wrote: 'It is the gold of our inner nature, buried beneath the mud of outward sense-cravings.'

This joy is not in you, it is you. I remember being deeply moved by a passage in A *Course in Miracles* that highlighted this idea. It states: 'It is hard to understand what "The Kingdom of Heaven is within you" really means. This is because it is not understandable to the ego, which interprets it as if something outside is inside, and this does not mean anything. The word "within" is unnecessary. The Kingdom of Heaven is you.'

A more accurate perception of happiness, then, is that it is the nature of your unconditioned Self. Hence . . .

> **when you're truly happy,**
> **you are being your Self.**

Rumi, the Holy Grail, and Your True Identity

Rumi, the great Sufi mystic and poet, once told a story of how he knocked on the door of his beloved God:

> 'Who's there?' came the answer.
>
> 'It is I, your lover, Rumi,' he said.
>
> From inside came the voice, 'Go away, there is no room for the two of us in here.'
>
> Rumi left, completely dispirited. He meditated and prayed, and later he returned to the house of his beloved once more and knocked again.
>
> 'Who is it?' the beloved asked.
>
> 'It is You.' With a welcome, the door was thrown wide open.[10]

When we chase happiness, we're really chasing our unconditioned Self, for the experience of true happiness is really the experience of the Self. The world, with all its transitory pleasures, cannot make up for that which is always within you. The more you can accept the idea that happiness is your nature, the more joyful your experience of the world will be. *With fewer needs, you will be more free.*

Author John Pepper wrote a beautiful passage in his book, *How to be Happy,* which I cannot improve upon. He stated:

> What we do know is that when we have travelled the world over in search of the Holy Grail, ransacked the texts of the saints and sages for clues as to its whereabouts, pleaded with the night to yield it to us, abased ourselves in rituals, followed the light paths

of romantic love and relationship and the dark ones of drugs and disorder, and done the million and one things it appears we have to do before finally we grind to a halt in exhaustion, our happiness still tantalisingly out of reach; then we see with a snort of absurdity that there is nowhere left to reach out to; that all the words have gone. The running, brother and sister, is done. The answer is contained here in this frail being in this dark night on this lasted heath; here or nowhere. The Holy Grail is us.[11]

Every time you say yes to happiness, you're saying yes to your unconditioned Self. By making it your intention to be happy, you're throwing off all of the defences, doubts and fears you've learned to value. You're letting go of the pain of your past, pain that would keep you in your past and would prevent you from experiencing happiness *now*.

Over the years, I've created many prayers and affirmations that help to strengthen the intent to be happy and free. Intention is the key. One prayer that's a particular favourite of mine is addressed to the God that sits in the centre of your unconditioned Self. It reads:

Dear God,
I know not by myself how to be truly happy.
Teach me, in this moment, how to allow the
spirit of true happiness to shine through.
In this moment, I give to You all my fearful
misperceptions of happiness.
In this moment, I give to You all the false
conditions I have placed between myself
and happiness.
And in this moment, I give to You my fear
of happiness.
Teach me, Dear God, to accept happiness
easily, effortlessly, and naturally.
Teach me, Dear God, to radiate happiness
easily, effortlessly, and naturally.
Teach me, Dear God, to accept and radiate
happiness in equal measure.
So be it.

Welcome to the Laughter Clinic!

About three years after setting up the Stress Busters Clinic, I was ready to make a radical change in my work, which had so far been very problem-focused. Until then, I had followed a philosophy of: *First resolve all problems and see about happiness later.*

Now, a new philosophy was emerging of putting happiness first. I was beginning to see that . . .

**making a wholehearted commitment
to being happy is a powerful medicine.**

Happiness is not just the absence of problems; happiness is the power that helps you heal your problems. And if illness and disease are symptoms of unhappiness, then surely a return to happiness *now* will help you to heal. I was beginning to see that, just as a block of ice will melt if you expose it to the sun, so too will our fears disperse before our inner happiness. Above all, happiness helps us to be unconditional and free once more.

The upshot of this change was that in September 1991 I opened the doors to the first-ever official Laughter Clinic in Great Britain. I received the backing of the government and the National Health Service to set up a clinic that focused first and foremost on natural, unconditional medicines of love, laughter, happiness and joy.[12]

Our approach was fourfold: (1) We would run at least one workshop a week for members of the public on anything to do with unconditional happiness; (2) we would collect, collate and make available as much research on happiness as possible from the fields of medicine, psychology, philosophy and religion; (3) we would hold professional training events for any health professionals who would like to develop their work; and (4) we would spread messages of love, joy and laughter through the world's 'more bad news' media of television, radio, and the press.

Within a month of opening, the Laughter Clinic had received more than 500 enquiries. This compared to fewer than ten during the first month of the Stress Busters Clinic. We were overwhelmed by the enthusiasm and interest. The Laughter Clinic had caught people's imagination and was obviously appealing. The Laughter Clinic ran for four years before it became known, as it is today, as The Happiness Project.

The workshops were an instant success. More than 1,000 events have now been run through The Happiness Project, addressing audiences of 5 or 6 people to 1,000 or more. Several workshops became very popular, such as *Angels Can Fly Because They Take Themselves Lightly,* which looks at the art of Self-acceptance; *How to Be So Happy You Almost Feel Guilty, but Not Quite!* which looks at the relationship between happiness and self-esteem; *Happiness Is a Way of Travelling,* which focuses on happiness *now;* and *Let There Be Laughter,* which looks at the relationship between spirituality and joy.[13]

More than 20,000 doctors, nurses, psychologists, counsellors and other therapists have attended professional training held by The Happiness Project. We've also contributed directly to several thousand media features around the world.

One of the peak experiences for me personally was in August 1996, when the BBC broadcast a 40-minute QED documentary on my work entitled 'How to be Happy', which followed three volunteers, Carol, Dawn and Keith, as they took my 'Eight-Week Personal Happiness Programme'. (The QED series was popular on the BBC for many years and comprised scientific programmes on numerous topics.) Approximately five million viewers tuned in that night to see the progress Carol, Dawn and Keith each made, as verified by independent scientists who conducted a battery of extensive physiological and psychological tests.[14]

I've enjoyed great help and support through the years. In the beginning, my then wife, Miranda, helped to evolve the project in countless ways. More recently, my brother, David, has helped to manage both The Happiness Project and another of our projects called The Deep & Meaningful Training Company. The Happiness Project is also blessed to have great workshop facilitators in Ben Renshaw and Alison Atwell. The list goes on!

The Happiness Project has been, and still is, a most marvellous journey. I now see how the study of happiness is really a most intimate journey of Self-discovery. By looking so closely at happiness – particularly the desire for it and at times the resistance to it – we can help ourselves and others no end.

❖ ❖ ❖

CHAPTER THREE

Being Good Enough

Claire had spoken most eloquently for 45 minutes about everything that was wrong with her. Eventually, I was moved to interrupt her pattern of thought: 'What do you *love* about yourself Claire?' I asked.

'What?' she replied.

'Objectively speaking, what is there to love about you?' Claire looked stunned. Now there were no words, only a bemused smile. 'Can you answer my question?' I asked.

'I don't know,' she said. 'No one has ever asked me to think that way before.'

I've seen many hundreds of clients over the years through my work with the clinics, my private practice, and The Happiness Project. In one way . . .

**every client has been different, and yet
in another way, they're all the same.**

Someone who's experiencing alcoholism, for instance, looks very different from someone who's experiencing anorexia. Similarly, someone who's dealing with depression looks very different from someone who has just survived a heart attack. And someone with agoraphobia looks very different from someone who feels totally stressed, and so on. They all look different, their conditions have different names, and yet, deep down, their illness is the same.

No *dis-ease* happens by itself. Alcoholism doesn't happen by itself. Alcoholism is an effect, not a cause. It is a symptom, not an illness. Alcoholism is not the primary dis-ease; the primary dis-ease *is* the excessive self-judgment and constant self-criticism that pressures someone into taking a drink in the first place. The same is true, in one degree or another, for depression, stress, burnout, and every other dis-ease ever 'named' by the medical and psychology professions. *Self-judgment is the dis-ease.*

It has been my experience that behind every pain, illness and form of unhappiness there is, hard at work, a fearful, relentless level of self-judgment – a distinct lack of love and acceptance that perpetuates and complicates symptom after symptom. We don't get ill when we're wholly joyous because our joy is free of fear and judgment. Illness does ensue, however, when we judge, berate, and criticise ourselves too harshly. In one way or another, we are all the same in that . . .

we all 'suffer' from the highly critical
condition of C.S.J. – Constant Self-Judgment.

Your unconditioned Self, being completely whole, has no need to judge. What is there to judge if all you know is wholeness and love? You know for yourself that when you feel completely happy and whole, you don't think to judge. Wholeness is joyful, not judgmental. Thus, self-judgment isn't natural to your unconditioned Self. It is learned. It belongs to the conditioned self, the ego, which suspects that 'everything good is outside' and fears that 'something is missing'. It wonders, 'Am I whole?'

You've learned to judge, criticise, and condemn yourself. No matter how hard anyone else has ever judged you, you judge yourself the hardest. In fact, you *save your most severe standards, judgments, criticisms and punishments for yourself.* This constant self-judgment is something you've learned. It isn't natural to you. Once, you were completely accepting of yourself and you were free, but now . . .

no one is harder on you than *you* are!

While your unconditioned Self continues to be free, your ego continues to judge and imprison itself. Your ego-self accepts nothing and judges everything, including happiness. Judgment is more than a habit; it is a way of life. Your judgments stain the windows of your perception. They filter everything you see so that, in truth, you *see nothing as it really is; you only see your judgments.* Thus, you don't see your own beauty, wholeness and Light within; you only see that you 'could do better' and 'be more'.

Your conditioned self, or ego, judges, pushes, drives and punishes you so incessantly to compensate for its fear that deep down you're inadequate and incomplete – that is, *your happiness is somewhere else.* This is not the truth, but you've learned to believe that it might be. Your ego is an addict. Indeed . . .

the belief in 'not being good enough' is your ego's greatest addiction.

The addiction to this belief feeds all other addictions, including over-dependency in relationships, extreme competitiveness, punishing social comparison, envy and jealousy, pained perfectionism, constant self-judgment, lack of assertiveness and a desperate never-ending pursuit of happiness. This addiction also feeds other more physical addictions that provide temporary comfort and escape, such as overeating, alcoholism, compulsive sex and illegal drugs.

Health, love and wholeness cannot flourish where there is constant self-judgment. The starting point, then, with any of my clients, isn't necessarily the 'named' dis-ease – that is, stress or depression – it is to address the underlying fears and judgments that may have given rise to that dis-ease in the first place. What I often end up prescribing *is a course in kindness, love and true self-acceptance* as an antidote to the learned criticism, fear, judgment and self-hatred of the ego. This is real healing.

> **In all my years, I've never had a client who suffered from being too kind to him- or herself!**

The ego-self resists kindness, for it believes that judgment buys you something. It is convinced that without judgment you will 'fall behind' and become complacent, slack, disadvantaged, and, in particular, 'wrong', 'bad', 'nothing', and 'not good enough'. *The cycle of constant self-judgment can only end with love.* In order to be well, we must learn to love again. All illness and unhappiness is, therefore, a call for love.

Like my client Claire, I was equally stunned when I was first asked, 'Robert, what do you love about yourself?' I was a delegate at a seminar on health and healing at the time, and I remember vividly how that simple question seemed to set a million chemical reactions bursting instantaneously and simultaneously through my body. My throat went dry, my heart skipped several beats and I stopped breathing. I began to perspire, my stomach churned, my bladder felt full all of a sudden, I couldn't speak, and for all I know, my ears probably started to flap as well!

Self-acceptance is as natural to your unconditioned Self as constant self-judgment is to your ego. You must choose between your conditioning and your freedom. Until you're willing to accept your Self – your unconditioned Self – you won't be able to accept all that you long for. The happiness, the peace and the love you crave cannot happen without Self-acceptance.

Home Alone: Horror Film or Love Story?

'All men's miseries derive from not being able to sit quiet in a room alone.'
– Blaise Pascal

We all experience moments in our lives that become turning points. I had one such turning point one weekend while in my second year of studying Communications. I was 19 years old at the time, and what happened to me that weekend was to change my life forever.

Weekends are everything to students. It's a time for dates, dinners, parties, friendship, bands, going home, romance, being cool, being wild, being whatever you want. Looking back, I recall how during most weeks, from Wednesday afternoon onwards, attention would turn to the forthcoming weekend. 'What are you going to do?' 'Who are you seeing?' 'Have you been invited to the party?' and so on.

I think it was one Thursday morning when I first began to panic a little. My friend Avanti told me he was going to be away for the weekend because he was taking a trip to London. I also found out later that morning that Philip was going home to Lancashire, James was off somewhere and Paul was going to an all-day 'Fight for Peace' rally. By Friday afternoon, I realised that all of my friends, without exception, would be out of Birmingham for the weekend. Now I was really panicking.

I remember going home on Friday afternoon and phoning around, looking for anybody to spend some time with that night. First, I tried the 'A' list of friends, then the 'B' list, and then the list of people I barely knew – 'Hello, it's Robert here. Robert Holden. Robert Holden with dark hair, six foot tall, sits at the back in psychology class . . .' No one – absolutely no one – was available. Around 7 o'clock that evening I eventually had to face what to me was a terrifying prospect – *time alone with myself.*

The idea of a little bit of time 'home alone' l could handle, but an entire weekend, an entire 65 hours until my first class on Monday – that was terrifying! Until now, I had deliberately planned my entire life in such a way as to ensure that I was never left alone with myself for too long. Initially, I was afraid, then I became a little panicky and finally I was completely terrified. It was like I was in a horror movie!

I remember thinking to myself, *Something isn't quite right here. Surely I shouldn't be this frightened to be with me!* It also occurred to me that if I found the prospect of spending time with myself to be so very awful, why would it be reasonable to expect anyone *else* to find that same prospect appealing? I knew that I was in deep trouble.

It was the decision I made next that was to change my life forever. I decided to stop running from myself. I took the plug out of the TV set, the radio, the stereo and the phone. I then went and lay on my bed and stared up at the ceiling. Immediately I felt bored. Totally bored. The loneliness was intolerable. I wasn't enjoying myself. I soon began to cry and cry and cry. I cried for so long that I remember having to drink water to rehydrate! I felt wave upon wave of what I can only describe as self-hatred wash over my body. My stomach in particular felt awful. I barely slept that night.

All through Saturday morning, I continued to struggle and wrestle free from my own company. The temptation to watch television, listen to the radio, or call my family was at times overwhelming, but I somehow knew that this would only be a distraction. I felt as if these feelings of self-doubt and self-hate had been chasing after me all my life, and now, finally, I didn't want to run any more.

I took one breath at a time and one feeling at a time. I simply decided to watch every awful judgment and feeling I'd stored up against myself. I decided there would be no more defences and no more distractions. The supply of awful judgments and criticisms seemed inexhaustible. Still, I took one breath at a time and one feeling at a time. I also said a lot of prayers.

It was on Sunday afternoon, when time had already become a blur, that I eventually began to experience what I would call a miracle. I became aware of a stillness in the flat. I was also feeling strangely peaceful. This peace seemed to emerge from the same place in my belly where all the pain had come from. As each moment passed, I felt more and more peaceful. For some reason, I no longer felt lonely being on my own.

For the first time in my life, I found my own company to be totally acceptable. I wasn't just putting up with me; I was actually *liking* being with me. I even remember thinking how lovely it would be if Monday morning could be put back a little! I emerged that weekend from what felt like an emotional fever in which I faced, with grace, some very dark fears. At last I knew what it felt like to be happy with myself.

You and the #1 Happiness Principle

The story of my weekend serves to illustrate a most fundamental principle of happiness, one that is at the heart of The Happiness Project's philosophy. This principle states that . . .

unless you're happy with yourself, you will not be happy.

This principle quite clearly has some far-reaching implications. It is pivotal to the whole subject of happiness. To understand it better, it's possible to divide the #1 Happiness Principle into four main parts. Each part throws light on the fundamental importance of Self-acceptance and inner peace for experiencing happiness now.[1]

1. What You Do

Part I of the #1 Happiness Principle predicts quite unequivocally that . . .

unless you're happy with yourself, you won't be happy with what you do.

Your ego projects its self-judgments onto every one of your achievements, without exception. Thus, your judgments about yourself and about what you do will always be identical. If, therefore, you judge yourself as 'not good enough', whatever you do, no matter how good it looks to others, will never ever be quite 'good enough' to you. No amount of achievement can change this.[2]

In my 20s, I was what you might call a typical 'high achiever'. Two clinics, four published books, deputy editor of the country's leading holistic-health journal, my own radio call-in show, thousands of media features worldwide, and hundreds of keynote conference speeches and workshops were all added to my personal résumé, which, like a bodybuilder's biceps, bulged a bit too big!

Like many high achievers, it was my sincere hope that enough achievement would someday bring me a bit of peace and happiness. Some of my achievements were literally for the joy of it all, but most of them were driven by a need to prove myself. Indeed, all through my 20s, I was so busy proving myself that I had no time to accept myself.

Success seemed like salvation. So I set out to be a success, hoping that enough of it would drown out the noise of my ego. Achievement was meant to offer respite from my constant self-judgment and 'not good enough' script. At the very least, achievement kept me busy. Being busy is like a behavioural Valium – you don't feel your feelings and you don't notice your judgments when you're busy 'doing'. You *have* to keep 'doing', though, or the self-hatred returns when you try to rest.

Achievement for the joy of it is healthy, for your motive is love and your worth is never questioned. Achievement because you *need* it is problematic. What I've slowly come to learn, only to forget again periodically, is . . .

**no amount of 'doing' can compensate
completely for a lack of 'being'.**

Over the last few years, I've had the privilege of working with many highly accomplished people, particularly in the world of business (and their résumés bulge even bigger than my own). Time and time again I've witnessed how massive amounts of personal achievement still amount to 'nothing' as long as there is little or no Self-acceptance. Achievement, it seems, can be a wonderful boost to the ego, but . . .

in no way is achievement a complete
solution for low self-esteem.

Go ahead and achieve, by all means. It can be great fun, especially when you do so for the joy of it. But make no mistake – 'X' amounts of achievement will not buy you 'X' amounts of happiness. Indeed, no amount of achievement will do for you what you're not prepared to do for yourself – that is, accept your Self. Achievement can be fun, but it is not salvation.

Happiness occurs naturally when you change your mind about yourself, when you give up your conditioning and accept your Self – your whole Self. Once you can accept that you are indeed 'good enough', all of your achievements will also be 'good enough', but not until then.

2. Where You Are

The second part of the #1 Happiness Principle focuses on the relationship between happiness and environment. It states that . . .

unless you're happy with yourself,
you won't be happy with where you are.

Dawn was one of three people who agreed to be filmed by QED on my Eight-Week Happiness Programme for the BBC documentary *How to Be Happy*. During our first meeting, Dawn told me how she had moved some 13 times in recent years in search of happiness. 'I first moved to get as far away from my family as I could,' she said. 'I hoped that if I put some physical distance between me and my pain, I would be free again, but wherever I moved, my pain came with me.'

Dawn had decided to take the Eight-Week Happiness Programme because, in her words, 'Everywhere I moved to I was really happy at first. But then the novelty would go, and the happiness soon wore off. The only problem with each new place was that *I kept turning up there!* I wasn't happy with me. I can see now that until I'm happy with me, nowhere will be good enough.'

I explained to Dawn during our times together that . . .

> **healing is not about changing your address;**
> **healing is about changing your mind about**
> **yourself – that is, giving up your self-judgments.**

A beautiful mansion adorned with priceless antiques may very well inspire happiness initially, but this change of address cannot compensate completely for a lack of inner peace. It's certainly true that an environment may *encourage* peace of mind, but no environment can *give* you peace of mind.[3]

Why is this the case? The answer lies in understanding that *perception is projection.* How you see anything external to you is exactly how you see yourself. Each judgment about yourself muddies the lens of your perception so that everything you see is stained with that judgment. It was the philosopher Immanuel Kant who wrote:

> **'We see things not as they are, but as we are.'**

For as long as you judge yourself 'not good enough', then no mansion, garden, luxury yacht or five-star hotel will be totally satisfactory. At first, all may appear well, but that's because you're in wonder and have forgotten to judge yourself. Once you're settled and everything becomes familiar, then the self-judgments will darken the lens of your perceptions once more.

We search the world for a heaven on earth, yet heaven is not a physical place and neither is hell. Heaven and hell are states of mind. Guilt is hell, fear is hell, judgment is hell; heaven is love and Self-acceptance. Heaven and hell are in your mind, and your mind goes with you wherever you go. It was the English poet John Milton who wrote: 'The mind is its own place, and in itself, / Can make a heaven of hell, a hell of heaven.'[4]

It is precisely for this reason that the mystics of old kept telling their disciples . . .

> **to change the world, first change your mind.**

My work with The Happiness Project does focus on one place in particular – not a physical place, but a spiritual place – a place right in the centre of your being. This place is your unconditioned Self. It is where the happiness you long for resides. In *A Course in Miracles*, this place is referred to as 'The Changeless Dwelling Place':

> There is a place in you where this whole world has been forgotten; where no memory of sin and of illusion lingers still. There is a place in you which time has left, and echoes of eternity are heard. There is a resting place so still no sound except a hymn to Heaven rises up to gladden God the Father and the Son. Where Both abide are They remembered, Both. And where They are is Heaven and is peace.

3. Who You Are With

Part III of the #1 Happiness Principle offers a sobering thought about happiness and relationships, a thought that I expand upon in Chapter 7 of this book. It states that . . .

**unless you're happy with yourself,
you won't be happy with who you're with.**

This is a particularly sobering thought, especially for romantic relationships, because often the very reason we desire to be with a partner is because we're not happy on our own! We search the world over, desperately looking for a partner who has a better opinion of us than we do. When we eventually find someone, we demand that this person love us even if we don't love ourselves, and here we enter a Catch-22 because, as long as we can't love and accept ourselves, we find it impossible to accept their love for us.

Relationships are deeply personal – far more personal than we often realise. The bottom line is . . .

**your relationship with your Self sets
the tone for every other relationship you have.**

To put it another way, *the way you relate to yourself ultimately determines* (1) *the way you relate to others,* and (2) *the way others relate to you.* Your relationship with others perfectly mirrors your relationship with your Self. In particular, you project your own self-criticism onto others constantly. Usually, at first, you experience a honeymoon period with new friends, lovers, children and colleagues, where they can do no wrong. Eventually, though, any unresolved self-judgments will resurface and project outward, causing much mayhem and separation.

When you feel whole and blissfully happy, you forget to judge other people. This is because you're not judging your Self. As soon as you lose sight of your own wholeness, however, you judge yourself and everyone else. For as long as you believe that you're 'not good enough', you'll try to improve yourself and everyone else around you. In particular, your lover, your children and your friends will not be safe from you as you make it your mission to 'correct their faults'. How many sons have paid the price for their father's wretched self-esteem? How many partners have been abused because of their partner's own self-hatred? How perfect your loved ones are already, and how perfect you are already . . . if only you could but see.

Deep down, every opinion you have about somebody else is really only a projection of an opinion you have about yourself. Therefore . . .

**eventually everyone must pay for your own
self-hatred; either that or you
change your mind about yourself.**

You may find that every now and then a new person will enter your life who appears to love you even more than you love yourself. I remember vividly how it happened to me when I met my first wife, Miranda. Very quickly, it became clear to me that she thought more highly of me than I did myself. Ironically, it was also clear to me that I thought more highly of her than she did herself. We tried so hard in those early days to sabotage our relationship and push each other away. The love we experienced was so great it shook our self-doubt and self-hate to the very core. Eventually it all came down to a simple choice – accept our Self and love each other . . . or hate our Self and separate.[5]

4. What You Have

Part IV of the #1 Happiness Principle takes us back to the idea that happiness is not in *things;* happiness is in *us*. It states that . . .

> **unless you're happy with yourself,**
> **you won't be happy with what you have.**

Nothing is enough as long as you judge your Self to be 'not good enough'. Nothing can make up for a lack of Self-acceptance. The ego, created by a thought of lack, can't ever be appeased and satisfied; it can only be dropped! You must leave behind your ego-conditioning if you're to return to the happiness of your unconditioned Self.

No amount of purchases, products or possessions can give you peace of mind. Once again, they may very well *encourage* you to be happy, but they can't actually *make* you happy. Deep down we know this to be true, yet we still keep trying to find a special 'thing' that will 'make' us happy.[6]

The world is seriously into shopping! Shopping is now our number one pastime. It is a great entertainment, an art form, even. But shopping is not, contrary to popular opinion, a purpose, a raison d'être, or a means to salvation. No amount of shopping can purchase joy – for *joy is not for sale*. When it comes to true joy, the truth is . . .

> **true joy is not about changing your wardrobe;**
> **true joy is about changing your mind –**
> **that is, giving up your self-judgment.**

No single possession in the world can make you peaceful. Peace of mind is something you must choose for your Self. Most of us do not believe this at first. This is why I encourage people to take what I call 'the BMW Test'. Most people long to own a BMW (or a BMW equivalent – a Harley-Davidson, a horse, a villa, a Versace tie). My advice is, don't resist! Try it. Go for it! Don't hold back! Do it so that you can prove to yourself that the world cannot by itself make you happy. Herein lies the key to freedom.

Remember the phrase 'What profiteth a man if he gaineth the whole world and loses his soul'.[7] The 'things' of this world are in no way 'bad' or 'wrong' or 'sinful' as some claim; they simply are not enough. Joy is not about accumulation or achievement; it is about acceptance – Self-acceptance.

In fact . . .

Joy is Self-acceptance –
it is freedom from self-judgment.

When you accept your Self, you accept joy naturally. Joy is like an inner Light that radiates upon and enlightens everything you see. When you're happy, there is beauty and purpose in everything. You are kind, philosophical and instantly forgiving. When you're miserable, however, even your favourite ice cream tastes sour and 'not good enough'.

Joy is miraculous. It can colour everything. What price joy? Sometimes I think that what we really need is a different type of credit card – not one for shopping, but a card that credits us with enough inner joy and inner peace to last an eternity. To be happy, all you really need do is give your Self, your whole Self, credit!

So What's Your Story?

Toward the end of his life, English philosopher Aldous Huxley gave an interview to a young journalist who was eager to extract gems of wisdom from the great man. When asked to sum up his lifetime's work, Huxley paused for a moment, and then smiled.

'It's a bit embarrassing,' he said, 'to have been concerned with the human problem all one's life and find at the end that one has no more to offer by way of advice than "try to be a little kinder."'[8]

Your ego and your unconditioned Self both have a story to tell, each very different from one another.

Your ego sees itself in you. It is a thought of limitation and lack, and believes, therefore, that you are in essence, *the Presence of Lack*. The ego is never at peace – it cannot afford to be while it believes 'everything good is outside'. It attacks and criticises you in order to motivate and strengthen. It believes that judgment buys better protection and better performance. The ego's learned chatter-chatter sounds like the rap of a megalomaniac sports coach who's constantly barking, 'You can do better', 'What's wrong with you?' 'Come on', 'Get a grip', 'Work!' and 'Try harder'.

Your unconditioned Self is a thought of complete wholeness and believes that you are, in essence, *the Presence of Love*. It sees no need for you to improve upon your wholeness; it merely wants to be whole! Quite clearly, then, your unconditioned Self sees things very differently from your ego.

In fact . . .

**your ego and your spirit have a
different view on everything.**

If the ego's prayer is always *'Look out!'* then your spirit's prayer is always *'Look within!'* for both your ego and your spirit have a different story. Your ego cries *'Look out!'* because it's afraid and because it believes 'everything good is outside'. Your spirit sings *'Look within!'* because it knows that you're complete and whole and happy already. These stories couldn't be more different. Which will you believe?

The ego compares itself to everything and comes off badly. Having researched the thinking of the ego for many years now, I've come to the conclusion that the ego's disparaging judgments follow four main patterns. Each pattern creates a story of (1) 'I'm not good enough'; (2) 'I'm wrong'; (3) 'I'm bad'; and (4) 'I'm nothing'. In truth . . .

> **none of the ego's stories about you are the truth,**
> **but that doesn't mean they don't feel true.**

There's no inherent power in any one of these ego storylines. They have no power at all, other than the strength of your belief. The more powerful your belief, the more powerfully each of these storylines appears in your life. Indeed, it's possible to become so conditioned by your own storyline that you eventually lose sight of the fact that you're the one who is perpetuating this fiction.

The key is to remember that every event in your life can encourage you to feel 'not good enough', 'wrong', 'bad', and 'nothing', but no event can make you feel that way – only your judgments and fears can do that. Ultimately, then, it is your belief that either strengthens or undoes each of these ego storylines.

1. 'I'm Not Good Enough'

Clive was a young, single, 29-year-old bank manager. He was five minutes late for our first appointment.

'I'm so sorry, Mr. Holden. It really isn't good enough,' he said. Not being good enough was the story of Clive's life. He was born into a poor family with barely enough to go around. There was never enough clothes, food or money, but they managed just fine.

Clive's family comprised a mother, father, older brother and younger sister. Dad wasn't home enough; he was always working. Clive's older brother, David, sounded like an absolute superstar. The way Clive described David, I was surprised he wasn't Managing Director of planet Earth by now. Clive always felt he was in David's shadow while growing up. Being the middle child, he felt he never really got enough attention.

Clive told me that his school years were okay but nothing special. He got good grades, but not good enough to go to the university he wanted. He had a few good friends and liked sports but was never good enough to make it his living. He was quite shy, particularly around girls. He played violin for a national youth orchestra but had stopped playing. He felt that his parents had never really given him enough encouragement for anything.

Clive finally found work at a local bank. He had obviously done very well at his job, judging by the number of rapid promotions he got. He didn't really see it that way, though. To him, he'd done all right, but he could have done better. Clive was obviously very competitive. He supported the underdog in everything. His confidence was low, but it was improving.

'I'm getting there,' he told me. Behind Clive's mild-mannered exterior, there was a perfectionist dictating the play. He denied this, however.

Clive had originally come to see me for some therapy to boost his confidence. I suggested to him that I probably wouldn't be able to do a good enough job unless we took a look at one thought he'd expressed – 'I'm not good enough.' Together, we looked at how this single thought had shaped Clive's personal story – that is, his history. I explained to Clive that until he was willing to change his mind about himself, his life would always fall short of being 'good enough'.

The inner taunt of 'I'm not good enough' is, if we're honest, a common experience. Both consciously and unconsciously, we're constantly haunted by doubts and fears that who we are, what we have, and what we do is 'not enough'. As a consequence, we wander the globe in search of a treasure called 'enough'. Sometimes we find what looks like 'enough', only to end up disappointed and let down. The fact is, we will always be disappointed until we change our mind about our Self.

> **Nothing is ever enough
> if you determine that *you* are not enough.**

How do you know if 'I'm not good enough' is running through your personal story? There are many signs, which include:

- You actually tell yourself, 'I'm not good enough.'

- According to you, your best is never quite good enough.

- You demand perfection of yourself, but you don't think you ever achieve it.

- You believe you never get enough approval or recognition from others.

- You compare yourself unfavourably to everyone who matters to you.

- You don't think your self-esteem is as high as others'.

- Envy and jealousy abound.

- Physically, you think you're not tall enough, not short enough, not light enough, not heavy enough, not pretty enough, and so on.

- Mentally, you think you're not intelligent enough, creative enough or clever enough.

- You consistently dismiss and overlook your personal successes and good fortune.

- Your needs, compared to others', aren't important enough to be shared.

- You never have enough of anything – money, time, rest – whatever.

- You attract people into your life who make you feel 'not good enough'.

- Deep down you believe that you have no right to your place in the world.

- You overachieve in an effort to prove to others and yourself that you're good enough.

2. 'I'm Wrong'

I had a client, Susan, who had convinced herself she was 'wrong'. Susan believed, for instance, that she was an 'unwanted child'. She also believed that she was the wrong sex because her parents had always wanted a son and had never had one. Susan told me she was originally supposed to be called Angela, but her mother determined that she wasn't pretty enough to be an 'angel', so she was called Susan instead.

Both her mother and her father were unloving towards her. She felt that they made each other unhappy and that they weren't suited to each other. Her father was a stern man who continually punished her for getting 'everything wrong'. Susan described her entire life as a catalogue of mistakes, accidents and disasters, with everything always 'going wrong'.

Now, in her early 40s, Susan felt very lonely and depressed. She described herself as a 'misfit'. She had never married ('I never found Mr. Right!'). As a young adult she was very rebellious, and she often mixed with the wrong people. Now she was just keeping to herself. Also, she always apologised for herself and had become very cynical. 'Everything always goes wrong,' she said.

Susan's sessions with me centred on forgiveness. She was angry at her mother, her father and, most of all, herself. This unresolved anger perpetuated her story of 'I'm wrong.'

'I know you've been encouraged to think you're "wrong" and "not enough", but this isn't true,' I explained. Over time, Susan began to understand that her belief of 'I'm wrong' was a self-fulfilling prophecy. 'Wrong decisions are made by people who believe in wrong decisions,' I told her. Susan learned to change her mind about herself.

Common signs of the 'I'm wrong' ego storyline include:

- You often tell yourself, 'I'm wrong.'

- You're afraid of getting things wrong.

- You believe things will always go wrong, and then they do.

- You feel cursed.

- You feel that you're a misfit.

- You feel like an impostor.

- You feel misunderstood, believing that people take what you say 'the wrong way'.

- You feel very uncomfortable when things appear to be going really well.

- You fear that everything is your fault.

- You feel like the black sheep – in the wrong family and the wrong place.

- You're convinced that you're living in the wrong time and on the wrong planet! Nowhere feels like home.

- Your theme song is: 'If There's a Wrong Way to Do It!'

- You're clumsy and make a lot of mistakes.

- In relationships, you're attracted to 'Mr. or Ms. Wrong.'

- When things are 'going right', you worry about what can 'go wrong'.

- You overcompensate by insisting that you're always right and never wrong.

3. 'I'm Bad'

Our greatest fear is that our core is rotten. The ego, or conditioned self, has learned to believe not only that 'everything good is outside', but also that 'everything bad must be inside'. The fear of 'I'm bad' is a vicious rumour that tries to convince you that not only did Adam eat a bad apple, but that *you are that bad apple*. We prefer not to look within our Self, just in case this rumour holds some truth. Hence, the rumour lives on.

The 'I'm bad' ego storyline can take many twists and turns. It gives rise to much superstition replete with devils, demons and dangerous, angry gods. Bad dreams, bad experiences and bad endings are common, for as long as we believe that we may be 'bad', our life must inevitably reflect this. Once again, if we change our minds about ourselves, we will change our life experience.

Common signs of an 'I'm bad' ego storyline include:

- You often tell yourself, 'I'm no good.'

- The best you feel is 'not bad'.

- Your life is constantly in a 'bad spot'.

- People treat you badly.

- You treat yourself even worse.

- You were a 'naughty' child.

- You are a rebel with a 'bad attitude'.

- You have 'bad days' when your mood is very dark.

- You are always in somebody's 'bad graces'.

- Someone is always in *your* 'bad graces'.

- You feel guilty about everything.

- You believe that you're a sinner.

- You commit crimes and do 'bad' things.

- You have an aversion to any type of criticism.

- You're attracted to people who are 'bad' for you.

- You never commit to anyone because you fear 'bad endings'.

- You believe all good things must come to an end.

- You over-compensate by always having to 'do good' and 'be good', whether you like it or not.

4. 'I'm Nothing'

All of your fears about being 'wrong', 'bad', and 'not good enough' are 'nothing' in that they are not the truth about you. They are a lie. They only feel like 'something' because of the power you give to them. Withdraw this power, and 'nothing' of these fears is left, for they're illusions. The ego is 'nothing,' and it's not surprising, therefore, that the ego's greatest fear is 'I'm nothing.'

The 'I'm nothing' ego storyline is based on a fear that if you don't become 'somebody,' you'll end up a 'nobody.' According to this storyline, there is no unconditioned Self. You have no substance, no spiritual Self. It's because you believe this that when you look for your spiritual Self you find 'nothing.' This is also the reason why when you pray and meditate, 'nothing happens' and you 'feel nothing.' As you change your mind, you'll change your experience.

Common signs of the 'I'm nothing' ego storyline include:

- You often tell yourself, 'I'm nothing.'

- Whatever you feel, 'It's nothing.'

- You feel like 'a nobody'.

- Growing up, you were the invisible child.

- You fear that your life will 'amount to nothing'.

- You feel that 'nothing much' happens in your life.

- 'Nothing' ever works out the way you hope it will.

- You often get depressed.

- You often feel overlooked.

- You believe that 'nothing and nobody' can ever help you.

- There is no God and there is 'nothing' to believe in.

- You often feel like a doormat.

- You attract people who make you feel 'like nothing'.

- You have no time for yourself.

- You dream of being a 'somebody'.

- You overcompensate by always being an exhibitionist, very public, and always getting noticed.

'I'm wrong', 'I'm bad', 'I'm nothing' and 'I'm not good enough' are four common storylines that have emerged from the thinking of your ego, or conditioned self. These storylines, and others, all reflect the ego's fundamental fear of lack, guilt and unworthiness. No matter how strongly you've learned to identify with these storylines, the fact remains, they're untrue, and . . .

you are not your ego!

Can You Forgive Yourself?

Forgiveness is the choice for wholeness.

Many times in your life you may have felt 'not good enough', but it's a mistake to say, 'I'm not good enough.' Similarly, it's one thing to judge a behaviour as 'not good enough', but it's quite another to judge *yourself* as 'not good enough'. Accordingly, you may think you get things wrong, but it's a mistake to say 'I am wrong.' You may judge a decision as 'bad,' but it's a mistake to say, 'I am bad'; and although you may appear to have 'nothing', it's a mistake to say 'I am nothing.'

You cannot be a victim and be happy. You cannot judge, criticise and berate your Self and be happy. You may judge that you've made mistakes in your past, but they are *not* your identity. No matter how many mistakes you think you've made, *you are not your mistakes*. To be happy, you have to know that this is true.

To be truly happy, you must be willing to give up the story of your ego. In other words, you have to be willing to give up your identity with the self 'that has been wronged', 'that did not get the love', 'that doesn't feel good enough', 'that grew up poor', 'that was once abused', 'that is unlucky', 'that always has to fight', 'that was unpopular', 'that was bullied', 'that failed at something', 'that is a slow learner', 'that nothing good ever happens to', 'that gets everything wrong', 'that is shy', 'that was once rejected', and so on. These experiences do not define who you really are.

The process for undoing your self-judgment, self-doubt and self-hatred (that is, your ego conditioning) is *forgiveness*. Most often, when we talk about forgiveness we talk about 'doing' something to someone else. The forgiveness I'm speaking of is quite different and much more personal.[9] For me, true forgiveness is a self-healing process that starts with you and gradually extends to everyone else. In essence . . .

true forgiveness is a willingness to change your mind about your Self.

Forgiveness is the process of giving up your limited self-concept for your whole Self. The willingness to forgive yourself is really the willingness to replace thoughts of fear with thoughts of love, thoughts of condemnation with thoughts of kindness, thoughts of doubt with thoughts of trust. Forgiveness is transformational – it gives you back you wholeness in exchange for all your learned fears. The unconditioned Self is remembered as you forgive yourself for all your fearful self-doubts and self-judgments.

What will you value more – the story of your ego, or the story of your unconditioned Self? Forgiveness is like a cosmic eraser that rubs out the pencil marks the ego has drawn upon your mind. Forgiveness works in the present. It teaches you that (1) you are not the pain of your past, and (2) the pain of your past is over now. Ultimately, *forgiveness undoes illusions of weakness and limitation; through forgiveness you become whole and joyous once more.*

With forgiveness, you choose to forget your conditioning and remember the truth about your unconditioned Self.

Forgiveness leads to enlightenment – that is, reclaiming your inner Light.

Who is the 'Light of the World' if it's not you? Through forgiveness, you wipe away your fears, you undo your doubts, and you wash away all darkness to reveal the Light of your unconditioned Self once more. *Forgiveness gives you back your freedom.*

The following process is a typical example of a forgiveness meditation used at The Happiness Project. Take a moment to be still and to sit with this process as you read it either out loud or quietly within your mind. This process will allow you to relax, and release and let go of your fears. It offers you a chance to forgive yourself for the times you've attacked, criticised and judged your Self.

Breathe freely, and allow each inhalation and exhalation to be easy, effortless and natural. As you read, take a moment to pause and to breathe fully after each sentence.

'I forgive myself for all the times I have been so hard on myself.'
'I forgive myself for all the times I have condemned myself.'
'I forgive myself for all the times I have been cruel and unkind to myself in any way.'
'I forgive myself for all the times I have criticised and betrayed myself.'

'I forgive myself for all the times I have told myself that I'm not good enough.'
'I forgive myself for all the times I have told myself that I'm wrong.'
'I forgive myself for all the times I have told myself that I'm bad.'
'I forgive myself for all the times I have told myself that I'm nothing.'

'I forgive myself for being afraid.'
'I forgive myself for feeling unworthy.'
'I forgive myself for all my judgments.'
'I forgive myself for all my mistakes.'

'Through forgiveness, I am ready to remember the truth about my Self, no matter how beautiful it is.'
'Through forgiveness, I am ready to remember the truth about my Self, no matter how wonderful it is.'
'Through forgiveness, I am ready to love and trust again.'
'Through forgiveness, I am ready to trust in love again.'

'I am willing, now, to accept I am not my fears.'

'I am willing, now, to accept I am not unworthy.'
'I am willing, now, to accept I am not guilty.'
'I am willing, now, to accept I am free.'

'Through forgiveness, I am free to enjoy love.'
'Through forgiveness, I am free to enjoy peace.'
'Through forgiveness, I am free to enjoy happiness.'
'Through forgiveness, I am free to enjoy my Self.'

'I am willing, now, to forgive and be free.'
'I am willing, now, to forgive and be happy.'
'I am willing, now, to forgive and be free.'
'I am willing, now, to forgive and be happy.'

❖ ❖ ❖

CHAPTER FOUR

Practising Acceptance

In the early days of The Laughter Clinic, I designed a wealth of exercises and techniques called 'Creative-Growth Games', which helped to cultivate a greater awareness and acceptance of joy and happiness.[1] Many of these games were made up quite spontaneously and are still used to this day in The Happiness Project. The following involves three of these games.

One afternoon at the clinic, I gave the participants a creative-growth game for homework called *Happy Days*. The challenge of this exercise is to dedicate one day a month to one's own personal nourishment, wellbeing and happiness. When asked for further information, I suggested that people might want to use this time to be kind to themselves, to rest, to have an adventure, to try something new, or simply to practise gratitude. Everyone loved the idea, and there was a sense of real excitement as people went home.

One month later, I asked the group to share their experiences of *Happy Days*. A rather awkward silence followed. It turned out that not one of 30 people had given themselves a *Happy Day*. A 'lack of time' seemed to be the chief obstacle. A whole day of happiness on top of a career, housework, the children, grocery shopping and gardening was asking a little too much.

Not to be deterred, I came up with another exercise for homework called *Happy Hour*. 'Once a week, I would like you to take one hour – a *Happy Hour* – to nourish yourself with love, treats and kindness. I want you to feed your spiritual bank account,' I said. The next week, I suggested we begin with a round-up of *Happy Hours*. More silence. No one had done the exercise. Once again 'lack of time' was cited, and also 'too much to do', 'the children,' 'I forgot', and 'I was too tired to do anything.'

'I have a new exercise for you,' I said. 'It's called *An Ecstatic 60 Seconds!* The challenge of this game is to give yourself one minute a day to stop everything and simply *be happy.*'

'What can you do in just one minute?' someone asked.

'You can smell a flower, smile for no reason, say thank you for something, breathe in peace, recite a favourite prayer, say an affirmation like "I accept happiness easily, effortlessly and naturally," massage your head, whatever you like,' I suggested.

One week later – you've probably guessed by now – I learned that not one single person had been able to enjoy *An Ecstatic 60 Seconds* for each of the seven days since we last met. Some had managed one or two brief bouts of joy, but that was all. When I asked why this was the case, many of the participants tried to convince me that *An Ecstatic 60 Seconds* isn't always practical, and that some days are much better suited to it than others.

This series of events was a turning point for me in my work. It really showed me in no uncertain terms that . . .

lack of time is never a real obstacle to happiness.

Life has certainly been speeding up. That I acknowledge. Do you remember, for instance, how as a young teenager your summer holiday felt like an eternity? Those six weeks or so were an absolute lifetime! And do you remember how, when you were four or five years old, every day felt like it went on and on? Something obviously happens to us when we hit 21 – it's as if life goes on fast-forward, and all of a sudden the months go by like the weeks used to, and the weeks go by like the days used to.

For many of us, life is faster than ever, we're busier than ever and we work longer hours than ever. We live our lives on the run – juggling duties, meeting responsibilities, always waiting in a queue for something, paying the bills, catching up on our 'to do' lists, and so on. We're in a race against time. Time is precious, so we 'buy time', 'steal time', and 'make time', but still . . . 'time flies'. No matter what we do, it appears that we're simply too busy to be happy.

The question is, though, how much time does it really take to *be happy?* Happiness is of the moment – it is timeless – and, therefore, each of us surely has time enough to be happy. I suggest that . . .

> **it takes as much time to be happy as it
> does to be depressed or resentful.**

Happiness requires no extra time. In fact, it requires no time at all. As I've already stated, happiness waits on welcome, not on time. The exercise *An Ecstatic 60 Seconds* proved to me beyond a doubt that 'lack of time' is not an authentic obstacle to happiness. 'Lack of time' is a smokescreen – it hides the real obstacle, the only obstacle – to accepting happiness now.

Happiness and Self-Acceptance

A little bit of pleasure every now and then – an occasional 60 seconds of joy – is for most of us quite acceptable and much appreciated. After all, it more than makes up for the work, the toil, the suffering and the sacrifice that went before. We're comfortable with life's little pleasures; we're less comfortable, however, with prolonged happiness, full-blown joy and everlasting bliss.

Ask yourself, 'How much happiness can I really handle?' One hour, perhaps? A week, a month, a year, a lifetime? For how long can you live with happiness and joy before you begin to question and doubt what is happening? For how long can you completely accept being peaceful before you become restless and anxious? For how long can you unconditionally enjoy someone's love and attention before you grow uncomfortable? For how long can you accept and trust the feeling of complete freedom, before you decide it must end?

The real issue isn't time; it's acceptance and, in particular, Self-acceptance. Happiness and Self-acceptance go hand in hand. In fact, your level of Self-acceptance determines your level of happiness. The more Self-acceptance you have, the more happiness you'll allow yourself to accept, receive and enjoy. In other words . . .

> ### you enjoy as much happiness as
> ### you believe you're worthy of.

Happiness is natural, easy and effortless when your Self-acceptance is high, but happiness is blasphemous when your Self-acceptance is low. When you feel low, you dream of being happy, but you also secretly fear that maybe you're not worthy of happiness, so you question, doubt, resist, test, defend against, overlook and push away invitations to be happy.

To withhold Self-acceptance is to judge that you're not worthy of happiness. You cannot, however, have low Self-acceptance *and* happiness. To persist with a judgment of unworthiness and also accept happiness is too much of a contradiction – one that will leave you feeling guilty. How can you accept happiness and also believe that you don't deserve it?

You attract what you believe you deserve. Thus, not only do you enjoy as much happiness as you believe you are worthy of, but . . .

> ### you suffer as much pain as you
> ### believe you're worthy of.

Self-acceptance (that is, Self-worth) is the key to both happiness and unhappiness. If you can accept yourself as whole, worthy and well, then happiness is natural and acceptable to you. If, however, you judge yourself as 'not good enough', then you're not good enough for happiness. Indeed, for as long as you judge that you're 'not good enough', you must always throw happiness off for fear of guilt.

Happiness and the Guilt Thing

The most popularly attended workshop at The Happiness Project is called *How to Be So Happy You Almost Feel Guilty, but Not Quite!* This should come as no surprise to you, for the greatest obstacle to accepting happiness is our guilt, and we have plenty of it.

What is guilt? Well, simply put, *guilt is the belief that you do not deserve happiness.* It is the belief that you are 'not good enough', 'wrong', 'bad', and 'nothing'. This belief is learned. It is not natural to your unconditioned Self. It is a thought of lack, and all thoughts of lack belong to the ego – that part of you that hopes for happiness but ultimately has learned to believe that you're not really worthy of it.

We long for happiness, but we also judge that we're far too guilty to accept it. We like the idea of happiness; it feels good. But we also fear that maybe it's selfish, wrong, inappropriate and that it comes with a hidden cost. We've learned to believe that happiness demands a payback – some suffering, labour or sacrifice, perhaps. Guilt isn't just about happiness, however. Have you noticed, for instance, that . . .

> **whatever you most desire is what**
> **you feel most guilty about!**

The ego feels guilty about happiness because it feels guilty about *everything*, particularly nice things. Take pleasure, for instance. Pleasure is happiness of the body; it is enjoyment of the senses. Pleasure is about beautiful colours, rich aromas, wonderful music, a healing touch and exotic tastes. We've also learned to believe, however, that pleasure is of the devil.[2]

Somehow we've learned to believe that pleasure is 'so good it's a sin'. We fear that too much pleasure can kill off all morals, subvert all virtues and ruin all values. All by itself, pleasure can, apparently, lead to hedonism, laziness, selfishness, anarchy, war, damnation, the end of the world and the downfall of the government!

Sex is pleasure. The idea that sex is natural, good fun and healthy sounds really great, very logical, objective and mature, but most of us still feel 'guilty as hell' talking about 'you know what'. Personally, I still vividly remember how all through my teenage years I felt absolute angst about the 'nudge-nudge, wink-wink' issue. In particular, I remember the agony of visiting the chemist to buy condoms. My planning was military. I used to think days ahead. Most often I would pick a drugstore out of town, where nobody knew me. Also, the cashier could not look like my mum, my dad or my biology teacher. Attractive women cashiers were also to be avoided at all costs!

I eventually lost count of how many times I visited the pharmacy to buy condoms, only to leave with yet another tube of toothpaste. Please don't judge me too harshly. Remember, I'm English, and my conditioning has been most thorough. Indeed, to the rest of the world, the idea that the English actually reproduce sexually is completely unbelievable! Our secrecy betrays our shame.

Sex, 'in the biblical sense', was apparently what got us all into trouble in the first place. If Adam hadn't got all hot and bothered about Eve, maybe we would still be whole and worthy of happiness. Religion and mythology teach us to be guilty about sex. For young boys, this guilt is forever reinforced, particularly at bath time when parents impart such wisdom as 'Play with it and it will fall off' and 'Do that again and you'll go blind.' Young girls go through something similar, I'm told.

We've learned to feel guilty about everything we like. Food is 'naughty, but nice'. Money is the 'root of all evil'. Peace and rest are dangerous, for 'the devil makes use of idle hands'. Laughter 'will end in tears'. Success will ruin you. Indeed, our learned response to success and happiness has many parallels. For instance, have you ever experienced 'fraud guilt', the belief that your success is really a mistake and that you don't deserve it?

The real test is to find something you're not guilty about. Guilt is so widespread, however, that I would have to say that . . .

> **guilt is not so much an emotion –**
> **it is more a way of life.**

Guilt is a way of life built upon a conditioned belief of *unworthiness*.[3] For as long as you judge yourself to be *unworthy,* you will never be able to freely accept happiness. You will attempt to bargain, barter, pay for and exchange happiness for something less pleasant, but even then, without Self-acceptance, happiness will feel uncomfortable.

Self-acceptance and happiness are both impossible while you believe in guilt – that is, that you do not deserve happiness. If you replace the phrase 'Self-acceptance and happiness' with 'Self-acceptance *is* happiness', then maybe you'll see more clearly how important it is to let go of guilt. Ultimately, letting go of guilt is undoing the ego.

Undoing Your Ego

Our world is littered with man-made myths, superstitions and stories of creation that tell tall tales of our descent from heaven, our fall from grace and our separation from God. According to these myths, Creation did not really begin with Light, but with *guilt* and *unworthiness*.

The mythologies of Egypt, Greece, Rome, Scandinavia, the Celtic Lands and the Bible are full of fearful stories – ego nightmares – of drunken, sex-crazed, violent gods full of anger and disdain for their creations. The story of Adam and Eve and their rejection from Eden is well known, for instance. Another story, from Egypt, tells how humans were first born as fish inside the tear of an angry and disillusioned god; the tear dropped to earth and formed the oceans.[4]

The Christian tradition reflects a confusion that exists in many other major religious and philosophical traditions. On the one hand, there are Christians who believe in a God of Love and who believe in man's *original blessing* – that is, that you and I are, in essence, whole, worthy and well.[5] On the other hand, there are Christians who ask God to bless bombs, who fear God's vengeance and who believe in original sin – that is, that you and I are guilty.

The Catholic Church is known to many as 'The Guilty Church'. I remember one ex-client of mine, a Catholic, who once told me, 'I know I'm guilty – I just don't know what I'm guilty of.' Guilt is not exclusive, however, to Catholics, contrary to what some Catholics might think. The Jewish faith is riddled with guilt. The Hindus have their 'karma'. The Muslims are constantly atoning. Guilt is quite clearly non-denominational!

I remember giving a talk called *How to Be So Happy You Almost Feel Guilty, but Not Quite!* to a group of orthodox Christians. We met in a village hall, in the middle of the countryside, on a dark, wet and windy winter evening. In summing up the great teachings of Jesus Christ, I reminded my audience how Jesus himself said, 'These things have I spoken unto you, that my joy might remain in you, and that your joy might be complete.'[6] I also mentioned how the Bible speaks of the 'joy of thy Lord', of 'joy [as] the fruit of the spirit' and of heaven as 'a kingdom of joy'.

My audience appeared to enjoy these references, and the young priest who had invited me especially enjoyed them. The old priest looked quite stern, however. I went on to remind my audience that Jesus also said, 'You are the Light of the World'[7] and 'Ye are Gods.'[8] I talked of original blessing and of the idea that heaven and Eden are really the unconditioned Self in all of us. The audience looked to the old priest for guidance.

Next, I suggested that the best way to accept the joy of God is to stop defining yourself as a 'sinner' and accept your role as the 'Light of the World'. At this point, *all hell broke loose*. 'It is because I am a sinner, that I know I will one day be happy with God,' said the old priest.

I replied, 'It is because I know you are *not* a sinner that you can be happy with God right now.' The applause was somewhat muted at the end of my talk!

From an early age, then, we're encouraged to think that our essence is not love, but guilt. We're taught strange ideas such as:

- Guilt is natural.
- Guilt is good.
- It's bad to feel not guilty.
- Without guilt, anarchy rules.
- Guilt makes you act 'good'.
- Guilt shows that you care.
- Guilt shows that you're sorry.
- Guilt stops you from sinning.

Of course, the reason we sin so much – that is, act up and play 'bad' – is because we feel so guilty in the first place. Guilt begets guilt.

Guilt cannot take you to love, peace, or happiness.

In our childhood, our parents sang hymns of guilt to us, such as 'Now look what you've done', 'You should be ashamed of yourself', 'We're very disappointed in you', and 'How could you do this to us?' Other great hymns of guilt include, 'Do you know how much we've sacrificed for you?' 'You are *so* selfish', 'You'll be the death of me', and 'You'll send me to my grave.'

Children are quick learners. We made up some good hymns of guilt, too, such as 'It's so unfair', 'You don't love me', 'Why can't we have one, too?' 'We never go anywhere', and 'Please, just this once.'

At school we're told by our teachers: 'What would your mum say?' At church we're reprimanded with 'What would God think?' At Christmastime we're interrogated with 'Have you really been a good boy all year?' At work, our boss gives us another 'Whatever you do, don't screw up' pep talk; and back in the apparent safety of our own home, our lover tells us, 'You never take me out' and 'You don't love me.'

You can begin to undo your ego and let go of your conditioning right now if you can accept and adhere to a most fundamental key to happiness:

**You cannot teach others that they're guilty
if you're to be free of guilt yourself.**

It's important to understand that, on the level of consciousness, thoughts are never given away; they're always shared. Therefore, if you teach others that they should be guilty, you're simultaneously teaching yourself that you should be guilty, too. Also, when you judge someone as unworthy of happiness, you are in that very same instant telling yourself that *you* are also unworthy.

The reverse of this principle is that every time you affirm others' goodness, their inner light, their original blessing, their innocence, you're affirming these qualities for yourself, also. The truth is, either we're all free or none of us is. You can't buy your freedom at anyone else's expense. Happiness would have you commit to the idea that you are, in essence, not guilty and neither is anyone else.

You Don't Deserve Happiness

The following story is one I often tell at The Happiness Project:

There once was a monk who travelled from village to village, smiling. His name was Ananda, which translated means 'joy' or 'bliss'. He had no home, no money, and no possessions to speak of. He wore a saffron robe, some beads, and a wonderful smile that he gave away to everyone he met. So warm, so loving and so infectious was his smile that everyone else would also smile in his presence.

One day the monk met a boy, also called Ananda. The boy walked beside the monk along a winding path. He asked the monk, 'Are you a holy man?'

The monk smiled. 'I am as holy as you are.'

The boy smiled. 'Why do you not own anything?' he asked.

'My smile is my own,' the monk replied.

'But what about money, a home, a horse?' asked the boy.

'The world cannot give me my smile – my smile is between me and God,' said the monk.

The boy and the monk walked along in silence. Eventually the boy asked, 'Who are you, monk?'

'I am the smile that went around the world,' explained the monk, 'and my gospel is a gospel of smiles.'

'Do you always smile?' asked the boy.

'Yes, even when I'm asleep,' laughed the monk.

'How do you manage to smile always?' asked the boy.

'Smiling is easy because I believe in happiness, and I also believe in you,' replied the monk.

Now the monk and the boy were both smiling.

This story illustrates two very important points. First, if you are to be happy, you must accept your holiness, or, if you like, your *wholeness*. In other words . . .

if you are to accept happiness, you must believe in your Self!

To be happy, you must be willing to accept that you are created perfectly whole, and that you're not, therefore, fundamentally guilty, lacking or unworthy. You may make mistakes, but you're not a sinner. As you learn to love and forgive yourself for your fearful beliefs and self-judgments, you automatically connect consciously once more to the everlasting joy of your unconditioned Self.

Second . . .

if you are to be happy, you must believe in happiness.

The monk, Ananda, could afford to smile all day long because he believed that happiness is natural to him *and to everyone else*. He saw happiness as a natural experience, not a peak experience. For Ananda, there was no mountain to climb, no sacrifice to make, no work to do in order to be happy. He simply chose to be happy. He had no 'happychondria' and he was also perfectly Self-accepting.

Again and again I've witnessed how our fearful limiting beliefs about happiness deny us our natural *right* to happiness, and also cause us so much extra suffering. The most damaging erroneous belief about happiness is, of course, that *happiness is somewhere else* – that is, it is not with you. After that, the next most painful and limiting belief about it is that *happiness has to be deserved*.

The belief that *happiness has to be deserved* has led to centuries of pain, guilt and deception. So firmly have we clung to this single, illusory belief that we've almost forgotten the real truth about happiness. So busy are we trying to *deserve* happiness that we no longer have much time for ideas such as: *Happiness is natural, happiness is a birthright, happiness is free, happiness is a choice, happiness is within* and *happiness is being*. The moment you believe that happiness has to be deserved, you must toil for evermore.

One of my clients, Jenny, once illustrated perfectly how many of us feel about happiness:

> 'Everything feels so pointless,' she told me.
> 'How do you mean?' I asked.
> Jenny sighed. 'Well, no matter how hard I try to be happy, I get absolutely nowhere. I feel so frustrated, Robert, because I've done so much hard work on myself.'
> 'You sound angry,' I observed.
> 'No, I'm depressed *and* angry!' We both smiled, and then Jenny began to cry. 'I feel so doomed,' she said. 'I feel as if I'm being punished.'
> I asked her, 'Do you believe that you deserve to be happy?'
> 'Probably not,' she replied.

Ask yourself now: 'Do I deserve to be happy?' Be careful how you answer this question, however, for there's a catch. If you answer *no,* then no matter what you do, you will, like Jenny, not accept much happiness. If you answer *yes,* then you're subscribing to the idea that happiness must be deserved and you will, therefore, have to fulfill all sorts of criteria (set by you) before you can be happy. Both *no* and *yes* are dishonest answers. The point is . . .

you do not *deserve* happiness!

This is not a message of gloom; it is a message of hope! One of the greatest single steps you can take to happiness now is to let go of the belief that happiness has to be deserved. You do not *deserve* happiness, you *choose* happiness. Happiness is natural. It is freely available to all. It is unconditional. And when you're unconditional about happiness, then happiness merely happens! *Happiness happens, if you let it.*

The belief that happiness has to be deserved has no power, other than the power you give to it. The problem is, you've learned to give it a lot of power. This single thought not only reinforces your belief in guilt and unworthiness, but it also contributes to almost every other major fearful belief about happiness. It contributes, in particular, to the work ethic, the suffering ethic, and the martyr ethic – three ethics heavily endorsed by our society.

From an early age, we are all spoon-fed beliefs about how important it is to work for happiness, suffer for happiness and sacrifice for happiness. Generation after generation, this fearful and thoughtless conditioning is handed down in much the same way that physical weaknesses and ailments are handed down through the genes. The good news, however, is that . . .

it takes only one loving belief to undo an entire belief system based on fear.

Changing your fearful beliefs about happiness, particularly the belief that happiness has to be deserved, requires absolutely no labour, suffering or sacrifice on your behalf. It merely takes willingness: (1) the willingness to see that you're not unworthy and guilty, (2) the willingness to let go of your conditioned beliefs about happiness, and (3) the willingness to accept that happiness is natural to your unconditioned Self. Willingness is the key.

Healing the Work Ethic

According to the work ethic, happiness is not natural – happiness is a pay cheque you earn for putting in the hours. The work ethic is one of the most dominant ethics of our world.[9] When I refer to the work ethic here, I'm not talking about the *joy of work;* I'm talking about the compulsive *need to work*. Work and more work is the key to happiness, according to the work ethic. And if that doesn't work, try even more work. The work ethic supports the pursuit of happiness, and it states quite categorically: *Happiness will not happen unless you work for it.*

There are, in particular, four erroneous and fearful beliefs about happiness that help make up the work ethic:

1. Happiness has to be deserved.
2. Happiness has to be worked for.
3. Happiness has to be earned.
4. Happiness has to be paid for.

The work ethic is all about labour – birth is labour, life is labour, love is labour, happiness is labour, work is labour and death is rest. We labour, not for the joy of it, but because we've learned to believe we must. The purpose of the work ethic is to work hard so as to atone for your guilt and unworthiness and thereby 'deserve happiness' once more.

'Workaholism' is endemic, and for many of us our life is governed entirely by work. Once upon a time, we worked to live; now, we live to work. Any 'life' we do have is merely recovery from work. We work, recover from work and then work again. We go to the office to work. After work, we bring some work home with us. For rest, we go to the gym for a workout. Totally exhausted, we go to therapy to work through our problems – 'I've done a lot of work on myself,' we say. After all that, there's the housework! Finally, we go to bed, too tired to be happy, but our mind is still working and we can't sleep. No problem. Insomnia is a wonderful chance to get more work done!

The work ethic is motivated by the belief that anything worthwhile requires great work, effort and labour. According to the work ethic – creativity isn't inspiration, it's perspiration; love is a labour, not a joy; success is a marathon, it never comes easily; health is about a 'no pain, no gain' attitude; salvation is hardest of all – it is a wrestling match with the angels, just ask Jacob. Nothing comes easily, according to the work ethic.

Has it ever occurred to you that . . .

you're trying too hard to be happy?

Thich Nhat Hanh, the Vietnamese Buddhist author and teacher, offers a beautiful lesson to the world through his ministry of peace and Self-acceptance. He encourages us to continually give up trying to be happy and simply be happy. He writes:

> Do we need to make a special effort to enjoy the beauty of the blue sky? Do we have to practise to be able to enjoy it? No, we just enjoy it. Each second, each minute of our lives can be like this. Wherever we are, any time, we have the capacity to enjoy the sunshine, the presence of each other, even the sensation of our breathing. We don't need to go to China to enjoy the blue sky. We don't have to travel into the future to enjoy our breathing. We can be in touch with these things right now.[10]

We're too busy working to be happy, to actually be happy. In the last ten years, the average working week has increased by more than 10 hours to nearly 50 hours a week; the lunch break faces extinction; six out of ten men and four out of ten women work on Saturdays; Sundays are also a workday for many. To cap it off, when we dare to leave the office at 5 P.M., there's always one sad, brainless colleague who shouts out, 'Part-timer!' or 'Only doing a half day?' Guilt ensues.[11]

As a society, we spend more and more time as a *human doing* and less and less as a *human being*. Indeed, the work ethic despises rest and play. We hardly ever go out to play any more; instead we go for cardiovascular workouts, business lunches and corporate away days. According to the work ethic, rest is 'downtime' – nothing useful is happening. Too much rest and you lose your edge!

If you're resting, you're not achieving. This is a worry because . . .

the work ethic thinks of happiness as an achievement and not as a natural way of being.

The thinking that promotes the work ethic fails to appreciate the idea that happiness is free. According to the work ethic, life is about achievement and so too is happiness. The work ethic is ego-driven, for it is only the ego that believes that your Self-worth is zero without achievement. We suffer, therefore, from an *achiever fever,* which is essentially the desire to achieve *anything* so that we can feel good about ourselves and thereby deserve happiness.

Let me be clear – work itself isn't the problem. On the contrary, work can be a marvellous opportunity to serve, to develop skills, to be creative, to meet people, to travel and to grow. What I'm really referring to is the addiction to work; and, in particular, *an addiction to the belief that you have to work, earn, deserve and pay for happiness.*

How do you know if you're 'suffering' from the belief that you have to work for happiness? Here are some telltale signs:

- You believe that happiness isn't natural; it has to be deserved.

- You believe people must earn happiness; it isn't freely given.

- You believe that all happiness has a price.

- Your life is a never-ending 'to do' list.

- Your reward for completing a 'to do' list is to make another 'to do' list.

- You're lost without something to do. Without achievement, you're nothing.

- You can't relax. In fact, you believe that relaxation 'makes' you feel guilty.

- People who only do one thing at a time are, in your opinion, underachievers.

- You think exhaustion is a weakness and a failure.

- You feel far too guilty to take all of your holiday from work.

- You feel you must keep busy, you must fill every moment, and there's always more you could be doing.

- You suffer from 'hurry sickness' – there's never enough time for you to do everything.

- What you achieve is never good enough.

- Your friends don't ask 'How are you?' They ask 'Are you keeping busy?'

- At the end of a day of work, you don't get on with your life; you merely *recover* from work.

- You'd like to sleep in on Sunday mornings, but you get too restless.

- You only take time off work to be ill, and even then you manage to get a bit of work done.

- You feel guilty if you have too much fun.

- You're suspicious of good times, success and things that flow easily.

- You have no friends, only work colleagues.

- You have 'really great friends' whom you never get to see.

- Time with the family is, strictly speaking, time away from work.

- You promise your children more time soon . . . one day . . . maybe next week.

A few years ago, a good friend of mine, Graham Taylor-Chilton, suggested we play a game of golf together. 'It will have to be during the week,' he said. I'd been working hard, too hard, and I needed a rest. I was a non-confessed workaholic, and so I did the 'sensible' and 'mature' thing and turned him down once, twice, three times. The harder I worked, the more exhausted I became and the less I achieved. Finally, common sense (that is, my wife!) prevailed. I agreed to play.

I remember how, on the drive over to the golf course, I felt so guilty about taking time off in the middle of the week. I got stuck in traffic, I got lost, I arrived late, I was edgy all day, the weather wasn't great; I kept thinking about work, and I played poorly. *What a waste of time,* I thought. Now I felt even more guilty.

When I got home, I told my wife about my day. 'Something's not right,' I said to her. 'I'm probably the hardest-working person I know, so how come I give myself such a hard time for taking some time out?' The guilt had to be faced. So, I decided the best way to face the guilt was to arrange another round of golf with Graham for the most guilt-inducing time possible – Monday morning! I did it. And with the help of my friends, I continue to do it.

We work to pay off our guilt. The moment we stop working, we feel our guilt. So we start working again. The work ethic is a symbol not only of our guilt, but also of our confusion. In particular . . .

the work ethic confuses willingness with hard work.

Happiness only requires willingness, not hard work. In particular, it requires us to be willing to slow down, loaf, laze, relax, and be happy.[12] Just as the work ethic is about guilt, true willingness is about Self-acceptance – that is, the acceptance that (1) you're entitled to joy, and (2) joy is your unconditioned Self.

Healing the Suffering Ethic

My father brought my brother, David, and me up on suffering stories. Time and time again he took great pride in recounting how difficult and tough life was for him when he was as young as we were. He would repeat the same stories over and over again, and each time the suffering became more and more exaggerated!

Our father's face would light up when he told us his tales of hardship. In fact, the harder the suffering, the warmer his nostalgia would glow. The 'School Story', as it was affectionately known in our family, finally went something like this:

> We were so poor that we had to walk to school every single day. We couldn't afford a car; we couldn't even afford the bus fare. I had to walk six miles there and back, come rain or shine. I had only one pair of shoes, with no soles. I had only one set of school clothes in seven years, and even they were hand-me-downs.
>
> I never missed a day of school, ever. Even when I had a temperature of 108, I'd still go. You had to go or you were flogged. At school, we always behaved ourselves. If you didn't behave, you were punished and beaten. We also remembered everything our teachers told us or we had our knuckles rapped.
>
> With not a penny to our name, I had to share books, pencils, pens, ink even. Books were a luxury in my day. We worked in the cold – central heating hadn't even been invented. Food was one meal a day. And at Christmas we

were lucky if we got an orange and some nuts – there were no computer games in my day.

Other great lines I remember were: 'We had to clean the house twice for a penny', and 'Anything less than a B+ and we had to mow the sports field for a week.' Strange as it may sound, both David and I would say that some of the happiest moments of our childhood were spent laughing with Dad as he told us his suffering stories.

The suffering ethic is born of our perceptions of guilt and unworthiness. Like the work ethic, the suffering ethic teaches us that happiness isn't free; it has to be deserved. It indoctrinates us into believing that suffering is the path to happiness and all good things. Moreover, it dictates that happiness without suffering has no real value or integrity. This is, of course, absolute nonsense. While it's certainly true that we can learn from our suffering and thereby become happier; it's not true to say that we have to suffer first in order to be happy. The unconditional truth is that . . .

you do not have to know suffering in order to be happy.

And yet, the suffering ethic would try to convince you that suffering is a prerequisite for happiness. This ethic also insists that you cannot know love until it is lost; you cannot enjoy peace without conflict first; you must fail in order to succeed; you must be weak before you can be strong; and you must fall before you find real faith. The truth is, however, that peace of mind needs no conflict to define it, love needs no fear to define it, and joy needs no suffering to define it.[13]

Many people are heavily invested in suffering because they believe that suffering makes you a great person. Nothing could be further from the truth.

Suffering happens, but suffering doesn't make you a great person.

Suffering does happen, and it's regrettable that it does. All of us have suffered disappointment, loss, pain, failure, rejection, bereavement, and so on. In no way am I trying to belittle this suffering, but what I'm saying is that *no amount of suffering adds to your greatness*. Your Self-worth was established in the heavens the moment you were created. Your worth comes, therefore, from who you are, not what you've suffered.

As I've already mentioned, it was at my Stress Busters Clinic that I first noticed how people would pit their illnesses and sufferings against one another in a sad attempt to get more love, more attention, more anything. Often, the first step to healing is to understand that no amount of war wounds increases your innate worth. In other words . . .

> **you have to relinquish your identity as a**
> **'sufferer', a 'victim', or an 'ex-addict' in**
> **'recovery' if you're going to be happy.**

These days I notice more and more how people introduce themselves with their illnesses. Within the first few minutes of introduction, we often hear something about recovery, therapy, Prozac, codependence, life coaching, nicotine patches, emotional hang-ups, and just exactly why 'life's a bitch'. Moments after shaking hands, we hear 'I'm in recovery', 'I'm a depressive', 'I'm an agoraphobic', and so on. We never call ourselves 'ex-broken-arm patients', but it seems the fashion these days to announce: 'I am a sober alcoholic'.

Very recently, I counselled a young woman, Sarah, who had travelled from Russia to see me. She is 25 years old, tall, willowy, very thin, and for the past ten years she has experienced bulimia. The most poignant moment of our time together came when I asked Sarah a very upfront question, which was: 'Would you be able, Sarah, to stop calling yourself a bulimic?' Sarah's whole body shook at the very thought. 'I know you experience bulimia, but can you see that bulimia is not who you are?' I asked.

Sarah responded wonderfully well to this challenge. I somehow knew she would. 'I'm scared,' she said, 'but I can see what you mean. It's just that I don't know who I am or what I am without bulimia.'

I reassured Sarah as best as I could. I told her, 'I know you've suffered greatly, but I hope you can see that this suffering doesn't define you or your Self-worth. Beneath your fears, your tears and your suffering, your happiness still waits for you. Your happiness is perfectly intact, and you're still completely whole. The joy of your unconditioned Self awaits your welcome.'

Sarah smiled.

Two weeks after our meeting, I received a letter from Sarah which reads, verbatim:

> *Dear Robert, Thank You. Thank You. Thank You. You are the first person in ten years who has not treated me as a bulimic. You treated me as a whole person. I found this puzzling at first. I even resented you a little for it. But I am coming around to the idea. For the first time in a long time, I can see myself without bulimia. This thought is scary and exciting. Let's look at that thought next time we meet. I'll call soon. With love and gratitude, Sarah.*

The suffering ethic pins its hopes on the idea that suffering is both a suitable atonement for your unworthiness, and an adequate payment for happiness. The great hope is that 'X' amounts of suffering will earn, pay for, buy or help you deserve 'Y' amounts of happiness. The truth is, though, that . . .

no amount of suffering can buy you any amount of happiness.

Happiness cannot be bought because happiness is free. Also, there's no exchange rate between happiness and suffering. Suffering cannot be traded in for happiness. Similarly, no amount of pain, hurt, guilt, sacrifice, bad luck, hard work, tragedy, disaster or crucifixion can buy you an ounce of happiness. Happiness is not deserved. Happiness is free – there is no escape from this freedom!

How do you know if you are 'suffering' from the belief that you must suffer to be happy? Here are some telltale signs:

- You subscribe to the belief of 'no pain, no gain'.

- You believe that nothing valuable can be gained without suffering.

- You mistrust gifts that aren't earned by suffering – that is, 'Easy come, easy go.'

- You believe that there's no such thing as a free lunch – everything has a cost.

- You suffer a lot of ill health.

- If there's a hard way to do it, you'll find it.

- No one is harder on you than you are.

- You withhold praise because you believe that praise leads to complacency.

- You like to think of yourself as head of the class in the 'school of hard knocks'.

- Comfort, wealth, and luxury 'make you' feel uneasy and guilty.

- You're an inverted snob, always attacking people who have a comfortable life.

- Less suffering equals less self-worth.

- You think you're a 'real' man or woman because you continue to suffer.

- Life's a bitch and then you die. Ain't that the truth?

- You convince yourself that you're better than anyone who hasn't suffered as much as you have.

- You truly think that no one has suffered as much as you have.

- You confuse love with sympathy – suffering gets you sympathy.

- You're a 'drama queen or king' – if there's no drama, you're uneasy.

- Pain is your only learning curve.

- You confuse passion with abuse – all your romantic relationships are a struggle.

- Too much comfort causes too much guilt.

- You hope if you suffer enough, God will feel so guilty that He'll grant you leniency.

- You like to strive, but to thrive would increase the guilt factor too much.

- There must always be an enemy somewhere.

- You're always fighting and struggling against some-one or something.

- You have a blind spot with respect to easy options – you always make everything difficult.

- You believe you have to fight for what you want, so you get into a lot of fights!

- You like to compare scars.

Another major misperception of the suffering ethic is the idea that suffering brings enlightenment. On the contrary, it's not suffering that brings about enlightenment . . .

**it's the decision to *give up*
suffering that *brings about* enlightenment.**

Many of the world's religious and philosophical traditions have tried to promote suffering as a legitimate spiritual path that can buy you something. In particular, the teachings of Christianity have often been distorted to encourage you to suffer for your happiness. Medieval Christianity, in particular, was very severe when it came to happiness, officially denouncing laughter as 'the song of the devil' and attacking happiness as a threat to monastic self-control.

The image of Jesus suffering on the cross is known the world over. Very rarely, however, do you see any pictures of a resurrected Jesus Christ. This obvious imbalance prompted me, a few years ago, to start a new collection of pictures depicting Jesus laughing, smiling, and happy. I have quite a few now.

Whenever I'm passing by a Christian bookshop or church, I always ask if there are any pictures of a happy Jesus. Never could I have anticipated the responses I often get. Many times I'm greeted with such aghast looks of shock, horror and disdain, it's as if I'd just asked, 'Have you any pictures of Jesus picking his nose?' Jesus was *joy-full!* Think about it – no one would follow a morbid or miserable Messiah.

Christians often argue for misery. One old argument is that you should be careful not to laugh or smile too much because nowhere in the Bible is there any mention of Jesus laughing and smiling. My response to this is that nowhere in the Bible is there any mention of Jesus brushing his teeth, buying birthday presents or ordering pizza, but that doesn't mean *we* shouldn't do these things. And anyway, there are enough references to joy in the Bible to keep everyone happy. In one version of Ecclesiastes, for instance, it is written: *'Do not abandon yourself to sorrow, do not torment yourself with brooding. Gladness of heart is life to a man, joy is what gives him length of days . . . Beguile your cares, console your heart, chase sorrow away; for sorrow has been the ruin of many, and is of no use to anybody.'*

The only value suffering has is that it points out that you're running low on happiness. The function of suffering is, therefore, to remind you to choose happiness, choose love, choose healing, choose forgiveness, choose laughter and choose freedom. Thus, the most helpful response to suffering is to use suffering as a chance to hit the 're-set' button in your life, and commit once again to what is truly important.

To be happy, you must value joy more than pain. You will also want to remind yourself again and again that *suffering cannot buy me happiness.* Your ego believes that suffering somehow atones for guilt, but, in truth, guilt isn't real; it's learned. If you can believe this, for yourself and everyone, you will be free of suffering.

Healing the Martyr Ethic

Happiness is made to be shared.

The martyr ethic is built upon a number of erroneous and fearful beliefs about happiness, the major one being that *happiness is selfish.* Another great fear of happiness to the practicing martyr is that *my happiness denies others their happiness.* In other words, it appears to the martyr that there isn't enough happiness to go around. Other fears of happiness for the martyr include: *Happiness leads to conceit, my happiness has no value to others,* and *being happy is inconsiderate in a world where there is suffering.*

The fear that *happiness is selfish* is not only untrue, it actually couldn't be further from the truth. Psychology researchers find time and time again that it is the depressed people, and not the happy ones, who are intensely self-focused and self-absorbed. Happy people, by contrast, tend to be outgoing, sociable, generous, loving, and kind. They're also more tolerant, forgiving, and less judgmental than people who are depressed.[14]

The martyr ethic confuses genuine happiness with hedonism, trivial pleasure-seeking, greed, arrogance, boastfulness, swaggering and pretentiousness. It overlooks the fact that *the basis of true happiness is love.* And like love . . .

> **the first impulse of true happiness is to share itself;
> happiness is not selfish.**

I remember reading an interview about a woman who had lived as a hermit for ten years in the wilderness in South America. At one point in the interview she was asked, 'Were you ever lonely?'

'Yes,' she replied, 'I used to get very lonely. Not when I was down, but when I was happy because I had no one to share my happiness with.'

True happiness is never selfish.

The history of martyrdom began with good intentions. The original goal of the martyr was to give up the 'ego' so as to remember the 'spiritual Self'. Spiritual martyrdom was, therefore, originally about giving up illusions of lack, guilt and separateness. It was not about loss, but about wholeness.

Many of the spiritual traditions of the world promote muddled messages about martyrdom. Indeed, ego-martyrdom (as opposed to Spiritual martyrdom) is all about struggle, suffering and sacrifice. For this reason, it's nearly impossible to be a saint and be happy in the Christian tradition. The great hope of ego-martyrdom is that enough sacrifice will buy happiness. As with the suffering ethic, though, the truth is that . . .

> **no amount of sacrifice will buy
> you any amount of happiness.**

True happiness asks you to sacrifice one idea – the idea that you must sacrifice something real to be happy. True happiness is, therefore, not really about sacrifice; it is about Self-acceptance – the acceptance that you're not guilty and that you're created whole, worthy and well.

I once counselled a lady named Joy (her real name) who came to see me from London over several weeks. Joy was in her 40s, an artist, recently divorced, trying to turn over a new leaf in her life, and, in her own words, 'a depressive'. Joy was brought up Roman Catholic. She'd gone to school in a convent where she was taught the 'value' of sacrifice and martyrdom.

'Sacrifice was the primary teaching of the convent,' she told me. 'We were all taught we were sinners and that penance and sacrifice was all we were good for.'

'How did you sacrifice?' I asked.

'We had to take cold showers daily to mortify the flesh; we had to open windows in winter; we had to skip dinners; we had to sleep without pillows; we had to give up anything we enjoyed . . .' The list went on and on. 'And because I wanted to be good, I became the best martyr I could, but it was never, ever enough,' said Joy.

Joy noticed that every time she attempted to be happy, it appeared as if the universe conspired to make her miserable. 'Recently, I tried to go for an aromatherapy massage for the first time in my life,' she told me. 'I felt so guilty, so wrong, but I wanted to do it. But when I got there, the aromatherapist was ill and she had gone home. Her colleague told me she has never been ill before.'

Joy went on to tell me, 'Last week, I decided to go to an opera, as I've never done anything like that. Just as I arrived, there was a bomb scare and the performance was cancelled. Earlier this year, I went on my first holiday for 20 years, and I got ill and spent the next two weeks in the hospital.'

I suggested to Joy that all of these failed attempts at happiness were definitely not God's doing, they were definitely not the universe conspiring against her, and they were definitely not coincidences. Joy's story was too similar to the martyr's story to be coincidental. 'I know this might be a stretch for you, Joy,' I said, 'but until you give up your belief in the value of martyrdom, I think you will attract even more disappointments like this into your life.'

'You mean they're not coincidences?' she asked.

'No,' I explained. 'They are effects – effects created by your ardent belief in your guilt and the need for sacrifice.'

Step by step, we began to challenge all of Joy's learned beliefs about her own *guilt* and *unworthiness*. She had to change her mind about herself before she could change the way her life was going. 'You've learned about lack and sacrifice,' I told her, 'and now we must learn again about wholeness and joy, for Joy is your name, is it not?'

Joy keeps in touch every now and then, and she continues to make good progress.

Most martyrs are 'kill-joys', although they would deny this heavily. Martyrs are so afraid of 'any happiness' that they tend to put the dampers on anyone being 'too happy'. Happiness is a major dilemma to anyone who believes in martyrdom because *you cannot be happy and guilty*. A martyr must decide, therefore, what he or she values most – happiness or guilt?

Martyrdom stems from *guilt* and *unworthiness,* and it inevitably ends in *guilt* and *unworthiness*. Most martyrs end up very unhappy because they feel that they never get the sympathy they think they deserve. Also, most martyrs end up very manipulative, using their own guilt to levy guilt upon others. Martyrs learn to adjust to disappointment and loss, and although they may dream of joy and happiness, they feel very uncomfortable about receiving any. This is because . . .

to a martyr, to receive is a sign of the devil.

One very common symptom of the martyrdom ethic that you may notice in yourself is that every time you receive a compliment, a present or any gift of love, you're tempted to recoil. Learning to accept, receive and say 'Thank you' is quite a skill. The fear of martyrdom is that 'happiness makes you selfish', but, ironically, it is martyrdom that often leads to selfishness because (1) a martyr denies people the chance to give to them, and (2) you cannot give freely that which you do not accept freely.

Martyrdom is so wrapped up in illusions of guilt that it overlooks a most important truth:

***Your* happiness is your gift to the world.**

Jane was 28 years old, a single parent who lived in a block of flats, supported financially by social welfare. She had diligently followed her 'penance plan' for happiness, and along the way she'd lost sight of happiness altogether. She was a classic martyr who had been brought up with the classic martyr teaching of 'a woman's work is never done'. She felt she was a second-class citizen who didn't know how to ask for her own needs. 'And when I'm with people,' she said, 'I can't just relax. I have to be useful to them, always helping and always trying to please them.'

The turning point for Jane came when I was able to point out to her that every time she abused and neglected herself, her young baby would cry, get ill and be unhappy. Jane saw the link immediately. Within a few days, she said to me, 'I get it. I have to be nice to me, because when I'm nice to me, my family gets the benefit, too.'

'Yes,' I told her.

'So happiness isn't selfish. Happiness is okay,' she said.

In truth, your happiness is more than okay. Your happiness is also a great gift. It is a total inspiration, a wonderful example, and a great service to the world. Your happiness contributes so much more to the world than your suffering. By choosing to be happy, you are being the 'Light of the World'. At The Happiness Project, we celebrate the idea of happiness as a gift in this statement:

It is because the world is so full of suffering,
that your happiness is a gift.
It is because the world is so full of poverty,
that your wealth is a gift.
It is because the world is so unfriendly,
that your smile is a gift.
It is because the world is so full of war,
that your peace of mind is a gift.
It is because the world is in such despair,
that your hope and optimism is a gift.
It is because the world is so afraid,
that your love is a gift.

❖ ❖ ❖

CHAPTER FIVE

Living Unconditionally

Happiness is free – there are no conditions.

One of my clients, Annabel, was much too wrapped up in self-improvement to be happy. Annabel was in her 40s, a mother of two, divorced, a 'fitness fanatic', a 'health-food gourmet', and a 'self-improvement nut'. In fact, she once told me that she lived 'for self-improvement'. Annabel had even made a career out of it. She was the author of several books in that genre, and she'd made many appearances on radio and TV.

I came to learn that Annabel's description of herself as a 'self-improvement nut' was entirely accurate. Every day began with meditation, affirmations, a health shake for breakfast and a power walk. Each week her basic routine included acupuncture for energy, a deep-tissue massage and ongoing therapy. She also read at least two self-help books a week. Her best friend was her fitness trainer, and she called herself a 'workshop junkie' because she attended every self-improvement seminar in town.

Such was Annabel's dedication to improving herself that it clearly came as a shock to her when I suggested that . . .

to be happy, you have to give up self-improvement.

Annabel's ardent desire to improve herself was motivated not by joy but by guilt, the belief that she wasn't already worthy of happiness. I explained to her that until she changed her mind about herself (that is, gave up her guilt) no amount of self-improvement would bring her any real, lasting peace of mind.

Annabel listened intently. 'I suppose I'm living proof that self-improvement can't make you truly happy,' she said.

I replied, 'I'm not asking you to give up trying to improve your life, your career, your health or your skills, but what I'm asking you to see is that true happiness demands no self-improvement, no special conditions, no intelligence test, no financial status, no elaborate sacrifice . . . no nothing. Happiness is freely available, always, everywhere to everyone.'

I told Annabel that her story was very similar to my own. In particular, I shared with her a 'severe case of life' I experienced the day after my 30th birthday. This 'severe case of life' proved to be the catalyst for another major turning point in my life, for it was at this time that I finally decided to give up self-improvement once and for all.

My 30th birthday 'ended in tears'. The celebrations that I had enjoyed enormously were abruptly and rudely interrupted by a soundtrack in my mind that was playing well-rehearsed anthems and marching songs, like, 'You're good enough', 'You could do better', 'You could have done more', and 'You've done nothing with your life'. My ego just had to have its say.

I remember I was halfway through another chorus of 'You've done nothing with your life', when I suddenly stopped the song and yelled out loud, 'Why do I still feel so awful?!' As I scanned a period of 12 years, I estimated that I'd read more than 200 self-help books (some of them several times), listened to nearly a hundred self-improvement talks, attended countless workshops, performed thousands of affirmations, meditated for up to five hours a day, prayed constantly, and so on.

As I continued to add up all my efforts on behalf of improving myself, it occurred to me that if I'd put the same amount of work and dedication into something physical, like bodybuilding, I would probably be 'Mr. Biceps of the Universe' by now! In fact, I reckoned that I'd be so muscle-clad that I would have to walk through doors sideways. Why, then, if I'd done so much, did I feel that there was still so much more to be done?

Tears rolled down my cheeks. I felt utterly broken. I prayed for help. An inner dialogue began almost immediately, and with it a new awareness dawned. I realised, for first time, that . . .

no amount of self-improvement
can make up for a lack of Self-acceptance.

Happiness doesn't demand self-improvement; it asks only for unconditional Self-acceptance – that is, the willingness to accept that your unconditioned Self is whole, happy and well already. In other words, *while self-improvement is the ego's greatest hope for happiness, Self-acceptance is, ultimately, giving up the ego* – that is, giving up your learned beliefs in inner lack.

Here, then, is your essential choice: (1) Improve your ego; or (2) let go of your ego and accept your Self – your whole, unconditioned Self. As of my 30th birthday, The Happiness Project has offered no more courses on self-improvement. We no longer encourage people to believe that they first have to prove or improve themselves in order to qualify for happiness. Instead, we help people give up self-improvement with a small 's' for a greater practice of Self-acceptance with a capital 'S'.

Self-acceptance is the key to the treasures of the kingdom, the kingdom of your unconditioned Self. I often use the following meditation at The Happiness Project. It reads:

Without Self-acceptance, peace is impossible; with Self-acceptance, peace is yours.
Without Self-acceptance, love has to wait; with Self-acceptance, love is made welcome.
Without Self-acceptance, there is no happiness; with

Self-acceptance, you know happiness.
Without Self-acceptance, truth hurts; with Self-
acceptance, truth heals.
Without Self-acceptance, you can accept no one fully
into your life; with Self-acceptance, you can.
Without Self-acceptance, you are always hiding; with
Self-acceptance, your spirit is gliding.
Without Self-acceptance, nothing is enough; with Self-
acceptance, you are enough.
Without Self-acceptance, you are not free to grow; with
Self-acceptance, your potential is free to flow.
Without Self-acceptance, there is no chance; with Self-
acceptance, you always have a chance.

Being Happy, Doing Nothing

The following story is asking you what has to happen –
according to you – before you let yourself be happy:

It was a beautiful, hot, lazy summer day and Billy was
fishing by the river. After a while, a stranger in a suit and
tie walked by. 'How are you doing?' asked the stranger.

'Being happy, doing nothing,' Billy replied.

'Catch any fish?' asked the stranger.

Billy hadn't stopped to count. 'Maybe ten, but I let
them all go back in again,' said Billy.

'Ten fish! Why, you should have kept them and sold
them,' said the stranger.

'Why?' asked Billy.

'You could have made a profit, and then invested that
profit in a better rod.'

'Why do I need a better rod?' asked Billy.

'Well, with a better rod you could catch more fish.'

'Why would I want more fish?' asked Billy.

'Well, more fish equals more profit, and with more
profit you could have your own refrigerated truck,' said
the stranger.

'But I like it here, just being happy, doing nothing,' said Billy.

'Okay, but with a great big truck you could make even more profit,' said the stranger.

'And then what?' asked Billy.

'Who knows? You could, with enough hard work, end up opening your own fish restaurant one day!' said the stranger.

'And what then?' asked Billy.

'Well, by then, you'd be so rich you could come fishing here whenever you liked!' said the stranger.

'Aren't I doing that already?' smiled Billy.

The fishing is a symbol for simply being.[1] Billy is your unconditioned Self, completely relaxed and happy . . . being, doing nothing. The stranger, in suit and tie, is the ego – the little voice that tells you that before you can simply be happy, you absolutely must, ought and should toil and struggle.

When Self-acceptance gives way to self-improvement, you often end up denying yourself happiness now because you believe there are certain conditions that first 'must', 'ought', and 'should' be met. In this way . . .

you make yourself miserable by your constant demands of 'must', 'ought' and 'should'.

The unconditioned Self makes no demands for happiness – it is unconditional. The ego-mind, convinced of its own lack, performs once again like a megalomaniac sports coach, shouting out a long list of 'musts', 'oughts' and 'shoulds' that it believes 'must' be met before you can be happy.

For example, the judgment 'I'm not good enough' spawns 'shoulds' like 'I should do more'; the belief that 'I'm bad' fuels 'musts' like 'I must always be good'; the thought that 'I'm wrong' leads to 'oughts' like 'I ought to get everything right'; and a fear that 'I'm nothing' creates 'shoulds' like 'I should do something.' The lists are never-ending.

Cognitive psychology has been particularly effective in identifying the highly irrational and illusory thinking of the ego,
which makes up the 'musts', 'oughts' and 'shoulds'.[2] Albert Ellis,
the founder of Rational Emotive Behaviour Therapy, deliberately
pokes fun at this ego-thinking by referring to it as 'musterbation'.[3]
Laughter is wonderful at helping to dissolve and let go of learned
fears.

Common examples of 'musterbation' include:

- 'To be happy, I must be liked by everyone.'
- 'To be happy, I must always be right.'
- 'To be happy, I must always be good.'
- 'To be happy, I must always be in control.'
- 'To be happy, I must be treated fairly by everyone.'
- 'To be happy, I must deserve it.'
- 'To be happy, I must work for it.'
- 'To be happy, I must never get angry.'
- 'To be happy, I must be perfect.'
- 'To be happy, I must always be on time.'
- 'To be happy, I must never let down my guard.'
- 'To be happy, I must hide my feelings.'
- 'To be happy, I must never be vulnerable.'

You may find it helpful to make a list of the 'musts', 'oughts'
and 'shoulds' you've invented for yourself. Some of your 'musterbation' may be so set that it has become unconscious and auto-
matic. This is when the 'musts', 'oughts' and 'shoulds' feel more
like universal laws than personal illusions. You do yourself a service every time you . . .

> **uncover, let go of, and smile at your
> 'oughtism' – remember, happiness is free!**

The ego saves most of its judgment, condemnation, 'oughtism'
and self-improvement for the body. Every day is a war against cellulite, grey hair, split ends, wrinkles, love handles, sagging breasts,
beer bellies, calories, and acne. How can you be happy when your

cholesterol is high?! Again and again the ego tries to prop up its fragile happiness with cosmetic surgery, sensuality boosts, face masks and high-energy workouts.

The ego's regime includes the following 'oughtism' and 'musterbation':

- 'To be happy, I must weigh less.'
- 'To be happy, I must weigh more.'
- 'To be happy, I should develop more muscle tone.'
- 'To be happy, I should have a smaller stomach.'
- 'To be happy, I ought to exercise more.'
- 'To be happy, I shouldn't eat chocolate.'
- 'To be happy, I must get rid of cellulite.'
- 'To be happy, I must get a facelift.'
- 'To be happy, I must get another one.'
- 'To be happy, I should eat less.'
- 'To be happy, I should eat more.'
- 'To be happy, I ought to have bigger breasts.'
- 'To be happy, I ought to be at least a size 8.'

Over and over you promise yourself that after this last 'must', 'ought' or 'should', you will be completely happy forever. The trouble is, without Self-acceptance, there is no end to self-improvement and to 'oughtism'. The ego is addicted to 'oughtism' because it's also addicted to the idea that happiness requires perfect conditions. Furthermore, the ego, by its very nature, is never, ever satisfied. You cannot appease the ego; you can only let go of it.

The choice is, therefore, either that you try in vain to first take care of all your 'oughtism' and then be happy, or you just decide to be happy anyway! You can do this with Self-acceptance, the acceptance that happiness is free to you always.

Three 'Mirages' of the Ego!

> *'Joy is not a carrot.'*[4]
> – Linda Carpenter

Think of your ego as the White Rabbit in *Alice in Wonderland*, always late for a very important date, forever dashing, running and chasing after some imaginary carrot. The White Rabbit first makes its entrance by disturbing Alice's peace as she rests by the babbling brook. A lazy, timeless moment is shattered by the White Rabbit's hurry, flurry, panic and pandemonium.

How often do you catch yourself, like the White Rabbit, living life on the run? How often do you experience peace of mind, or a mind in pieces?

'Faster, faster!' cries the ego, convinced that everything good is outside, and equally convinced that something is missing on the inside. The inner peace of your unconditioned Self holds forever true. It can never be broken, but it can be overlooked.

Until you can accept that true happiness exists within you, you'll be forced to bounce around from place to place, searching the world in vain for some external replica. The ego pins all its hopes for happiness on three very vague goals: that of 'more', 'there', and 'next'. Happiness is possible, according to the ego, with 'a little bit more', when we 'get to there', and when we 'take the next step.' The point is, however, that . . .

**happiness requires no next step;
it is already here!**

Living life in the fast lane, we constantly overlook and fail to appreciate what we already have as we chase after 'more'; we sacrifice what is possible now for what we hope may come 'next'; and we throw away all that is available to us 'here' as we sprint over to 'there.' And yet, without Self-acceptance, the happiness of 'more', 'next', and 'there' fades just like a mirage fades before a thirsty traveller lost in the desert.

1. 'More'

Happiness – the more we chase it, the more it flees.

The 1980s was the decade of 'more', in which a 'ready, steady spend' society tried to buy happiness once and for all by acquiring more 'stuff'. The world became a giant department store, shopping became the number one national pastime, and rampant materialism offered apparent salvation. Suggestions that the 1990s gave birth to a post-materialistic age are premature, but it's true that more and more people are beginning to realise that . . .

more 'stuff' cannot buy you more happiness.

In recent years, more than 500 extensive pieces of psychology research have shown quite conclusively that, since the 1950s: (1) We have more things and more wealth than ever before; and (2) we are more depressed, more violent, more suicidal and more stressed than ever before.[5] The research indicates that 'more equals less' – that is, as we acquire more, we become more demanding and less satisfied.

'More' is the ego's promised land. 'More', or 'the Oliver Syndrome', as I affectionately call it, is the ego's hope that 'more stuff' will somehow magic a rabbit out of a hat and you'll be happy.[6] The ego is never satisfied, though – how can a thought of lack ever be satisfied? Clearly, we don't need more stuff; we do, however, need more Self-acceptance. We have to learn that although *more stuff can encourage you to be happy, more stuff cannot make you happy.* Zero peace of mind plus lots of 'things' will still leave you wanting more. Self-acceptance is the key. To put it another way . . .

'more' is never enough until you choose to be happy.

Do you remember how, ten years ago, you promised yourself that you'd be happy once you started earning what you do now? Are you happy now? Do you remember how you convinced yourself that your last promotion would make you happy? Are you? And now that you're more successful than, say, five years ago, are you more happy? And isn't it amazing how your most recent successes have seemed to create more work for you and not less?

What are you currently convincing yourself you need more of before you can be happy? What 'more' do you think you need to be good enough, happy and successful? Is it more money? Read the research! Maybe you're after more horsepower, one more qualification, more recognition, more cupboard space, more time, or maybe a home with one more bedroom? Whatever it is, the 'things' of this world are mere toys. They're great fun. Play with them all you like, but don't think for a moment that they *are* your happiness.

True happiness is unconditional – it requires nothing 'more' than itself to exist. No amount of 'more' can make you 'more happy'. Happiness is not consumed; it is chosen.[7]

2. 'Next'

Happiness is present time – it has nothing to do with the future.

At home, I have a very precious clock that was presented to me after I gave a talk at an annual conference for The LIFE Foundation. This clock is a 'now clock.' It is like any other clock, except that where there are normally the numbers 1 through to 12, there is simply the word 'now', 'now', 'now', 'now'. This clock helps me to keep the time! The demography of happiness, according to extensive psychology research, states that your 20s won't make you happy, your 30s won't make you happy, and neither will your 40s, 50s, 60s, 70s, or 110s! In other words, there's no special time, age, or stage of life that brings with it happiness.[8] In effect . . .

happiness has nothing to do with time;
it has everything to do with 'now'.

Contrary to popular belief, time does not heal, time does not fly, time does not do anything. Time has no consciousness. It does nothing for you. The key to happiness *now* is what you choose to do with your time right now. Are you, right now, making the most valuable use of your time? This moment is, after all, the time of your life. Your choices are what make each moment.

The White Rabbit in *Alice in Wonderland* carries a large clock so as to keep time. In his hurry to get to where he's going 'next', he repeatedly fails to look at the clock. Not only does he 'lose time', he also loses the moment. How often do you miss out on happiness *now* as you chase the clock? Are you really so sure that 'next' is really any better than 'now'?

Every day I make a point of slowing down my train of thought so as to appreciate the moment. 'Next' can wait for the moment. Now is here, and I want to give it my full attention. It's a funny thing, but time and time again I have found that . . .

> **the more you give to *now*,**
> **the more you get from *now*.**

With the help of my '*now* clock', I take the time to enjoy the moment. It doesn't take much to do this. Sometimes a deep, long, slow exhale is enough. A smile works well. 'Thank you' is prayerful. Wonder and awe also work well. When I'm outside and hear a bird sing, I stop to look for the bird. When I see a beautiful flower, I name the flower, greeting it as I would a dear friend. Happiness makes you eccentric like that!

The ego's goal of 'next' is in keeping with the ego's belief that *happiness is somewhere else*. It's all about living in the *not now*. I often catch myself living in the *not now*. In particular, when I sit down to eat lunch, often my first thought is not for the lunch, but 'what will we eat tonight'. Also, there's a member of my family, who shall remain nameless, who goes on holiday with bags full of brochures to plan her 'next' holiday!

The fantasy of 'next' often prevents you from giving your very best to *now*. We kid ourselves that happiness will happen soon and that we'll give our very best to the 'next time', the 'next job', and our 'next partner'. The truth is, however, if you don't change first, then 'next' will be no different from *now*. In other words . . .

> **time cannot make you happy; your attitude can.**

Until you can accept that happiness is about a choice and not a clock, then what comes 'next' will be no more helpful to you than what is here now. Time is not your answer. Consciousness, and the decision to be, are your answers. Time will not save you, but changing your mind about yourself can. Slow down a while, cease to hurry for a moment, and let the inner happiness bubble up. In this way, *now* becomes an ideal preparation for what comes 'next'.

> *'When from our better selves we have too long*
> *Been parted by the hurrying world, and droop,*
> *Sick of its business, of its pleasures tired*
> *How gracious, how benign, is Solitude.'*
> – William Wordsworth

3. 'There'

Happiness is a way of travelling, and not a final destination.

One of the biggest causes of stress in our society is that we've set happiness upon the horizon instead of in our heart. In doing so, we've tried to make happiness into a destination, a place, a point to arrive at, and a final sanctuary. All of a sudden, to be happy we have to travel across space and time to get 'there'.

I remember the first time I asked a group of people at the Laughter Clinic, 'What is happiness?' As we looked at each other's answers, mine included, we became aware that almost every answer involved long-distance travel! The answers included: 'Happiness is Miami Beach and a piña colada', 'Happiness is the stars', 'Happiness is a deserted island in the Indian Ocean', 'Happiness is a carnival in Brazil', and 'Happiness is Hawaii'.

The ego's goal of 'there', or the 'Greener Grass Fixation', as I call it, pins all your hopes of happiness, peace, love and salvation on geography. The point is . . .

geography can't make you happy.

Geography can certainly *help you* to be happy, but it cannot *make* you happy. And there's no amount of geography that can make up for a lack of Self-acceptance. Everywhere is hell while you feel like hell, but everywhere can also be heavenly when you feel whole and well inside.

New locations can certainly help inspire new thoughts, new perceptions and new beliefs. There are times, therefore, when it makes sense to change your location or job, for instance, in order to secure a fresh start. But because the world does no more than mirror your state of mind, 'there' will end up being just like 'here' if there is no more Self-acceptance.

Sometimes, as the French novelist Marcel Proust once wrote: 'The voyage of discovery lies not in finding new landscapes, but in having new eyes.'[10] To be happy, we must be willing to see things differently and to see ourselves differently. The ego, being a thought of lack, cannot see wholeness. Thus . . .

the ego has 'been there, done that' and it still ain't happy!

Can you give up the ego? In other words, are you willing to believe and to see that you are whole already, happy already, worthy already? Dare you entertain the possibility that you carry within you all the wonders that you search for outside of yourself? To the ego this sounds blasphemous, but to your unconditioned Self this is merely a natural way of thinking.

Laughing at the Cosmic Joke

What if you stopped searching for happiness?
And what if you then discovered you were already happy?

Before I reveal the cosmic joke, I'd like to share a piece of writing with you. It's called 'Question Time':

'Am I close, God?' pleaded the pilgrim.
'Close?' enquired God. 'What does "close" mean?'
'Close – near to you – towards the front of the
queue – chosen – special,' pleaded the pilgrim.
And God could not understand, and yet God
spoke, 'You are Me – You are as close to God
as You can get.'

'How soon, my Lord?' prayed the monk.
'Soon?' enquired God, 'What does "soon" mean?'
'Soon – quick – fast – how long to go before at
last I am One with you?' prayed the monk.
And God could not understand, and yet God
spoke, 'Nothing can happen sooner or later than
now. Is now soon enough for You?'

'Am I forgiven, Father?' begged the nun.
'I have heard this word many times,' said God.
'What does it mean?'
'Forgiven – loved – paid up – sins forgotten –
apologies accepted – in good standing,' begged
the nun.
God understood none of this, except for love,
and thus, He spoke, 'Love is what You are, and
all I know You by – nothing else is real.'

'Am I deserving?' the disciple asked.
'And what is this word, "deserving"?' enquired God.
'Deserving – good – worthy – in the money – a
bit of luck my way – well thought of by You,
God,' the disciple explained.
And God was puzzled once again, and yet
God heard Himself say, 'Whatever is worthy
of Me is worthy of You; anything unworthy of
Me is unworthy of You.'

'Will I be saved?' the priest called out.
'Oh dear,' God sighed. 'Here is another word
I understand not.'
'Saved – safe – protected – the lost and found
department – defended,' the priest cried out.
And God replied, 'Save your worries, save
your fears. You are saved because, in truth,
you were never lost – confused, I grant You –
but never lost!'

Beneath all the fearful, guilt0, and unwise dogmas that so pollute and stain the spiritual traditions of the world, there is, at heart, a rich untouched seam of joy, bliss, happiness and laughter, as typified by stories of the joyful Christ, the laughing Buddha, the playful Krishna, the singing angels, and others.[11] For us, also, beneath our own fear, guilt and pain, there is, at heart, a rich, untouched spirit of total joy that is constantly at play. Herein lies the cosmic joke.

Simply stated, the cosmic joke is really a touch of cosmic irony. All the great spiritual teachers, including Buddha, Jesus and Krishna, started out, like you and I, as searchers of happiness, love and God. When the truth was revealed to them, they laughed. They laughed for joy, and with relief, for their searching was finally over. They now understood that what they'd searched the world for was within them all along. In other words . . .

YOU ARE **what you seek!**

When the Zen master Po-chang was asked about seeking for the joy of the Buddha, he answered, 'It is much like riding an ox in search of an ox.' The Chinese philosopher Menicus, from the 4th century B.C., said, 'The Tao is near and people seek it far away.' An ancient African proverb on happiness states: 'Why tell animals living in the water to drink?' The 18th-century French writer Voltaire said, 'Paradise is where *I am*' – 'I *am*' being your unconditioned, universal Self. And, for good measure, the American humorist Josh Billings put it like this: 'If you ever find happiness by hunting for it, you will find it, as the old woman did her lost spectacles, safe on her own nose all the time.'[12]

Imagine how funny it would be if you were to overhear the mighty sun praying for light, the ocean praying for water, the wind praying for a breath of fresh air. Imagine, if you can, a dark sun, a dry ocean, a wind without air, and, for that matter, a universe cramped for space, eternity rushed, infinity feeling slightly hemmed in. And what could be funnier than you and me, made of joy, praying to God for more love and more happiness!

You are what you seek. The cosmic joke challenges you to give up your fears, your guilt, your conditioning and your doubts, and accept the truth about your unconditioned Self. You are not a body, you are not a fearful mind, you are not separate, you are not small – you are the Presence of Love, you are happiness incarnate, and peace of mind is always with you. True Self-acceptance is the realisation that . . .

the soul is joy!

Our greatest fear is that we are, at heart, wrong, bad and not good enough – the devil incarnate. The laughter of the cosmic joke is really relief that this nightmare of mistaken identity and confusion is not the truth. The laughing Buddha laughs because he can afford to. He knows he is safe and that we are all safe. To get the cosmic joke, though, you must be prepared to change your mind about yourself.

Another way of stating the real truth about you, according to the cosmic joke, is to say that . . .

> you are truly happy 100 per cent of the time;
> your only problem is that you are not
> always aware of this.

Yes! Amazing as it may sound, your happiness is with you 100 per cent of the time. The reason you do not always feel happy is because you let the sunshine of your spirit get eclipsed by clouds of fear, doubt, guilt, illusion and mistaken identity. In truth, you can afford to laugh, however, because no matter what happens to you in the world, your spirit is safe and sound in the heaven of your unconditioned Self. Happiness cannot leave its source!

When troubled, therefore, don't pray: 'God, grant me happiness!' 'God send me Your Love!' or 'God, give me peace!' Can you see how each of these prayers presupposes and reaffirms that what you want is not already with you? Instead pray, 'God, reveal to me my joy', 'God, heal my fear that Love is not here', or 'God, teach me to feel again my peace of mind.' Remember . . .

> **real prayer is not a cosmic DHL delivery**
> **service; real prayer is receiving that**
> **which is already given.**

The cosmic joke encourages you to laugh out loud at illusions of lack, guilt, and the false conditions and obstacles in the way of your salvation. That is what the poem 'Question Time' is all about. Your inner fears, if not healed, are always projected out onto that which you seek – that is, God, love and happiness. By letting go of your fears, all projections disappear, and only joy remains.

One of my favorite lines in *A Course in Miracles* is: 'God does not forgive because He has never condemned.' This is quite a brilliant insight. God is unconditional, and so too is love and happiness. Thus, the fears that happiness has to be worked for, suffered for and sacrificed for are truly laughable. Holy laughter pierces through all illusions.

Uncovering the 'Joy' of Happiness

When St. Francis of Assisi was asked by Brother Leo, 'What is perfect joy?' he replied with the following story:

> Imagine that I return to Perugia on the darkest of nights, a night so cold that everything is covered with snow, and the frost in the folds of my habit hits my legs and makes them bleed. Shrouded in snow and shivering

with cold, I arrive at the door of the friary, and after calling out for a long time, the brother porter gets up and asks:
'Who is it?'

And I respond: 'It is I, Brother Francis.'

The porter says: 'Be on your way. Now is not the time
to arrive at the friary. I will not open the door for you.'

I insist, and he answers: 'Be on your way right now.
You are stupid and an idiot. We are already many here and
we do not need you.'

I insist once more: 'For the love of God, let me in, just
for tonight.'

And he answers: 'Not even to talk. Go to the leper col-
ony that is nearby.'

'Well, Brother Leo, if after all this I do not lose patience
and remain calm, believe me, that is perfect joy!'[13]

What St. Francis was trying to teach Brother Leo was that true
happiness is unconditional in that it is ultimately unaffected by
the world. Joy is, ultimately, not of this world; it is quite clearly
very different to worldly pleasure and life satisfaction (see Table
C). Essentially put, pleasure and satisfaction are conditional ego-
states; joy is unconditional – there is no ego.

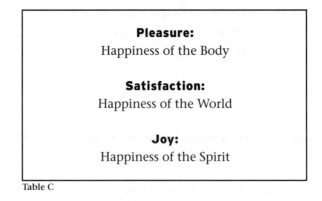

Pleasure:
Happiness of the Body

Satisfaction:
Happiness of the World

Joy:
Happiness of the Spirit

Table C

Pleasure is happiness of the body. It can be thrilling, warm, wet, fuzzy, funny, physical, sexual, exciting, deeply restful and highly arousing. Pleasure is sensual and highly transient in that it quickly comes and goes. Pleasure doesn't exist on its own – it must always have an external spark or stimulus, such as sound, aroma or touch. Pleasure is also non-universal – that is, the same stimulus does not elicit the same pleasure in everyone. For instance, I enjoy star-gazing, you may not; I listen to Barry Manilow songs, you may not; I like spicy foods, you may not; I appreciate the rich smell of farmyards, you may not; I adore the feel of silk, you may not.

Satisfaction is happiness of the world. It implies a mental judg-ment, usually favourable, about the 'contents' of the world around you. For instance, 'I'm happy because my house no longer leaks', or 'I'm happy because my body is the right shape', or 'I'm happy because my car is the right shape.'

Satisfaction always requires a because – that is, a reason. You're happy because you judge that 'this is good', 'this is okay', and 'this is right'. You're happy because the world looks a certain way – it fits your picture. This satisfaction with life is very fragile, though, for it hangs on how the world looks. Your contentment is threat-ened, therefore, each moment the world changes, and the world is changing each moment! Certainly, circumstances can help you to be happy, but it's a mistake to think that you need a precise form or a precise set of circumstances to make you happy.

Joy is happiness of the spirit. It is 'true happiness' in that it always stays true. This is the happiness that goes with you wher-ever you go. Whereas physical pleasures and life satisfaction are born and then die, joy is eternal and timeless – it is happiness *now*. This joy is inward, it is deeply intimate, a part of the fabric of your soul, and it is the amazing grace of your spirit. As such, it is constant.

This joy is natural. It is 100 per cent unconditional, non-judgmental and free. Wherever you go, there It is. It is not empty, It is full. It is Loving. It has consciousness. You can relate to It. You can ask It for guidance. You can ask It to shine Its Light upon your problems. You can sing to It, pray to It and dance with It. You can meditate on It. You can draw with It, write with It and heal with

It. You can ask It to bless your relationships, your life, your career, everything. *Let It be!*

Being Unreasonably Happy!

And all of a sudden I was out
of my mind;
And I lost my head;
And I forgot to remember;
And I could no longer make up
my mind.

And I was so unreasonable –
Happy, loving, ecstatic, for no
reason at all.
I smiled, I laughed, I loved, I
was generous for no reason
at all.
I sang, I danced. 'Hello,' I
cried.
I was happy – happy for no
reason at all.

And I was so thoughtless –
Free to fly without any thought
of fear at all.
Free to go without judgments,
plans or the need to know;
Free to live without any thought
of 'what if', 'watch out', or
'how so?'
I was really not myself.

And try as I might,
I still cannot think straight.
I have still not come to my senses.

Being sensible has lost its appeal.
I live, now, in a world of innocence,
And in no sense at all do I
regret the day
I gave way
And lived totally out of
control.

Can you remember a time in your life when you were happy for no reason at all? All of a sudden you were surprised by joy. It bubbled up as if from nowhere. Your smile was almost too big for your face, your heart wanted to leap out of your chest, and your whole body rang like a bell. 'I'm happy!' you cried. *I wonder why?* you thought. 'I must know why?' you demanded. And just then, the joy appeared to die.

Children are often happy without reason – it is part of their charm. Often you can catch a child laughing for the sheer joy of it, smiling for the sake of smiling, playing happily with happiness. It both amuses and saddens me to think that when a child laughs for no reason at all, we think it's wonderful, but when an adult laughs for no reason at all, we immediately fear for his or her health. The point is . . .

who ever said happiness needs a reason?

'Thoughtless', the poem above, describes my own experience of what I call 'joy', or 'unreasonable happiness'. Joy is unreasonable happiness in that it requires no reason, no stimulus, no special conditions, no controlled effort and no down payment. This joy is beyond time, beyond space and beyond this life we know; and yet it is fully alive, fully present, fully possible now. This can only be, however, if we accept that happiness is free.

There's an old joke I picked up at psychology school that goes like this: if a psychologist came across two doors, one saying 'Heaven' and the other saying 'Lecture on Heaven', the psychologist would walk through the door to the lecture!

Honestly, which door would you walk through? Maybe . . .

> **your greatest downfall is that you believe you**
> **have to understand happiness before you can be happy.**

Can you accept happiness unconditionally, without even understanding it? If you can, then happiness is yours unconditionally. Happiness is never grasped; it is simply let loose. In truth, happiness needs no reason. A smile needs no reason. Love needs no reason. Kindness needs no reason. There are gifts for free – life's true treasures. Can you cope with that?

Being Spontaneously Available

> *'The soul should always stand ajar, ready to*
> *welcome the ecstatic experience.'*
> – Emily Dickinson

My friends Tom and Linda Carpenter have taught me as much about happiness as anyone. They are dedicated teachers of *A Course in Miracles;* and they travel the world, quietly sharing their profound messages of love, truth and joy.[14] When they're not travelling, they live on a tropical flower farm on the Hawaiian island of Kauai.

Tom, Linda and I will sit and talk about truth, God and the universe for hours on end.[15] It is our joy to do so. I remember once asking Tom, 'What is happiness?' His answer moved me so deeply that it has since become a central principle of my work with The Happiness Project. He said:

> **'Happiness is being spontaneously available**
> **to your spirit.'**

Spontaneously available! What a beautiful phrase that is. The moment he said those words, it reminded me of a very famous story of a meeting between a Zen master and a distinguished university professor. The professor, who taught history and philosophy, had requested a meeting with the Zen master while travelling through Japan. The Zen master agreed to the meeting.

'I have come to learn from you what is truth,' said the professor.

'Would you like some tea?' said the master, who was smiling from ear to ear.

'Thank you,' said the professor. 'I have little time, but I am keen to learn all that I can.'

The master began to pour the tea.

'You see,' said the professor, 'my entire life has been a search for truth.'

The master continued to pour.

'That's plenty of tea, thank you.'

The master kept pouring.

'Master, the cup is overflowing – no more tea will go in.'

The master smiled. As he still poured, he said, 'My dear professor, like this cup, you are full of your own beliefs and theories. How can I show you Zen unless you first empty your cup?'

Think of the professor as a symbol of your ego, or conditioned self – full of plans, theories, beliefs and ideas about happiness. The Zen master is a symbol of the unconditioned Self, entirely empty of hypotheses and schemes. The master neither searches for happiness nor tries to understand it; he is simply happy. He's happy because he's spontaneously available to the joy of his unconditioned Self. *Spontaneous availability is full acceptance.*

Happiness isn't an intelligence test. You don't have to *understand* happiness before you can *be* happy. Indeed, you cannot understand happiness first. Rather, you must first choose to be happy, and only then will you understand. In other words, you cannot *think* your way to happiness. Happiness is not a formula of thought. If anything, happiness is the relinquishment of thoughts, theories and theses;

**to be happy, you have to give up all
concepts of happiness.**

This is particularly true if you're currently unhappy, for the thinking that makes you unhappy now cannot make you happy later. You have to be willing, therefore, to be spontaneously available to fresh insight, fresh wisdom and fresh inspiration. The message is: *Be fresh!* Now is new. It is not the past. Your mind is full of 'old tea', so you must first empty the cup – that is, be willing to let go of limited fears and ideas.

The mystics of old continually beckoned their students to give up concepts of God, love, heaven and joy. They explained that your thinking is at best like a finger that points to the moon, but it is *not* the moon. Stop pointing! Stop theorising! Be willing to be available to the joy of your soul. Say, 'I am available.' Affirm, 'I am available.' Sing, 'I am available.' Listen, be open, be clear, be empty. Take a leap! Jump for joy!

To the intellect, simply choosing to be happy isn't enough. It's a silly idea. Sometimes, though, the silly ideas are the best. When I was researching my book *Laughter, the Best Medicine,* I discovered that the word *silly* comes from the old European words 'seely' and 'saelig', both of which mean 'blessed', 'happy', and 'joyful'.[16] When you're silly, you're creative, open, fearless, and, above all, you are unconditioned.

When I asked Tom to expand on his idea of spontaneous availability, he reminded me of a phrase in *A Course in Miracles* that reads: 'A healed mind does not plan.' He then went on to say . . .

'Your plan for happiness will not work.'

Tom's teaching of spontaneous availability moved me deeply because I'm a 'recovering planner'. Ever since I can remember, I've lived my life to a plan. All through my 20s, in particular, I diligently followed my five-year plan, my three-year plan, my one-year plan, my one-month plan, my one-week plan, and my daily plan. My whole life was planned out. I was very focused, but I was also rigid, inflexible, unavailable and preoccupied. Have you heard the saying 'Life is what happens to you while you're busy making other plans'?

What Tom implies by 'your plan for happiness will not work' is that happiness requires no plan. If you think that happiness needs a plan, then your thinking is off. Happiness need not be planned for; it is here already. Sometimes, though, we're simply too busy planning our future happiness to enjoy happiness *now*. Can you let go of your plans and accept peace now, love now and joy now? Can you move past your conditioning and accept happiness unconditionally? Can you be spontaneously available?

You Only Live Once . . .

> *Your whole life is not in front of you – it is here – NOW!*

After years of studying stress, I've concluded that one of the biggest causes of stress is that we wait for happiness to happen. We think happiness is not for now; rather, we see it as a reward we work towards, struggle after and suffer for, in the hope that one day it will happen. Following this erroneous train of thought, today becomes a day for well-behaved hardship, noble suffering, mild martyrdom and quiet desperation, and tomorrow, maybe, we might be happy. I believe, however, that . . .

to be happy, you have to lose the 'wait problem'!

Conditions will get no better in the future for as long as you're waiting around to be happy. Indeed, it's only when you stop waiting that conditions begin to improve. I remember how all through my teenage years and early 20s I had this fantasy that life would get better in about 18 months' time or so. I remember how I used to think that I'd be less shy, more confident, more successful and probably world famous! I was convinced that something wonderful and special would happen to me.

I had nothing concrete to base these feelings upon; I just hoped that when 18 months had passed, life would have ironed out its problems for me and I'd be a lot happier. What I experienced, however, was that the 18 months never came any closer – no matter how much time elapsed, the 18 months always seemed 18 months away. I finally, painfully, began to realise that, in order to be happy, I had to participate more fully in my life – now. In other words . . .

to be happy, you have to give up 'when' for 'now'!

A good exercise is to take two pieces of paper and write on the top of one: 'I'll be happy when . . .' and on top of the other, 'I'll be happy if . . .' Now complete the list. When do you think you'll be happy? 'When' are you hanging on for? And what 'if' has to happen before you choose to be happy? Keep writing and writing, and see how many conditions you've tried to convince yourself you need before you can start smiling.

'You only live once . . .' has a double meaning. It refers to the idea that this moment in time will only ever happen once. Make a point, therefore, of knowing what the date is today, because this date is a one-time thing. Today will never, ever happen again. Bearing this in mind, how will you choose to live today? Today isn't a practice run – the game is on already!

'You only live once . . .' also refers to the 'wait problem' and the fact that we're always *preparing* to be happy instead of *being* happy. In other words, you only start to really live once . . . work is over, it's Saturday night, the holidays are here, you have some money, you fall in love, you get married, you buy a home, you buy another home, your mortgage is finally paid off, your pension plan matures, and so on. But even then you still can't be happy . . . not until the grandchildren get a good education!

What are you waiting for before you give yourself fully to this world? More support, maybe? More confidence? More authority? More opportunity? More qualifications? Can you see that . . .

While you wait, happiness waits.
While you wait, love waits.
While you wait, peace waits.
While you wait, freedom waits.
While you wait, opportunity waits.

While you wait, the world waits.
While you wait, we all wait.

The 'wait and see' sickness is simply fear. 'What if I stop waiting and go for it, and then I fail?' By waiting, you fail. By giving yourself fully, you'll get all you once waited for – all the support, confidence, authority and opportunity. It happens when *you* happen.

Happiness happens when you give yourself fully!

Why wait for what is already here?

Recently I experienced one of my most profound psychotherapy sessions ever. Paul is in his 40s, a tall man, quite lean, eyes set back in a soft and kind face. He'd been on my 'Eight Week Happiness Programme', during which he'd shared with all of us the fact that he was recovering from alcoholism. In our one-on-one session, Paul told me how he had tried 'everything' to be happy but 'nothing' had worked. In particular, he described to me how, every time he appeared to take a step closer to happiness, happiness took one step further away. Happiness was always on the horizon, and the horizon was always out there somewhere.

'I've given up chasing happiness, and now I'm just waiting to be happy,' Paul told me. Without really knowing why at the time, I asked Paul to close his eyes and picture the happiness he spoke of.

'What do you see?' I asked.

'I see a small light in the distance,' replied Paul.

'How small and how far away?' I asked.

'Very small, like a little light at the end of a very long tunnel.'

Again, without really knowing why at the time, I asked Paul to imagine that this light was beginning to travel towards him, slowly at first. 'Can you picture that?' I asked.

'Yes,' he said.

As the light travelled towards Paul, I could see that his body began to tremble. 'Take a breath, Paul – breathe deeply and slowly. Let the light come even closer.' As he did so, silent tears spilled down both his cheeks. 'How far away is the light?' I asked.

'I don't know – about ten feet, maybe.' Paul wanted to open his eyes.

'Keep your eyes closed, Paul, let the light approach, and keep breathing,' I whispered.

Inch by inch, in Paul's mind, he allowed the light to come closer, and each time it did, his body trembled more and more, and tears fell to the ground. Eventually, the light was right in front of Paul and covered his whole inner vision. Following my intuition, I then asked Paul to take the light back inside himself. As Paul did this, he sobbed and sobbed – he cried tears that seemed to come up from the very pit of his stomach. At that moment, I don't mind admitting, I cried, too. We eventually held each other.

I suppose what we'd gone through together was a type of time travel. By bringing the light closer, we were bringing the future closer. We were exchanging 'when' for 'now', 'there' for 'here', and 'outer' for 'inner'. Paul's trembling body signalled his resistance to this. His tears – and mine, also – were for the grief of denying this inner happiness, and for all the years of looking for happiness in all the wrong places. Without travelling anywhere, Paul's journey was complete.

Paul had, in that moment, accepted happiness unconditionally and the waiting was finally over. A week later, he was still 'over the moon'. Two weeks later, however, Paul found that he was pointing at the moon again. The old doubts, fears and conditioning had returned. Before Paul could condemn himself too badly, we embarked upon 'The Journey of Light' exercise again. At the time of this writing, we continue to do this meditation together as a way of constantly reminding ourselves that true happiness is here and now.

❖ ❖ ❖

CHAPTER SIX

Healing Unhappiness

Life is actually bad for your health, or at least that's how it feels sometimes. When we're 'in good health', life is great, everything is great. We acknowledge life to be a blessing – full of beauty, awe and wonder. We value life and we do everything we can to 'get a life'. But we also have moments when we probably wouldn't recommend life to anyone under any circumstances. *Life feels deadly.*

It seems as if one moment you can be dancing gracefully, beautifully, with effortless ease; and the next moment you wish someone, somewhere, had the decency to tell you that your shoelaces are untied. You know about laughter, but you also know about tears. You've loved much, but you also have your fears. You enjoy highs; you endure lows. You can be warm; you can be cold. Sometimes you're in tune; other times you can't even hit a note. Oh, for a drop of hindsight; oh, for a bucketful of foresight!

Life can be trying. The tests are sometimes easy, sometimes difficult; sometimes obvious, sometimes hidden; sometimes multiple choice, sometimes a 2,000-word essay that has to be handed in *now!* Sometimes you pass the tests, sometimes you have to take the tests again. And sometimes life is simply too much to bear. Then the tests really stack up and you fear you might not have what it takes to come through.

My friend and colleague Alison Atwell faxed me a passage by Stuart Wilde a while ago. He's the author of *Weight Loss for the Mind*,[1] among other books. On top of the fax, Alison wrote: 'Is this life or what?!' I met Stuart soon afterwards at a conference and asked him if I could share his words, and he readily agreed. The passage reads:

> *We have to embrace infinity inside a mortal body.*
> *We have to believe in a god we can't see.*
> *We have to learn to love in a dimension where there*
> *is so much hatred.*
> *We have to see abundance when people constantly*
> *talk of shortages and lack.*
> *We have to discover freedom where control is the*
> *state religion.*
> *We have to develop self-worth while people criticise*
> *and belittle us.*
> *We have to see beauty where there is ugliness.*
> *We have to embrace kindness and positive attitudes*
> *when surrounded by uncertainty.*

This passage sums up the challenges of life quite beautifully. It illustrates the maze of mystery, uncertainty, paradox and duality that appears before us on our life's path. The world is like a chrysalis and we are the butterfly; and somehow it's up to us to emerge from the world, free again, wholly joyous and loving. In spite of it all, we must *not* stop loving.

Sh!t Happens!

> *Sometimes we get frightened.*
> *And sometimes we lose our way.*

Unhappiness can be frightening, not the least because it feels so permanent. How ironic it is that when we're happy we immediately fear that it can't last, but when we're unhappy, we instantly 'know' it will last forever. When we're depressed, we rarely think, *This will be over by lunchtime!* Instead, our perception collapses, our thoughts freeze and our focus stays fixed on the pain. Thus, the illusion of unhappiness is that it feels so final and so forever, when, in truth . . .

> **although unhappiness feels so permanent,**
> **it is always transient.**

Unhappiness has a way of collapsing time and space. Thus, when we're unhappy, we not only feel that it will last 'always' and 'forever', but we also believe that 'everything' about our life is 'wrong', 'bad', 'not good enough', and 'nothing'. We generalise, we 'awfulise,' we experience what one of my clients once called 'humoroids' – that is, *hardening of the attitudes that cause piles of problems!* Hence, unhappiness blackens perception and blots the mind with thoughts of despair, hopelessness and more fear.

When unhappy, we lose the art of being specific. One of my clients once illustrated this with great humour. 'I am so dreadfully unhappy,' Mary said. When I asked her why, she folded her arms tight across her chest and said, 'I'm just so afraid.'

'What are you afraid of?' I asked.

'Everything!' she replied.

'Can you be specific?' I asked.

Mary then smiled, and yelled, 'I am being specific!'

The principal reason unhappiness is so frightening is that . . .

> **unhappiness is fear!**

The story of your unhappiness – that is, the events, people, reasons and circumstances – may appear different from my story, but the source of our unhappiness is the same. *Every form of unhappiness is a manifestation of fear.* Thus, fear and unhappiness are inextricably linked – they are the same thing. The same is also true of fear and grief, fear and anxiety, fear and depression, and fear and the pain of failure.

Unhappiness is born of fear and it gives birth to fear. When we give our power to unhappiness, we automatically side with fear, and we automatically become very afraid of everything. *Fear is afraid of everything because fear can only see itself in everything.* Think for a moment. *What is fear not afraid of?* To make matters even worse, fear's 'solution' to everything is more fear, more panic, more doubt and more defence.

Fear is frightening. It plays tricks with the mind. I once read somewhere that . . .

F.E.A.R. actually stands for *False Evidence Appearing Real.*

I've also read that F.E.A.R. stands for *Forgetting Everything is All Right.* And another translation I once read is*: Fuck Everything And Run!* No matter which one you relate to, fear is frightening.

Although you've managed to live through every type of fear, failure, grief and disappointment in the past, there's a part of your mind that always says: 'This time it's different.' Welcome to your ego! Your ego, full of fear and doubt, is blind to the strength, power and love of your unconditioned Self. It believes, therefore, that every new episode of unhappiness is terminal. Indeed, according to the ego, not only are you about to die, but you're going to die alone!

Most frightening of all is the loneliness of unhappiness. We feel so separate, so isolated and so cut off from everything, especially our unconditioned Self, when we're unhappy. Happiness feels like it's a lifetime away, a million miles away . . . when we're unhappy and afraid. We feel small, weak and vulnerable; and the ego quickly kicks into action, reinforcing the fears with commentary such as 'No one can help', 'Nothing will work', 'It's no use', 'There's no answer', and 'There's no hope.'

Our fears, doubts and loneliness attempt to talk us into even greater unhappiness. It's as if the ego conspires, often in our most private moments, to make us feel as if we're here on the planet to endorse a special type of pain – so deeply personal, awful, and unique to us. Surely no one suffers the way we do.

The truth is, you can walk up to anyone, on any street, in any city, in any country, in any culture, and on any continent, and if you say, 'I'm so sorry to hear about your problem', their reply to you will most likely be, 'Who told you?!' Unhappiness isn't so special! It doesn't make you unique – lonely, maybe, but not unique. We all know what pain is. We've all 'suffered', and we're all ready to heal . . . aren't we?

Give Yourself a Break

Happiness isn't just the absence of sadness;
it's also the capacity to love and heal your sadness.

My client Joanna's first words to me were: 'I feel totally stupid being here.' She went on to say, 'This is a total failure for me. I should be enjoying my life. I should be happy. I should be carefree. I'm 21, for Christ's sake. I'm 21 and I'm depressed. I haven't even started to live, and I'm depressed already.' We had barely introduced ourselves when she went on to say, 'I wish I could just pull myself together, but I can't find anything to pull.'

Joanna came to me for treatment for depression. Several courses of antidepressants hadn't worked. She was bright, clever, very aware and hypercritical. According to her, nothing she did was ever good enough. She had a natural flair for fashion design that she'd given up because she was 'useless at it'; she sang solos at church and had performed on TV, but 'really I'm an awful singer,' she told me. And so it went on.

I didn't treat Joanna for depression because that wasn't her problem; her problem was a constant, learned form of self-criticism – one born from a fear of being 'bad', 'wrong', 'nothing', and 'not good enough'.[2] Clearly, no amount of achievement would be good enough for her because deep down she felt guilty and not good enough.

The very first issue Joanna and I addressed was not her criticism of herself or her achievements, but her criticism of her emotions. She was so hard on herself that it wasn't safe for her to *have* any emotions. I explained a principle of healing that applies to everyone, which is . . .

> ### to heal unhappiness, you must make it safe to
> ### feel your feelings.

Joanna saved her most severe judgments for her emotions. Every emotion was, in Joanna's mind, completely dismissed as being either 'wrong', 'bad', 'stupid', 'crazy', 'pathetic', 'idiotic', or 'nothing, really'. I lost count of the times she said, 'I should be handling this better' and 'I shouldn't feel like this, but . . .' Joanna's excessive judgment about her feelings was really an attempt to control her pain. Alas, she found that *judgment does not control pain; it compounds pain.*

I almost always begin therapy by addressing my clients' response to their unhappiness and not the unhappiness itself, for I've come to learn that *it is the response to unhappiness that causes so much pain.* In other words . . .

> ### unhappiness is painful, but the response to
> ### unhappiness is often more painful.

We can be so brutal, so critical, so judgmental and so afraid of our emotions, particularly unhappy emotions such as grief, anger, sadness and depression. Every time we criticise and judge ourselves for feeling unhappy, we're simply adding fuel to the fire. With every self-attacking thought, the pain flares up and feels more real. The more we condemn, the more we identify with the pain itself. Soon, pain feels more real than joy.

The first step, then, to healing your unhappiness is a radical one. It is to trust that . . .

> ### unhappiness is not real.

When I say *unhappiness is not real,* what I mean is *unhappiness is not the truth about you.* The truth is that no matter how much you've learned to identify with your pain, *you are not your illness, and you are not your emotions.* It is a lie, for example, to say, 'I am an anorexic'; you may be experiencing anorexia, but anorexia is not *you*. The real you has no conditions – it is unconditional. Thus, you're not your anorexia, your alcoholism, your cancer, or any other illness, for these conditions are experiences and not identities.

Similarly, it's also a lie to say, as Joanna did, 'I'm depressed.' Yes, you may be experiencing depression, but you are *not* depression; you may be experiencing anger, but you are *not* anger; you may be experiencing grief, but you are *not* grief; you may be experiencing fear, but you are *not* fear. Once again, no matter how much you've learned to identify with these feelings, they do not, in truth, define you. Emotions are experiences; they are not who you are.

For centuries the Buddhists have taught followers to say 'I am with anger', as opposed to 'I am angry'; 'I am with sadness', as opposed to 'I am sad'; and 'I am with unhappiness', as opposed to 'I am unhappy.' This practice of naming the emotion you are *with* helps you to not confuse your identity with the emotions you feel. It's also very good for keeping perspective, staying centred, honouring your emotions, practising peaceful acceptance and healing unhappiness. Try it.

Unhappiness and fear have a way of distorting vision and making *false evidence appear real*. In the Taoist Bible, the Tao Te Ching, it explains that when you're unhappy and afraid:

> The way that is bright seems dull;
> The way that leads forward seems to lead backward;
> The way that is even seems rough;
> The highest virtue is like the valley;
> The sheerest whiteness seems sullied;
> Ample virtue seems defective . . . [3]

Unhappiness is Self-deception – it is not a truthful state. It has nothing to do with your joyous, loving, unconditioned Self; it has everything to do with the ego – the thought in your mind that believes that you're small, separate, unworthy, in exile, and have every reason to be afraid. The ego, born of fear, sees no spirit, no happiness, and no hope.

Unhappiness and fear feel real, but they're not. They appear to eclipse the joy of your spirit, but they cannot destroy the spirit. Your spirit lives on, always free, loving and happy 100 per cent of the time. Unhappiness happens when you wander away from your true Self and 'lose spirit'; true healing is simply a return to spirit, a return to love, a return to truth and a return to joy. In truth, then . . .

pain runs deep, but joy runs deeper.

Whatever pain you may be experiencing right now, it's good to know that your true unconditioned Self is okay and all is well. To realise this, you must first be prepared to give yourself a break – a break from the incessant self-judgment, and a break from identifying with the pain. *You are not your pain.*

Honesty Is the Best Policy

One day a man went to visit a doctor who was famous for his radical healing cures. 'What's your problem?' asked the doctor.

'I'm completely depressed,' said the man.

After a brief consultation, the doctor said, 'I won't give you tablets for your depression. The circus is in town this weekend, and I want you to go see the great clown Grimaldi.'

The man bowed his head and said, 'My dear doctor, I *am* Grimaldi.'

Psychology surveys on subjective wellbeing show conclusively that people tend to exaggerate their public reports of happiness.[4] We'll often fake happiness when we're low, such is our shame about unhappiness. We're also eager to keep up appearances; and to put on a brave face, a stiff upper lip, a mask, and a smile . . . for, like us, society doesn't tolerate unhappiness well. As the saying goes: 'Laugh and the world laughs with you / Weep and you weep alone.'[5]

'How are you?' we greet our friends. 'Not so bad,' they say. They're telling us nothing. They're neither happy nor sad, good nor bad. When I ask my clients how they are, the answer is often, 'Not so bad', and even, 'I'm well, thank you!' They are, apparently, not unhappy, but they've still made an appointment. Similarly, doctors greet their patients, 'How are you?' 'Well!' say the patients. 'Why are you here, then?' ask the doctors.

It's extremely rare for people to admit publicly to being sad, depressed, nervous, angry, jealous or unhappy – the shame of it would be too much. From an early age, we've learned to hide and be dishonest about our emotions, for fear of judgment and guilt. Common 'You should be ashamed of yourself' messages include:

- 'Big boys don't cry.'

- 'Take that look off your face.'

- '*I'll* give you anger.'

- 'How dare you . . .'

- 'Don't be a cry-baby.'

- 'What a song and dance!'

- 'You'll be smiling on the other side of your face in a minute.'

- 'Pull yourself together.'

- 'Who do you think you are?'

- 'Get a grip.'

- 'Stop crying.'

- 'Stop laughing.'

- 'There will be tears before bedtime.'

We've learned to be secretive. We hide our feelings. We suppress our emotions. Suppression, denial, rationalisation, and other defences all seem to work well at first, but they soon fail, for what felt like peace was only avoidance. We cry alone and in private. Eventually, when the pain of suppression and shame begins to scream unbearably, we jettison our pride and attend self-help groups with names like *Depressives Anonymous* – the shame and secrecy continue.

Being secretive about your emotions doesn't heal your pain; it exacerbates it. In fact, I'd say that . . .

**90 per cent of any pain comes from trying
to keep the pain secret.**

You can't keep a secret and truly move on with your life. By being dishonest about your pain, you stay in pain. Dishonesty may appear to help you get through your day, but it will always leave you in pain in the end. Healing is a process of truth, and you cannot get to truth via dishonesty. Dishonesty is, at best, a control tactic; it is not a medicine. It cannot give you peace.

To heal, you must be prepared to accept that *you are not wrong for feeling unhappy or being unwell.* You must surrender the temptation to use your unhappiness and illness as a verdict or as evidence to prove that you're guilty and 'not good enough'. *Your disease is not the truth about you.* It is not you; it is merely an experience.

Again and again, I have to remind my clients that being unhappy isn't a form of capital punishment. I tell them that . . .

unhappiness isn't a sin!

As long as you continue to judge yourself for feeling unhappy or being unwell, you'll feel shame. After judgment and shame, there comes punishment (see Figure 3). At the precise moment you most need love and care, you administer a course of personal abuse and neglect. By refusing to love and be kind to yourself, you're punishing yourself, playing out your guilt, atoning for your weakness and 'getting what you think you deserve'.

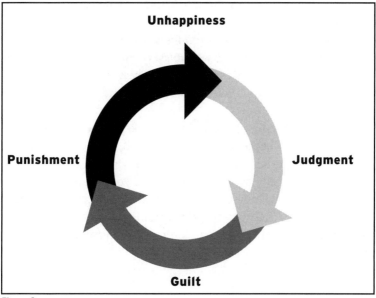

Unhappiness

Punishment

Judgment

Guilt

Figure 3

You cannot heal in secret. You must be prepared to tell the whole truth to someone, to God, to the Holy Spirit, to a healing agency. When it comes to healing, honesty is the best policy. Secrecy only adds to your pain, for . . .

secrecy feeds shame!

Where there is shame, there will be pain, and as long as you believe you're guilty, you'll continue to attract unhappiness. In fact, *you will experience as much unhappiness as you believe you deserve*. Honesty lets the truth out, and truth eventually dispels all shame. This is important because a belief in unworthiness creates a world of experience entirely different and separate from that created by a belief of true Self-acceptance. For instance:

Unworthiness attracts pain; worthiness is peace.
Unworthiness casts doubt; worthiness is certainty.
Unworthiness projects guilt; worthiness is freedom.
Unworthiness spreads fear; worthiness is loving.
Unworthiness fuels anger; worthiness is a smile.
Unworthiness is suffering; worthiness is rest.
Unworthiness demands sacrifice; worthiness is whole.
Unworthiness always falters; worthiness is true.

Honesty is the first freedom! It is the key to healing. Your ego cannot afford to be honest, but you can. By being honest about your most private self-judgments, the pain you feel begins to melt almost immediately; by being open about your shame, the agony is shared and quickly begins to fade; and by being truthful about your fears, their tight, fixed grip instantly begins to loosen. By being honest, you discover that you're no longer alone and help is now at hand.

Letting Down Your Defences

My encounter with my client Donald was to affect me profoundly. Donald was a short man in his late 60s with a small body, but his spirit was gigantic! His face was covered in character lines, and he had one eye, a full smile, a bushy black moustache and rosy cheeks. He always sat with his shoulders hunched, leaning fully forward towards me. It was in our third session together that he said to me, 'Robert, I think my real problem is that I've forgotten how to be honest with myself.'

'I can smile for you, Robert,' Donald said, 'but my smiles are fake. I can laugh for you, Robert, but I no longer know what it *feels* like to laugh. In fact, I can't feel anything very much.' Donald went on to tell me that the last time he'd cried was as a young boy, and how he was haunted by self-criticism and self-doubt. 'I want my real smile back,' he told me. Perhaps his request becomes all the more poignant when I tell you that Donald is a professional clown.

Donald had got straight to the heart of the matter when he told me, 'I've forgotten how to be honest with myself.' So afraid was he of his unhappiness that he'd decided to put up a barrier to defend himself from the pain. The barrier had seemed to work at first, dulling the pain quite well, but Donald soon discovered that by cutting himself off from his pain he had also, inadvertently, cut himself off from his joy.

Donald had discovered that defences are dishonest. He had hoped that his defences might somehow lessen the pain, but instead they only added to it. He felt cut up and cut off from his feelings. He also discovered that you cannot be selectively honest about feelings – that is, honest about joy but dishonest about anger, or honest about anger but dishonest about jealousy. In our discussions together, we arrived at the conclusion that . . .

what you defend against you attract!

All too often the language of medicine and healing is a language of war. We talk about 'tackling health issues', 'defeating depression', 'banishing the blues', 'killing cancer', 'overcoming anxiety', 'beating period pain', 'winning the fight against AIDS', and so on. I also contributed to this warlike language with my clinic 'Stress Busters'. Healing is not a war; it is a peace process. It's not about resistance; it's about acceptance. Acceptance is the key to peace, love and healing.

A feeling has only one ambition in life, and that is to be felt! Emotions want *motion*. Every time you resist and defend against an emotion, the pain will persist longer. You must be prepared to honour every feeling you experience – be it anger, jealousy, depression, sadness or hate. Honouring the feeling is the same as being honest about and accepting the feeling. *Ultimately you* *accept the feeling, not because it's real, but because <u>love</u> is real.* In other words, pain is always just a visitor. It is transient. It always ends. Meanwhile, your unconditioned Self remains intact, forever loving, truly whole, and free of pain. So . . .

acceptance is a setup for love.

Defensiveness won't heal, love will; condemnation won't heal, kindness will; judgment won't heal, forgiveness will; fighting won't heal, peace will; resistance won't heal, acceptance will. At The Happiness Project, I often share what I call 'The Declaration of Acceptance'. It reads:

> *Without acceptance, anger will enrage you.*
> *Without acceptance, guilt will shame you.*
> *Without acceptance, judgment will condemn you.*
> *Without acceptance, anxiety will torment you.*
> *Without acceptance, sadness will depress you.*
> *Without acceptance, fear will terrify you.*
> *Without acceptance, pain will hurt you.*
> *Without acceptance, loneliness will isolate you.*
> *Without acceptance, love cannot love you.*

Donald played with the idea of acceptance. 'Fighting my unhappiness has got me nowhere,' he said. As Donald became more and more defenceless, he discovered a new strength and a new freedom. At first he talked about his unhappiness without really feeling it, but one day the tears finally came. The day Donald cried was the day he began to smile again and really feel it. Donald's courage was exceptional. He was an inspiration to me. We would often hug and hold each other, crying and laughing. Together we gave each other the courage to accept, love, and let go of our pain.

Suppression, repression, denial, intellectualisation, rationalisation, avoidance, lying and every other type of defence are not the easy options they might first appear to be. Like a bad drug habit, defences keep asking more and more of you. It takes a lot of conscious and unconscious effort to keep the lid on unhappiness. Defensiveness is exhausting.

Medical drugs, if wrongly prescribed, can be another form of defensiveness that actually hinders the healing process. All too often in modern medicine, drugs are used incorrectly to suppress feelings. I think of unhappiness as a piece of information – it's like a red light on your car dashboard telling you to attend to your engine. Well, to follow this analogy, taking heavy sedatives inappropriately is a bit like taking the fuse out of the car dashboard so that the light no longer shows. No red light does not mean no problem.

Fortunately, more and more doctors are learning to prescribe their drugs more wisely. In particular, they're learning not to use drugs to simply 'shut their patient's feelings up'. Sedation isn't the same as healing. This short-term 'solution' is a false economy that eventually leads to more pain, not less. For too long, the medical profession has pondered *drugs or therapy*.[6] Sometimes both are necessary. Whatever is the most loving option is best.

Soon after Donald stopped coming to see me, I received a letter from him in which he'd included a passage written by the German poet Hermann Hesse. It reads:

Suffering only hurts because you fear it.
Suffering only hurts because you complain
about it.
It pursues you because you flee from it.
You must not flee, you must not complain,
you must not fear. You must love.
You know all this yourself, you know quite
well, deep within you, that there is a single
magic, a single power, a single salvation,
and a single happiness, and that is
called loving.
Well then, love your suffering. Do not
resist it, do not flee from it.
Taste how sweet it is in its essence, give
yourself to it, do not meet it with aversion.
It is only your aversion that hurts,
nothing else.[7]

Asking for Help

> *'Ask, believe, receive!'*

There's a story of a schoolteacher who told her class of young children the story of Moses. The children listened attentively, and after she finished, the teacher asked, 'Why do you think Moses wandered lost in the desert for 40 years?'

There was a rather long hush. Suddenly, a boy shot up his arm, obviously inspired by a genuine flash of insight: 'Maybe, Miss, Moses was afraid to ask for directions!'

Healing is restoration. It's about clearing away the rubble of your conditioned mind to reveal once more the wholeness of your unconditioned Self. As with true happiness, this restoration doesn't require excessive labour, huge sacrifice, endless struggle, heavy suffering or any large down payments. Healing asks nothing of you other than your willingness to *accept* healing.

The willingness to accept healing is the key to restoration, and part of that willingness also includes being willing to ask for help. For, in truth . . .

you cannot be healed alone!

Too many times we try to heal alone. We somehow have it wired up in our mind that *asking for help means we've failed.* We're either too proud or too guilty to ask for help. Selfishly, we deny people the opportunity to love and care for us because we feel too clumsy, too embarrassed, too undeserving, too selfish, too superior, or that we're being too much of a nuisance.

During my years with the Stress Busters Clinic, I found that most of my clients had suffered alone with their stress for an average of between two and ten years before they first asked for help. On a similar note, my friend Michael, an Anglican vicar, once told me, 'People love God so much they don't worry Him with their problems!' Healing and freedom must mean more to you than pride and guilt if you're going to be happy.

It is a classic symptom of stress to *discount solutions before you try them*. This is the 'Yes, but . . .' disease. Therefore, if your pride and guilt aren't getting in the way of your asking for help, maybe it's your cynicism. Cynicism is like a mental cancer. It attempts to kill all hope, light, adventure, growth and healing. Cynicism is a decision to be a victim. Apart from being unhelpful, cynicism is also never justified, never real, never true and never accurate.

Cynicism delays healing in a number of ways: (1) We don't ask because we already 'know' that 'it' won't work; (2) we don't ask because we believe that we 'can't be helped'; (3) we do ask for help, but we fully expect to get no answer – this suits our cynicism perfectly, because as long as we get no answer we can hold on to our imagined guilt and still play the victim.

In the Bible it is written: 'Ask, and it will be given you.'[8] What a deal! Don't you think, however, that it sounds almost too good to be true? It looks a little like a free lunch. Where are the hidden extras, I wonder? What's the flip side to all this? Check the small print. Easy come, easy go! Many times in my past I've waved my fist in the air, feeling angry, abandoned and aggrieved, quoting the Bible to God – 'I'm still asking. Where's Your answer?'

I have come to learn from my own experience that when it comes to asking for help . . .

**you cannot hold on to pride,
guilt and cynicism and be healed!**

When you ask for help, you will receive the answer you believe you deserve. This is the key to asking. Thus, the sentence 'Ask, and it will be given you', maybe makes more sense if you say, 'Ask, *believe,* and it will be given you.' You cannot be proud and open, guilty and open, cynical and open. For as long as you want to stay proud, guilty or cynical, you close the door on any real answer to your request for help.

When you ask 'for help', you have to be open and spontaneously available 'to help'. Therefore, before you ask for help, it's important to put aside all pride, guilt and cynicism. In other words, you have to surrender illusions for truth, past for present, resentment for hope. Ask – believe – receive!

To heal and be happy . . .

**you must be willing to ask,
and be willing to receive.**

I am currently practising to be a better asker. For too long in my life I've suffered from a condition I call B.M.S. – *By Myself Syndrome,* the main symptom of which is being too afraid to ask for help. For example, in a busy shopping centre I'll spend 40 minutes (not quite 40 years!) looking for a store, when I could easily ask one of a thousand people for directions. In a music store, I'll search over and over for a particular CD before thinking to ask for help from someone who's paid to help people who ask for help.

I'm told that *fear of asking is* unique to men! I believe, however, that both men and women know what it is to play the martyr, to refuse help, and to try to go it alone. Too often healing is delayed because we try to mend ourselves before, and not after, we've asked for help from friends, family members, counsellors, God and the Holy Spirit. We heal by being willing to ask and being willing to receive.

Stick to Your Strengths

*If you're unhappy, maybe it's because
you've abandoned your greatest sources of strength.*

My mother, Sally, recently experienced what could be called 'a severe case of life'. What started out as a routine treatment for a bout of depression became a close encounter with death after she was prescribed a combined course of sedatives, tranquillizers, antidepressants, and other drugs that almost killed her. Three different times my brother, David, and I said our goodbyes to Mother, believing she might die that night.

About six months into my mother's nightmare, I became completely exhausted. Travelling hundreds of miles to the clinic, often late into the night, four times a week, had taken its toll. The endless, fruitless attempts to communicate with clinic administrators and doctors didn't help either. And then there was also the fear and worry for my mother.

Fear is exhausting. Having no time for rest is also exhausting. But even worse was the fact that somehow, in the middle of this crisis, I had managed to abandon my true sources of strength when I most needed them. Bit by bit, without even noticing, I had cut myself off from all that nourishes and sustains me.

My sources of strength include morning meditation, prayer, God, my family, my friends, the gymnasium, a healthy diet and evening meditation. Well, my healthy diet collapsed immediately. Night after night I dined alone in my car driving to the clinic, eating vegetables (crisps, actually!), fruit and nuts (chocolate bars!), and drinking diet soft drinks. My morning meditation, which usually lasts an hour, somehow became 15, 10, 5 minutes long. Prayers were said on the run. Friends understood why I didn't call back. Completely exhausted, I 'vegged out' on videos. The idea of visiting the gym exhausted me even more. And I usually only remembered my evening meditation the morning after!

'Time is the problem,' I kept telling myself. The reason I had no time, however, was that I'd strayed from my sources of strength. There's never enough time if you have no energy. How ironic, then, that when I most needed my sources of strength, I completely deserted them. I remember promising myself constantly that once my mother was better, *only then* would I start meditating, exercising, talking to God and eating healthily again.

I was in a rut, and . . .

the strange thing about a rut is that you never consciously fall into one!

I bet you've never thought to yourself, *Here is a rut, I'll fall into this one,* or *That looks like a nice rut, I'll give it a go.* No! The psychology of ruts is more subtle and deceptive than that. Ruts are periods of Self-deception. They can last a week, a month, or several years. They are the times when you forget to be true to yourself and to what most strengthens and supports you.

The question is, are you clear about what your greatest sources of strength are? Can you name them immediately? Or do you need more time to think? Has it ever occurred to you that maybe you're unhappy or unwell because you're not clear what your greatest sources of true strength are? Or maybe you're suffering because you're being egotistical in trying to rely solely on your own strength?

Whatever your sources of true strength, I guarantee you that, like me, you'll be tempted to abandon them the next time you're stressed and unhappy. It is indeed a great irony that when we're under pressure or in pain, we move away from, rather than towards, our sources of strength. Just like the biblical story of Peter and Jesus, when Peter distanced himself from Jesus three times . . . we do exactly the same with our own sources of strength when we're in crisis.

Some strengths – particularly external ones like friends and family – come and go, live and die, for such is the nature of life in this world. The eternal spirit of your unconditioned Self is, however, always strong and true. You could say, then, that . . .

happiness is remembering not to lose spirit.

Beneath the pain that feels so very real, your spirit is still at play, blissfully free and unaffected by the dramas of the world. Stay close, surrender, be open, and let the strength and spirit of your unconditioned Self guide you, inspire you and heal you.

Do Not Control Your Own Healing

Be responsible: give up control!

The following story offers an excellent illustration of the dangers of trying to control your own healing process.

There once was a man who was trapped on the roof of his house while dangerous flood waters were rising up all around him. Clinging to the chimney, he feared for his life. Never before had he felt such a desire to live. He called for help, 'Dear God, I want to live. Please help!'

Instantly God replied, 'I will help you, my Son.'

Shortly thereafter, a neighbour came by in a canoe: 'Hop in old boy!' cried the neighbour.

'Thanks anyway, but God is on His way,' cried the man.

Time passed, and the flood waters still continued to rise. A complete stranger passed by in a motorboat, and this good Samaritan offered the man a lift.

'Thanks anyway, but God is on His way!' cried the man.

Soon the man was standing on top of his chimney, the waters still rising. Out of nowhere, a helicopter arrived with a rope.

'Thanks anyway, but God is on His way!' cried the man.

The man eventually drowned. Before entering Heaven he angrily confronted God, 'Why didn't You help me?' he cried. 'I would have thought that You of all people would have kept Your word!'

'Well, I tried,' said God, 'I came in a canoe, a motorboat, and a helicopter, but each time you turned me away.'

The man in this story is a symbol of the ego, which always wants to be in control of everything, including its own demise. The man asked for help, but he didn't receive. Three offers of help were made, but three times the man gave up his chance for safety because he had already determined in his mind what his rescue should look like.

The willingness to accept healing requires you to give up all temptation to control what you think your healing 'must', 'ought' and 'should' look like. The bottom line is . . .

you cannot control your own healing.

The temptation to play doctor and control your own healing can inhibit essential healing agencies such as trust, openness, surrender, spontaneous availability, possibility thinking and relaxation. Control is often motivated by fear, and it is fear that often prevents acceptance and willingness. Hence, healing happens when you give up control, not when you keep control.

Everything and anything can help you to heal once you're willing to accept healing unconditionally. Give up your prejudices, therefore. Listen with an open mind to every offer of help that comes your way. Don't discount solutions before you try them. Antidepressants have their place. Complementary medicine can work. Counselling and psychotherapy have value. The doctor may listen to you more than you think. Forgiveness may be the answer.

Willingness is like the electricity that makes all your household appliances work. Without electricity, your new phone, your 42-function washing machine, your super-duper computer and your 200-channel TV set are all useless. Similarly, without willingness, no healing treatment will work. Hence, the willingness to accept healing for yourself must come first. After willingness, anything and everything can work, especially if you give up control of the process.

Staying Open for Miracles

This is an ancient story from India:

One day a prince was out hunting when he was shot in the heart by an arrow soaked in poison. The arrow appeared to come out of nowhere. Physicians arrived immediately, but before they could begin to administer their medicines, the prince ordered, 'First, tell me what the poison is on this arrow.'

After the poison was identified, the physicians were about to begin their treatment when the prince ordered, 'First, tell me what type of material this arrow is made of.' After he was told, he then demanded to know who might have made the arrow. All the while, the poison on the arrow tip was spreading through the prince's body.

The prince began to weaken, but so enraged was he at being shot that he said to his doctors, 'Before you begin, I must first know who shot me. You must bring him to me so that I can ask him who he was sent by.' The prince then requested that his spiritual advisor be called. 'I need to know why this has happened,' he demanded. Eventually, the prince died with the arrow still in his heart.

In this story, the prince is a symbol of the ego. He's not ready or willing to accept healing. First, he wants to understand everything, and then he will let his physicians heal him. His stubborn insistence on understanding everything is eventually what kills him.

It's a common mistake to think that healing requires understanding. It does not. While understanding can certainly be helpful, it is not a necessary prerequisite for healing. All too often the healing process is blocked, delayed and complicated by an insistence (by both client and counsellor) to get to the root of all understanding first. Too much analysis, dissection, breakdown, separation and logic can close you down rather than open you up. Thus . . .

being *open* to healing is more important than trying to *understand* healing.

This is true for both client and therapist. When I first became interested in healing, I travelled to meet with many of the world's greatest healers. Over and over, I would ask them how healing works, and invariably they taught me that trying to understand logically how healing works can often block it. The key, they said, is to get your ego out of the way. Your job, then, is simply to be open to the miracle of healing. First, be open, and then you'll understand.

Healing is all about miracles – that is, seeing things differently. If you're unhappy or unwell, you're being asked to give up your current frame of mind so as to picture things differently. Healing is about giving up the thinking that led you to feeling unhappy or unwell; and being open to seeing differently, thinking differently, believing differently, expressing yourself differently, and acting differently.

One of the most important principles of healing at The Happiness Project is the idea that . . .

there's no such thing as a 'negative emotion'.

As long as you believe that something is 'negative' – such as anger, jealousy, unhappiness, depression, and other 'negative emotions' – you will not gain anything positive or helpful from these experiences. To heal, you must be open to dropping your prejudices, your conditioning and your judgments so as to see the Light.

Being open to miracles means being open to everything, including your pain, your fear and your guilt. When you're truly open and unconditional, you see that nothing is implicitly 'bad', 'wrong', or 'negative'. Everything, handled in a healthy way, can contribute to the value and enrichment of your own life.

Remember Joanna, the 21-year-old woman suffering from depression whom I mentioned at the beginning of this chapter? Well, after about three months of seeing her, I gave her an assignment for homework, which was: 'What is the wisest thing you've ever learned while handling your emotions?' Her answer was quite beautiful. It read:

> *I have never, ever had time for my emotions before now. I used to think emotions are a total weakness. The truth probably is I've been too scared to look at them. But the thing I have learned most recently is that perhaps my feelings aren't out to get me! Feelings are not punishments. Feelings are information. It is as if every feeling I have is trying to tell me something.*
>
> *I never thought I'd believe this, but I actually feel grateful for my depression. My depression has been a gift. I am ready to build a new life now.*

Joanna is thrilled to know that her words are included in this book. We've talked together many times about the 'gift' of her depression. We both understand that, in truth, depression isn't the real gift; the real gift is Joanna's courage to face her depression openly, with honesty and love. Her willingness to heal ensured that condemnation and fear eventually gave way to openness and forgiveness. A miracle had occurred.

Commit to Happiness NOW!

Don't wait until all your unhappiness is over before you commit to happiness. Commit to happiness *now!*

There's no better time to commit to happiness than when you're unhappy. Committing to happiness is, however, the very last thing you feel like doing when you're down to your last nerve, your muscles are set rigid, and your head is auditioning for a part in *High Anxiety!* Nevertheless . . .

**unhappiness undoes itself when you commit
to happiness 'now'.**

If, right now, you feel unhappy, I encourage you to pray out loud, 'I commit to happiness.' If, right now, you're experiencing conflict, affirm, 'I commit to peace.' If, right now, you feel depressed, sing, 'I commit to joy.' If, right now, you're experiencing resentment, state, 'I commit to freedom.' If, right now, you feel grief, declare, 'I commit to healing.' If, right now, you're experiencing anger, assert, 'I commit to love.'

I'm not asking you to deny that you feel unhappy. Pretending not to feel what you're feeling isn't honest, truthful, or helpful. What I'm suggesting is that you feel what you feel *and choose to commit to happiness.*[9] It is your commitment to freedom that will unlock the prison door. So:

When in fear, feel fear, and commit to love.
When in tears, cry tears, and commit to healing.
When unhappy, honour it, and commit to joy.
When in conflict, own it, and commit to peace.
When in pain, express it, and commit to freedom.
When angry, feel it, and commit to harmony.
When resentful, be honest, and commit to forgiveness.
When hurting, nurse yourself, and commit to laughter.
When down and out, rest up, and commit to success.

When you've committed to happiness, what then? The answer is: *nothing.* Perhaps the hardest lesson for us to learn in our own healing is that . . .

**there's nothing for you to do, other
than to accept healing for yourself.**

Healing isn't a task. It's not work. Remember, healing does not require labour, suffering, struggle, or any other great effort; it merely requires your willingness. Believe, above all, that your willingness is enough. Follow your willingness, let your willingness bless you, and allow your willingness to bring healing to you.

Love Is the Answer

Judgment is the source of all sorrow.

Depression is a call for love. Fear is a call for love. Anger is a call for love. Grief is a call for love. Jealousy is a call for love. Guilt is a call for love. All unhappiness is a call for love.[10] This becomes clear the moment you're willing to stop judging yourself and your unhappiness. Healing is all about a decision either to . . .

love or judge?

Unhappiness is energy plus judgment. Can you see that all unhappiness stems from a judgment of 'this is bad' and 'this is wrong'? Nothing, in itself, can make you unhappy, but the belief that what you're witnessing must be 'bad' and 'wrong' will certainly encourage grief. Redundancy, for instance, need not be 'bad' or 'wrong', but if you insist it must be so, then you'll suffer great unhappiness. Look at your judgments!

There once was a man who never once lost his smile. One day he was fired from his job.

'This is bad news,' said his colleagues.

The man smiled. 'It is,' he said. Within a week he found a job that paid double his previous wage.

'This is good news,' said his friends.

The man smiled. 'It is,' he said.

On the first day of his new job, the man who never once lost his smile spoke up to disagree with his new boss.

'This is bad news,' said his new colleagues.

The man smiled. 'It is,' he said. The next day, his new boss commended the man for being honest and forthright with his opinions.

'This is good news,' said his colleagues.

The man smiled. 'It is,' he said.

A month later, the man who never once lost his smile was badly injured in a terrible car crash. He was hospitalised for six months as a result.

'What bad news,' his friends said.

'It is,' the man said, still managing to smile. He received a five-figure settlement for his injury.

'What great news,' his friends said.

The man smiled. 'It is,' he said.

A year later, the man who never once lost his smile lost all his money as the stock exchange collapsed.

'Bad luck,' said his friends.

'It is,' the man said, and still he smiled. Soon after, he was laid off from his job.

'Bad times,' commiserated his friends.

'It is,' said the man, who had now lost everything except his smile.

His friends, amazed that the man was still able to smile, asked, 'How can you still smile when things are so "bad"?'

The man replied, 'I see nothing as "bad."'

His friends countered, 'But when we commiserate and say "Too bad" you say "It is," you agree.'

'No,' said the man. 'When you say "bad" or "good", I simply say "It is", and in doing so I'm practicing acceptance and freedom from judgment. It's because I don't get caught up in judgment that I can always afford to keep my smile.'

The problem with judgment is that there is no *is!* Nothing *is* because everything has to be 'good' or 'bad' and 'right' or 'wrong'. In other words, there *is* no acceptance. Everything you see you judge. Seeing is judgment. Thinking is judgment. You see nothing as it is; you only see your judgment of it. It is this lack of acceptance and openness that causes you so much pain.

Judgment isn't natural; it's learned. Judgment is an attribute of the ego, and the ego is always on guard, ready to dispense its judgments. While you continue to judge, there's no acceptance, no peace and no rest. Because you were once afraid, you taught yourself to judge, but now you find that judgment only increases fear. Similarly, because you once lacked trust, you taught yourself to judge, but now you find that judgment diminishes any chance of trust.

If you judge something as 'bad', you must inevitably feel 'bad'. If you judge something as 'good', you will feel 'good'. This is solid emotional mathematics. True freedom, however, comes from the willingness to give up judgment for love. This is particularly true when it comes to your judgments about emotions. When you're willing to give up judging your emotions, you're left with acceptance; and when you have acceptance, you also have love. Can you see that:

Fear, without judgment, is love.
Anger, without judgment, is love.
Guilt, without judgment, is love.
Depression, without judgment, is love.
Jealousy, without judgment, is love.
Hate, without judgment, is love.
Anxiety, without judgment, is love.
Sadness, without judgment, is love.
Pain, without judgment, is love.
Love, without judgment, is love.

Wisdom isn't judgment; wisdom is the relinquishment of judgment. Can you see that whenever you judge anyone or anything, *you* are the one who experiences the effect of the judgment? This is what is meant by the saying 'Judge not that ye may not be judged.' You may be angry at your mother, but it is *your* nervous system that feels the anger. You may be upset at your partner, but it is *your* mind that is unsettled. Judgment condemns and punishes everyone, including 'ye' who judges.

Giving up judgment is only difficult because you still believe that judgment will somehow give you peace. To give up judgment, you must first realise that judgment cannot and will not give you peace. In other words . . .

> **judgment won't make you safe;**
> **it will only make you afraid.**

Second, to give up judgment, you only have to understand that you don't know enough about anything to make an accurate judgment. In other words, all your judgments are half-baked opinions and not whole truths. In the manual of *A Course in Miracles*, there are some wonderful words that read:

> It is necessary for the teacher of God to realise, not
> that he should not judge, but that he cannot. In giving up
> judgment, he is merely giving up what he did not have. He
> gives up an illusion; or better, he has an illusion of giving

up. He has actually merely become more honest. Recognising that judgment was always impossible for him, he no longer attempts it. This is no sacrifice. On the contrary, he puts himself in a position where judgment through him rather than by him can occur. And this judgment is neither 'good' nor 'bad'. It is the only judgment there is, and it is only one: 'God's Son is guiltless, and sin does not exist.'

Third, in order to give up judgment, you can begin by not judging yourself for your judgments! I was recently interviewed for a magazine in which I was asked, 'Are you judgmental?' The most honest reply I could give was, 'I am as judgmental as I have ever been. However, I've learned not to judge myself for my judgments. I've also learned to take my judgments less seriously. Most judgments are fears, and I'm determined not to live my life by fear.'

Finally, judgment and love are opposites. By making a commitment to love and by cultivating a more loving outlook, judgment will automatically fall away. Love begets love; judgment begets judgment. The truth is . . .

you cannot judge and love!

The experience of your entire life boils down, then, to a simple decision: Do you love, or do you judge? Which do you value the most? You so hoped that judgment would give you strength and peace, but there is no strength and peace in a mind that constantly judges. Love is strong. It is strong because it is free of fear and judgment. Love will give you all the peace you long for.

❖ ❖ ❖

CHAPTER SEVEN

Lots of Love!

Where there is love,
pain breathes,
tears smile,
hurt softens,
guilt loses its edge,
judgment forgets to judge,
fear is no longer afraid,
separation is over.

Where there is love,
you are there.

One day a young boy who had wandered away from the crowd came across an old yogi dressed in gold, who was dancing and laughing all by himself in the middle of an open field. It was raining. There was no music and there were no other people, but still the yogi danced for joy. The eccentric-looking yogi transfixed the young boy.

After a while, the boy shouted out, 'Why do you dance alone?'

Without missing a step, the yogi replied, 'What makes you think I'm alone?!' The yogi continued to dance and laugh. The young boy soon joined in.

The wise mystics of old continually referred to this world as a place of illusion. They also said that the greatest illusion of all is that you and I appear to be totally separate from each other. This sense of separation increases and heightens each time you're afraid, hurt, unhappy or in pain. If, however, you have truly loved, for only a single moment even, then you too have felt the all-encompassing sense of wholeness and oneness of love that defies the information of your physical senses.

Love is bigger than anything. It's bigger than your body, your mind, your self, your fears, your guilt, your ego and your loneliness. Love is union. When you love, you join, you connect, and you feel as one. With true love there's no separation, no little 'me' or little 'you', no more than or less than, no distance, no lack, no limits. Love is wholeness and love is healing, for . . .

**happiness starts with love,
and sadness ends with love.**

Love is also bigger than romance! Therefore, the love I speak of isn't reserved for one special person and denied to all the rest. This isn't true love. True love is the intention to make love the basis of not only your marriage, but also all your friendships, your work and everything else in your life. Love is precious, not because it exists between two people, but because it is a part of all of us.

Love Is Heaven!

Fear is hell!

Picture the following scenario:

I'm in a hospital in the middle of England. It's late afternoon. I've just finished facilitating a one-day workshop on the connection between health and happiness to senior doctors, nurses, occupational therapists and administrators at the hospital. I've said my goodbyes and am now walking through a series of very long, dark, empty, cold corridors, searching desperately for 'Exit' signs as I go. I'm lost.

As I enter another long corridor, I see someone up ahead walking towards me. It is then that I embark upon a distinctly schizophrenic conversation in my own mind:

Voice 1: 'Here comes someone.'
Voice 2: 'It's a stranger.'
Voice 1: 'I'll ask him for directions.'
Voice 2: 'You don't know him.'
Voice 1: 'I'm lost – I need help.'
Voice 2: 'No, you don't. Keep quiet.'
Voice 1: 'I'll say "Hello."'
Voice 2: 'Are you mad?'
　　　Brief pause.
Voice 1: 'He looks friendly enough.'
Voice 2: 'He's wearing a white coat – he's probably a doctor.'
Voice 1: 'Good. I'll ask for directions.'
Voice 2: 'It's unprofessional to ask for directions.'
Voice 1: 'No, it isn't.'
Voice 2: 'Keep your head down, and avoid eye contact. Make it look like you're not lost.'
Voice 1: 'Asking for help will save time.'
Voice 2: 'You are mad.'
　　　Brief pause.
Voice 1: 'I'll smile, say "Hello," and ask for directions.'
Voice 2: 'He'll think you're a patient.'
Voice 1: 'No, he won't.'
Voice 2: 'He doesn't look friendly.'
Voice 1: 'I'll be friendly, and then he will be, too.'
Voice 2: 'You have no idea what you're talking about.'
Is this madness, I wonder? I think so! And I invite you to

laugh at my madness, for laughter is the most healthy response to this nonsense. However, before you sign any petitions to have my licence to practice revoked, look at your own thinking for a moment and check to see if you haven't already had an inner dialogue like this today. I do mean 'today'.

Voice 1 is the 'voice of love'; Voice 2 is the 'voice of fear'. The voice of love is natural, innocent, wholly present and unconditional. This voice is, according to the voice of fear, too friendly, too trusting, too loving, too open, too naive, too optimistic and too happy. In every situation, no matter how mundane or insignificant, your fear will always try to talk you out of love.

In any given moment of your life, you're either moving closer to heaven or closer to hell. In other words, you're either being loving or fearful. Love is heaven; fear is hell. When you're truly loving, you feel like heaven, but when you're afraid and cynical, you feel hellish.

> In h.e.a.v.e.n. all the letters stand together:
> Happiness next to Eternity; Abundance,
> Vision, and Ease joined to Now, as one.
>
> In h.e.l.l. all the letters stand alone: the
> Horrific Effect of not enough Love and
> Laughter, waiting to be undone.

Love and fear are more than mere emotions. They are two distinct frames of mind, two contrasting philosophies, two opposite intentions, each capable of creating a world of experience both entirely separate from one another. Love and fear are two different stories. Every day you walk out of the front door of your home, either into a world of love or a world of fear, depending on which story you most believe in. You choose the story.

At The Happiness Project, I often quote a passage from *A Course in Miracles*, which reads:

'Whenever you are not wholly joyous, it is

**because you have reacted with a lack of love to
one of God's creations.'**

When we love, all is well. When we use fear to get love, we end up feeling lonely, abandoned, guilty, cut off and afraid. Where there once was love, there is now fear, hastily built defences, walls of projection, a desire for absolute independence, a need for tight control, a lack of trust, paranoia, a fear of intimacy and a fear of rejection. When you go with fear, love is no longer realistic, heaven is a myth and happiness is but a dream.

Fear preys, Love prays! All the while, fear shouts, 'Look out!' Love sings, 'Look within.' Fear screams, 'Close your heart and be safe.' Love asks, 'Keep your heart open and be strong.' Fear says, 'Take what you can.' Love says, 'Give what you want.' Fear wants you to 'defend yourself'. Love wants you to 'stay open'. Fear advises, 'Be afraid!' Love advises, 'Be loving!' Fear preys, 'Love is weak.' Love prays, 'Love is God.' Love and fear each have a different opinion about everything and everyone.

Let Love Be Your God

If you dedicate your life to love, you will be happy.

My father died when I was 25 years old. Whenever anyone you love dies, it can change your life forever. It was a dark night. No moon. Heavy clouds. Horizontal rain was lashing against the windshield of my car. I'd driven nearly 200 miles, and it must have been nearly midnight by the time I reached the hospital. My brother, David, was already there, and he was the first to tell me that our father had died. He put his arms around me and said, 'Dad's dead. He's in peace now. There's nothing left for us to do here. Let's go home.'

As we drove away, I remember feeling both sadness and joy. The sadness was for me, for I would never see my father in his physical body ever again. The joy was for my father. I somehow hoped that death would be a fresh start for him. My father had left our home when I was 15 years old in pursuit of alcoholism. For years he lived rough on the streets, in hedges, under Waterloo Bridge. David and I worked half of any week to try to get him proper care. To me, my father was never an alcoholic, though; he was a warm, loving, beautiful man who had simply lost hope. Back at home that night after my father's death, David, my mother and I talked long into the early hours of the morning. *We had to because death feels so unreal.* I think I'm speaking for most people when I say that when somebody dies you just don't get it! For days, weeks, and months after my father's death, we still kept expecting him to walk into the room at any moment just like before. Until the actual funeral, death feels completely unreal; after the funeral, death just feels very unreal!

David and Mum finally went to bed. I stayed up. My mind was wide awake. Over and over I kept on thinking just one thought – *What's real?* In my mind I surveyed the world for something real, something reliable, something everlasting that doesn't die. Like a mantra, I kept on asking 'What's real?' I got my answer pretty much right away, but I didn't take it seriously until I realised it wouldn't go away. Every time I asked 'What's real?' the answer was . . .

'Love is real!'

It was shortly after my father's funeral that, for the first time ever, I consciously dedicated my life to love. I wanted to do this so that I could live my life as a mark of respect for my father, and to everyone else I've known who has died. I was grieving, and deep down I wanted there to be a point to it all. Again and again, the only thing that felt at all real about life and death . . . was love. I realised that *love inspires everything that is whole, that love animates life, and that, even after death, only love remains.* It took my father's death to show me that *we live for love,* and that . . .

love is the whole point of everything!

Each of us is so impressive, so attractive and so inspirational when we dare to open our hearts to love. It's as if we radiate when we love. Think of a time when you've been truly loving. Bring those feelings forward to now. Can you remember how you walked, how you talked and how you held yourself? Do you remember the light in your eyes, and the light in other people's eyes? And do you remember how much energy you had? Generous, creative, abundant, open, defenceless – the whole world was aroused by you!

It's as if you fulfil the purpose of your being each time you choose love. What higher purpose to life is there other than love? Can you think of a better reason to be alive other than love? Invent other reasons if you will, such as victory, fame, wealth, success . . . happiness even . . . but can you see how these lesser gods are but a pale reflection, a mere consolation prize, for the only real god, which is love?

There were many times, soon after my father's death, when I felt like giving up on love. It felt so tempting to give in, to give up, to become cynical, to cut off, and even to die. Cynicism was my protest march. Love was my acceptance speech. Daily, I began to call upon the power of love to inspire and guide me – with clients, seminars, talks, telephone calls, meetings, fun, play, family, rest – everything.

Love's power is unconditional – it is unconditionally wise and unconditionally available. People sometimes forget that they can pray to Love for help, strength, guidance and surrender. In my workshops, I often share one of my prayers called 'Let Love Be Your God.' It reads simply:

Love, and let
Love be your
God.

Pray to Love.
Worship Love.
Sing to Love.
Meditate on Love.

Walk with Love.
Talk with Love.
Look with Love.
Listen with Love.

Dedicate your
Life to Love.
Dedicate your
Relationships to Love.

Dedicate your
Work to Love.

Love, and let
Love be your
God.

Love and Be Happy!

To be happy, love must mean more to you than anything.

I was once reliably informed by a client of mine that the only place where happiness comes before love is in the English diction-ary! In real life, love comes first. Happiness is an attribute of love. One might even say that love is happiness. If your current plan for happiness doesn't put love first, don't think for a second that you'll be truly happy. To be happy you can't get around love; you can only go *through* it.

The fundamental principle upon which I base my entire life and work is very simple. It is: *Love and be happy.* These four words are my Bible of Happiness. I honestly believe that these words, plus the willingness to live by them, are enough to help build a life of unimaginable joy, healing, intimacy, wholeness and creativity. Love is the material that happiness is made from. Thus . . .

**your intention to love, no matter what,
is the absolute key to happiness.**

Think about it. Try, if you can, to hate someone and be happy.
Try to resent somebody and be joyous. Try to be angry at someone
and be peaceful. Try to judge someone and feel free. Try to control
someone and not feel controlled. Try to be fully independent and
intimate. Try to cheat somebody and feel safe. It can't happen,
because what you do to another you're doing to yourself. *Love
works!*

Fear begets fear. Make no mistake about this. Fear can only
offer itself to you. So often we try to convince ourselves that 'the
means justifies the ends' and that 'the destination will make up
for the journey', but we know this isn't true. The destination *is*
the journey, and fear cannot lead you to love. Fear leads to fear.
Similarly, guilt leads to guilt, judgment leads to judgment, and
punishment leads to punishment. Love, on the other hand, leads
to love. And love also leads to happiness.

Affirm, therefore, your intention to love. Make it your prayer,
your mantra, your meditation, your morning ritual and your evening ritual. Put love first – above everything. You'll find that as
you strengthen your intention to love, so automatically will the
temptation weaken to replace love with lesser gods like control
and fear. If you're prepared to stick with love long enough, you'll
discover for yourself that . . .

love is the key to real abundance.

First, love! *Love and enjoy everything!* If you're waiting to be
happy before you start being loving, then you'll find that you're
in for a very long wait. Similarly, if you're waiting to be successful before you're truly loving and generous, then you'll be greatly
disappointed and frustrated. There's no such thing as happiness
without love first, success without love first, health without love
first, peace of mind without love first, or freedom without love
first. *First, love!*

Love,
And you will enjoy abundance;
Love,
And you will enjoy success.
Love,
And you will enjoy peace;
Love,
And you will enjoy happiness.
Love,
Place love above everything.
Love,
And you will enjoy everything.

Love is your best bet for happiness. That being the case, I'm often asked, 'How do I know if I'm being truly loving or not?' Well, one acid test for checking to see if you're being true to love is – if you're being genuinely loving, you'll feel happy. Conversely . . .

if you're not happy, you'll know that you're *not* being loving.

Love and be happy is the key. Therefore, to say that love is your best bet for happiness is not strictly true. The whole truth must be that love is your *only* bet for happiness. Happiness cannot ever happen without love.

Love Never Leaves You

'You are never not full of love.'

Your unconditioned Self is always loving, unlike your ego, which has learned to always be afraid. Like happiness, love is natural to you. It is constant. Certainly, there are times in life when love can appear to be overwhelmed by fear and hurt – for all the world it can feel like love is lost – but in truth, love doesn't die, love doesn't fade, love doesn't change. Love is forever. Love is never destroyed; it is only eclipsed.

Love is the essence of your unconditioned Self, and love doesn't leave its source. Love never leaves you. If you were to take away your possessions, your history, your wealth, your conditioning, your pain and your glory, you'd be left with nothing – nothing but love. Love remains. Love is the inner god of your unconditioned Self. Table D gives you two profiles, one for your loving unconditioned Self, the other for your fearful conditioned self.

Unconditioned Self	Conditioned self
whole	split
oneness	separation
love	fear
joy	pleasure/pain
knowing	searching
trust	doubt
abundance	lack
acceptance	judgmental
free	defensive
infinite	small
eternal	temporal

Table D

By dedicating your life to love, you're attempting to change your mind about yourself. In truth, you're full of love, yet you've learned to believe that there's little or no love within you. The moment you scared yourself into thinking that love was outside you and not within was the moment your ego made love special, limited, scarce, weak, rare, and, above all, elusive.

Loving relationships are born of Self-acceptance – that is: (1) 'I accept that I have love to give'; (2) 'I accept the love of others'; and (3) 'I accept that love lives within.' Without Self-acceptance, truly loving relationships are impossible. Peace, joy and union with others happens only as you heal the conflict in your own mind. Self-acceptance is essential, therefore, because . . .

you cannot be loving and guilty!

The greatest contribution you can make to any relationship is to love and accept yourself. For as long as you insist on believing that deep down you're unworthy of love and not good enough, all of your loving relationships will eventually deteriorate into a fearful contract of needs. Thus, you'll find that you constantly have to change your friends and your lovers in order to give love another go.

Relationships are the experience of personal beliefs projected. In other words, you get the relationship you think you deserve. If, for instance, you judge that you're worthy of a little bit of love, you'll experience relationships that have only a little bit of love. If, however, you judge that you're entirely worthy of love, you'll experience relationships where love continually renews itself.

If you're willing, even just a little bit, to entertain the possibility that you are whole, worthy and well, you allow for the possibility of experiencing wholeness and joy in each of your relationships. As your belief in your own wholeness strengthens, so too will your experience of whole, healthy, loving relationships strengthen. In other words, by giving up guilt, you make yourself more available to love.

The Law of Projection insists that . . .

what you believe about yourself
you will project onto your relationships.

Therefore, if you judge yourself to be 'not good enough', you'll always find, eventually, that your partner and your friends are 'not as good as you first hoped'. Also, as long as you believe that something is missing in you, you'll experience something missing in your relationships. Similarly, if you judge yourself as 'bad', 'wrong', or 'nothing', then your relationships will turn sour, go wrong and amount to nothing, unless, that is, you're prepared to change your mind about yourself.

The love that inspires a relationship never leaves, but it can be overlooked. There is never 'no love', but there's often pain, conflict, separation, abuse, anger and a need for revenge that can appear to eclipse love's presence. If you're experiencing any pain in your relationships, the key to healing and happiness is to realise that . . .

**the source of the problem isn't
the relationship; it is projection.**

Unfortunately, none of us can keep our damning self-judgments and guilt to ourselves. We always attract people (consciously and unconsciously) into our lives who we can share (that is, project onto) our suffering and conflict with. When the pain and abuse is too much, you're not bound to stick around in a relationship, but it *is* a good idea to address why you might attract such abuse. This is vital for the health of all your relationships now and in the future.

It's always tempting to lay blame for all your relationship problems on 'the other person'. If healing, and not revenge, is your true intention, then you'll want to ask yourself: (1) What have I projected onto this situation? (2) What is my part in this conflict? (3) Why have I attracted this person into my life? and (4) What can I do to be loving here and now?

Blame is dishonest – no one is completely responsible for your pain.

When a relationship appears to be full of pain, it's because your relationship is full of projections. Sometimes we're scared to take responsibility for our projections because we fear . . . 'If I take more responsibility, I'll feel more guilty.' You take responsibility for your part, not to step into more guilt, but to take the first step into undoing your guilt. Honesty isn't about condemnation; it's about a willingness to be free, loving and true. By being honest about your fears, your projections and 'your part' in any conflict, you instantly create a possibility for more honest, loving relationships.

In your quest for happiness, you can never escape the fact that *you can only love another person as much as you're willing to love yourself.* There's no way around this. To be even more blatant, I could say that *unless you're willing to be loving to yourself, you can't be loving.*

So many relationships run into trouble because we expect our partners and our friends to give us something we're not willing to give ourselves – that is, love and acceptance. The fact is, however, that . . .

**no one can love you more than you're prepared
to love yourself and get away with it!**

The bottom line is that you won't let anyone love you if you're not willing to love you. When anyone turns up in your life wanting to love you more than you love yourself, you may very well be amused and excited at first, but your lack of Self-acceptance will eventually try to talk you out of love. Too much love and not enough Self-acceptance leads to too much guilt. Eventually, you must either change your mind about yourself (that is, drop the guilt), or you must change the personnel.

You will also find that *when people do love you, you won't allow yourself to see it unless you love you!* Have you ever been in a situation where your partner or a friend showers you with bouquets of 'I love you', 'You're wonderful', 'You're beautiful', 'You're amazing', and all the while you're thinking, *He/she doesn't really love me?* Or maybe you've experienced it the other way around, where no matter how much you tried to love someone, this person wouldn't or couldn't let you do so.

Projection is powerful. Whenever you're upset because you judge that your partner or friends don't love you enough, you can be sure that what you're really witnessing is the projection of *your own reluctance to love yourself enough.* Similarly, if you feel that you're not getting enough recognition from someone, you're really witnessing the projection of *you not giving enough recognition to yourself.* The more you love yourself, the more you're able to recognise how loved you are.

It's uncanny, but completely true, how over and over again, you find that . . .

people will treat you the way *you* treat you.

What you do to yourself, others will do to you, also. In other words, no one can do anything to you that you aren't already doing to yourself. Similarly, no one can make you feel anything you don't choose to feel yourself. There's absolutely no way around this. *Your relationships mirror your judgments.* Hence, you'll find that if you reject yourself, others will, too; if you condemn yourself, others will, too; if you distance yourself, others will, too; if you judge yourself, others will, too; and if you overlook and undervalue yourself, others will, too. Projection is the Law of 'Others Will, Too.'

If you want peace, first make peace with yourself; if you want love, first practise love on yourself; if you want kindness, first be gentle on yourself; if you want acknowledgment, first pay respect to yourself; and if you want faithfulness, first be true to yourself. Put another way:

Love thyself, so that you can love another.
Love thyself, so that you cannot project fear.
Love thyself, so as to let others love you.
Love thyself, so as to let people near.

The gift of relationships is that together we can encourage each another to believe once more in our innate wholeness. Although no one can *make* you happy, everyone can *encourage* you to be happy. The intention to love can work miracles. Through relationships we learn to practise forgiveness – that is, we make the choice for wholeness. As we forgive ourselves and one another for our fears and doubts, we strengthen our resolve to trust once more in the love that created us.

Unless you can accept your wholeness, all your loving relationships will become needy relationships. All pain in relationships has something to do with perceptions of personal lack – that is, needs. Without Self-acceptance, you'll always end up resenting and abusing any person you expect to meet your needs. This is true whether they meet these needs or not.

Wholeness has no needs. With wholeness, relationships are joyful, not needy. By being willing to love yourself, to accept your own wholeness, you open yourself up to an entirely different experience of loving relationships.

Love Has Never Hurt You

My wedding to my first wife, Miranda, was a truly happy occasion. We were married in my grandmother's English country garden, with acres of rich, green grass rolling down to a beautiful river below. We were blessed and honoured to have Edward Carpenter, now ex-Dean of Westminster, and his wife, Lillian Carpenter, begin our wedding ceremony. What followed was a profusion of Bach, harp, prayer, flowers, friendship and champagne. The whole event was a celebration of love – universal love.

There are so many wonderful memories of that day, but one very amusing one that we often recall happened during the receiving line, when the guests lined up to give us their congratulations. One by one, we received well wishes plus advice such as: 'Enjoy today – it doesn't get better than this', and 'Make the most of this – this is as good as it gets.' Other 'words of wisdom' included:

- 'It takes more than love, you know.'

- 'Enjoy love while you're young.'

- 'You can't just rely on love – you have to work at it, too.'

- 'You're young, and I know you think love lasts forever, but . . .'

- 'Love is hard.'

- 'Love is never easy.'

- 'Love isn't without its pain.'

- 'The first year is the hardest. Survive that and you'll be okay.'

- 'Remember, don't live in each other's pockets. Have lots of time apart.'

- 'You've done it – you're trapped now!'

- 'Be realistic – it won't always be this wonderful.'

- 'Don't let love stop you from having fun!'

On and on it went. It was as if, one by one, each person had plucked a thought of fear out of our minds and said it out loud. Now, to be fair, there were a hundred times more wonderful thoughts of love, and of hope for love! However, what we witnessed were two distinct attitudes to love – one very limited and fearful, the other very abundant and hopeful.

Your ego can only judge anything, including love, as it judges itself. Thus, because the ego is a small idea about yourself, it sees love as limited. Conversely, your unconditioned Self, being completely whole, accepts that love is whole. Once again, the ego and the spirit have a completely different point of view, as shown in Table E.

LOVE IS . . .	
Conditioned self	**Unconditioned Self**
limited	infinite
weak	powerful
dangerous	safe
not enough	everything
frightening	comforting
special	universal
hard	king
blind	true
painful	healing
a trap	freedom
a dream	real
death	life

Table E

Perhaps the greatest misperception of love is that *love hurts.*[1] Of course, nothing could be further from the truth. Any one thing can only give of itself, and in the case of love, love can only give love. What hurts isn't love itself, but your *misperceptions* of love, your fear of love, your giving up on love, and, in particular, your resistance to love. In fact, it's fair to say that . . .

most of all, it is your resistance to love that hurts you so.

For our wedding service, we chose six readings, one of which is a famous passage by Emmett Fox. It reads:

There is no difficulty that enough love
will not conquer;
no disease that enough love
will not heal;
no door that enough love will not open.
It makes no difference how deeply

*seated may be the trouble; how
hopeless the outlook; how muddled the tangle;
how great the mistake.
A sufficient realisation of love will
dissolve it all. If only you could
love enough you would be the
happiest and most powerful
being in the world.*[2]

The problem isn't that love doesn't work; the problem is that we don't trust that love will work. When loving feels difficult, we're easily discouraged, and we often give up on love too soon. Ironically, the moment you turn away from love is when you begin to feel let down by love. This, once again, is projection. We then search for love substitutes, most of which lead to loss, pain, sacrifice, fear and illusions of separateness.

We've become too accustomed to looking at love through the limited, fearful eyes of the ego instead of through the wholly joyous vision of our unconditioned Self. It is important, therefore, that when you're tempted to limit the power of love, or when you're finding it difficult to love, you call for help from your unconditioned Self, from love itself and from your God.

One prayer I once wrote for myself is called 'Consciousness of Love'. It reads:

*Beloved Creator,
Consciousness of Love.
Open me up to the Love that I am.
Let the Love that I am light up my
relationship with You, with _____,
with everyone.
Let the Love that I am sing constant
hymns of divinity to all of me, that
I might remember You in everyone.
Let the Love that I am relax me,
inspire me, help me to be, that this
world may enjoy the best of me.*

Let the Love that I am hold me,
guide me, casting out fear, healing
all pain, that I, the One and the
many, may feel Your beloved peace
once again. So be it.

By being willing to heal your misperceptions and fears of love, you're not only healing your relationship with love, but you're also healing your relationship with yourself and with everyone else as well.

Always Communicate Your Love!

Love is the most fun you
can have with anyone.

The following story serves as a reminder of how important it is to communicate from the heart at all times:

A husband and wife, both in their late 70s, decided that, after 55 years of marriage, it was high time they got a divorce. When their counsellor asked them why, the wife issued a catalogue of reasons: 'He never asks if I'm happy,' said the wife.

'I assumed you were,' said the husband.

'He never says he loves me,' said the wife.

'I thought you knew I loved you,' said the husband.

The wife continued, 'He never says I'm beautiful.'

The husband replied, 'I look at you every day and admire your beauty.'

'We rarely talk,' said the wife.

'I know you like to read a lot,' said the husband.

'I read because we don't talk,' said the wife. There was a pause. 'And we never go out,'she added.

'I thought you liked to stay in,' said the husband.

'I only stay in because I'm waiting to go out,' said the wife.

The counsellor continued to take notes.

'He's also very mean to me,' said the wife.

'In what way?' asked the counsellor.

'Well, at breakfast, three times a week for 55 years, he has always served me the crust of the loaf, and I hate the bread crust!'

The husband was distraught and wailed, 'I give you the crust, my dear, because that is *my* favourite part of the loaf.'

Did you know that the word 'assume' can make an 'ass' out of 'u' and 'me'?

I once gave a workshop to a group of nurses at a Royal Hospital in the middle of England. The workshop was about the value of love and laughter in the healing process. The morning had been truly joyful, creative and great fun. One hour after lunch, everyone in the room was in tears, experiencing profound grief. There were no handkerchiefs, so I placed an order for paper towels!

The trigger for all the tears began with a comment I made about how important it is for personal health and healthy relationships that we openly express the love we feel. 'Love shouldn't be suppressed and hidden,' I suggested. I talked, in particular, about my father's death and how, although I knew he was certain of my love for him, I still wished I'd told him 'I love you' more often.

I went on to say that after my dad's death, I undertook emotional surgery to remove my stiff upper lip and to heal my British conservative conditioning. From now on, I was going to express my love for everyone I knew. My mother and my brother, David, got it first! Then my close friends. And then everyone else.

'What could be more sad,' I said, 'than not having the courage to tell someone you love them?' It was at this point that I noticed the tears start to roll.

One by one, the health professionals shared their stories. One young nurse shared her grief that none of her family had ever said they loved each other. Everyone in the room, without exception, could relate to her grief. Another nurse said, 'My parents never directly praise, show affection, or say "I love you" to my face, but my sisters tell me that as soon as I walk out of the room, my parents don't stop talking about how proud they are of me.' We all smiled, for we recognised the pattern. 'I just wish we could be more honest,' said the nurse.

How many loving relationships have appeared to die because no one could quite bring themselves to say 'I love you'? It is indeed a common fear that as soon as you pronounce your love for someone out loud, fate must immediately issue a penalty calling for punishment, rejection or some other payment. This fear isn't natural. It can only be your learned guilt and unworthiness that breeds such fearful superstition. Out of fear, you decide to hide your love and play it safe. Yet . . .

by playing it safe you lose what you're trying to keep.

Talk joy! Talk love! Talk happiness! Too many relationships crumble simply because there isn't enough talk and focus on joy, love and happiness. If it's a truly loving relationship that you're committed to, then expressing your love will strengthen the love and not weaken it.

When counselling couples, I often ask each person to draw their own individual picture of happiness. It becomes clear when both pictures are being compared that, although both people want happiness for themselves and for each other, they have hardly ever taken the time to talk openly, honestly and directly about happiness. There's nothing stopping you from asking your partner or your friends, 'What is happiness?' 'How can we be happier?' 'Do you feel loved by me?' or 'How can I love and support you better?'

You Have to Jump for JOY!

Do you want to be independent or happy?

The 'Me Generation' is our society's most recent experiment in a catalogue of ill-fated attempts at the pursuit of happiness. It is about individualism, ego, separating out, making it on your own, setting your boundaries, doing your own thing, being unattached, being free of commitment and being fully independent.[3] The point is, however, that you're not independent! Independence is a complete and utter illusion, for you are inextricably connected to the entirety of everything.

In therapy circles and popular psychology, much is made of healing 'co-dependence', the addiction to apparent external sources of love. This is good work, except when it is mistaught and it leads to more boundaries, more defensiveness, more separation and unhealthy independence. Perhaps what we need now is a movement for 'recovering independence addicts' – one that helps people give up their separation, wounding and fear for a greater experience of joining and wholeness.

Independence is impossible – any environmentalist, biologist, quantum physicist, poet, spiritual master or little baby will tell you so. The English poet and cleric John Donne put it well in 'Iland Verse':

> *No man is an Iland, entire of itself;*
> *every man is a peece of the Continent,*
> *a part of the maine; if a Clod bee washed*
> *away by the sea, Europe is the lesse, as*
> *well as if a Promonterie were, as well as*
> *if a Mannor of thy friends or thine own*
> *were; any man's death diminishes me,*
> *because I am involved in Mankind; and*
> *therefore never send to know for whom*
> *the bell tolls; it tolls for thee.*[4]

The desire to be independent often betrays an attachment to old wounds. Hence, independence is a defence – a defence against fear, against hurt and against a commitment to love. Moreover, too much unhealthy independence can also end up blocking the possibility of attracting mutual happiness and love. How can you be independent and intimate? How can you be independent and receive? How can you be independent and experience the joy of sharing yourself wholly with another person?

Independence as a defence tends to stem from two fundamental fears in a relationship: (1) the fear of rejection, and (2) the fear of intimacy. Both of these fears are learned; they aren't natural. They have each become, however, heavily ingrained in our way of thinking. In a nutshell, then . . .

**every relationship must face
the fear of intimacy and the fear of rejection.**

Fear of intimacy and fear of rejection are all about imagined needs that arise from a perceived lack of wholeness. In other words, both the fear of intimacy and the fear of rejection stem from learned guilt and unworthiness. Thus, you're afraid that if you're intimate with others, they'll eventually judge you as severely as you judge yourself. And you fear rejection by others because you've already judged yourself to be unacceptable and you don't want to be reminded of the pain.

Where there is fear of intimacy and rejection, you may notice some of the following behaviours:

- You never commit fully, preferring to keep your options open.

- It may look like you commit fully, but you know you never do.

- You have many, many acquaintances, but no one knows you really well.

- You take a long time to get to know people, and you always begin by putting firm boundaries in place.

- You give people your time, your money and your attention, but never *You*.

- You're wary of commitment because it feels like a loss of freedom.

- When a relationship gets really good, you step back, you test it, and you sabotage it.

- You 'wait and see' if the relationship 'is going to go somewhere' before you hop on.

- You're afraid of rejection, so you try to reject others before they reject you.

- You find yourself needlessly upsetting, quarrelling with, and annoying your loved ones.

- You prefer the focus to be on others, never on you.

- You're afraid that what you give, you ultimately lose.

- There's no one you share all of your parts and all of your Self with.

For years I prided myself on being 'completely independent'. I was the proverbial 'one-man show' who would make room for a little bit of love every now and then – just enough to convince me I wasn't as miserable and as lonely as I felt. Dysfunctionally independent people tend to keep busy to prevent themselves from recognising their pain. Independence looks like safety, but the safety is sterile. Even now, I'm aware that when I'm hurt or in pain, my temptation is to pull away fast and be independent again. The fact is, though, that . . .

intimacy heals!

When loving is difficult, the key is to move in closer – nose to nose. The more you move away, the easier it is to project, numb out, separate, be safe and sterile, and be superior and lonely. If your intention is to love, no matter what, then you'll want to get close, let down your defences and be open. God knows, this can be difficult, for love brings up fear. But the more you can put love first, the less difficult this becomes.[5]

One important key to intimate communication is to *share the feelings; don't shoot the feelings.* In other words, for the communication to be safe and healing, you must commit to the truth that (1) there are no enemies here, and (2) your feelings must not be used as weapons. A relationship that's truly dedicated to love can afford to drop guilt, defence, attack and the desire for separation. To experience joy again, you must jump for joy. To do this, joy must mean more to you than vengeance.

Lose Control

Do you want to be happy or in control?

Love doesn't control. Control is not love, control is fear. You don't attempt to control a relationship because of joy, but because of fear. Control is meant to bring certainty and safety, but this so-called safety is so sterile it soon smells of fear and death, not love and life. Control is also meant to prevent losses, but whatever you try to control you'll ultimately end up losing.

Love and joy require freedom, not control. This is difficult to understand for those of us who have been brought up in and conditioned by a culture that demands that you try to control life. The ego always seeks to control everything; the unconditioned Self seeks to set everything free. Love and joy cannot be organised, controlled and dictated to, but can only be accepted, shared, and allowed to be.

> One day a young apprentice devil came running to the chief devil and said, 'Chief devil, sir, something awful is happening to planet Earth!'
>
> The chief devil frowned and growled, 'What's happening?'
>
> The young devil, very afraid, stuttered, 'There's a bloke called Jesus, and he's teaching everyone to love one another. He's also telling them that God is love and not fear.'

The chief devil was busy writing his book, *The Joy of Politics*. He told the young devil to keep an eye on things for him and report back later. The young devil soon returned looking even more worried than before. 'Chief devil, sir,' said the young devil, 'now Jesus is encouraging people to give up fear, hate, and resentment, and to start practising forgiveness.'

The chief devil was still busy writing. He was halfway through a chapter on 'Bureaucracy'. He frowned and growled at the young devil, 'Go away and watch for me.'

It wasn't long before the young devil returned again, looking totally terrified. 'It's got worse, chief devil, sir. Now Jesus is talking about joy and that the Kingdom of Heaven is within.'

The chief devil put down his pen. He had just finished the final chapter on 'Control'. He frowned and growled at the young devil, 'Why do you worry so? As soon as Jesus dies, we'll enlist people to organise, control, and make rigid his teachings. We will create another religion! And soon, the love Jesus speaks of will be lost in dogma.'

It was the poet William Blake who wrote:

> *He who binds to himself a joy*
> *Does the winged life destroy;*
> *But he who kisses the joy as it flies*
> *Lives in eternity's sunrise.*[6]

I remember how, soon after I fell in love for the first time, I became terribly afraid. At first we experienced what I call the Wonder Period. We were open, honest, loving, defenceless, and entirely grateful to be together. We both forgot to be guilty and unworthy of love. *And,* we were both entirely present – that is, we were focused on the love we felt for each other now. We weren't trying to plan, organise or dictate the future of the relationship. Eventually, doubts and fears arose, and so did the temptation to take control, to be defensive and to take precautionary measures – for a pre-emptive strike!

As you experience even greater levels of love and intimacy in a relationship, it will test your faith in yourself (that is, do I really deserve this?), in each other (that is, do we really love each other?), and in love itself (that is, does love really last?). When your faith falters, you'll experience the urge to take control. By doing so, you're attempting to create greater safety, certainty and strength. And yet, even more control often leads to even less happiness and aliveness. For this reason, my prayer for all my relationships is:

> 'Dear God, I give You my relationship with _____.
> I give you my desire to control this relationship.
> Let Love be my guide.
> Let Love bless us both.
> So be it.'

The truth is . . .

you cannot be in control *and* happy!

Control isn't only about the fear of loss. Although it may not look obvious, another reason for trying to control your relationships is because on one level you're afraid of too much love. The ego objects to too much love because more love means, ultimately, less fear, less judgment, less defensiveness and less separation. Where there is only love, the ego is out of a job. So, either the ego reasserts itself, or you change your mind about yourself – you love yourself and you accept your wholeness.

If you could accept that you're whole already, you would no longer fear loss or love. Fear leads to control, and control equals trouble. Have you noticed, for instance, that you experience the most pain with people whom you most try to control? Also, have you noticed that the more you control your partner, the less attractive he or she becomes? Furthermore, have you noticed how resentful and bitter you become whenever someone tries to control you? Like a butterfly caught in the clutches of a sticky hand, love's beauty is lost without the freedom to fly. The bottom line is . . .

you cannot love what you control.

Apologise Quickly!

Do you want to be proud or happy?

Every relationship, be it romance or friendship, begins with a honeymoon phase, or Wonder Period. The new person in your life can do absolutely no wrong. You're loving, accepting, and completely forgiving of the fact that this new person worships football, works late, has emotions, lives with Mother, is set in his/her ways, only likes fast food, forgets to flush, keeps stray animals, eats crisps in bed, and crunches popcorn too loudly at the movies. It's easy to love in the Wonder Period because you're in the present time.

After a while, relationships move into the second phase, which I refer to as the Now That You're Mine Phase, or the Familiar Period. During this time, the new people in your life become familiar to you, and they begin to 'sound familiar', to 'remind you of . . . ', and to 'behave in the same way as . . .' The ego is always looking for patterns to defend against; and now the emphasis shifts from present to past, imagination to memory, hope to doubt, love to fear, freedom to control. You recall now how, in the past, you appeared to lose out in love, so you become afraid and attempt to amplify love with a little more control.

Next, love gives way to a power struggle for control, dominance, sitting in the driver's seat, feeling superior and being right. This is the Control Period. Now, love is no longer natural. Instead, it becomes a learning curve. You'll inevitably make mistakes when you engage in a power struggle. You'll mess up, act bad, get things wrong, fight, attack, defend yourself, get hurt, get petty, lose it, and *feel guilty*. Neither you nor your partner or friend will want to enforce the guilt, however, if your relationship is consciously dedicated to love and truth.

There will be many opportunities for you to make an apology during the power struggle. Unfortunately, the goal of being happy often gives way to the goal of being right during the Control Period. In other words, being right means more to you than being happy. You have to ask yourself . . .

do I want to be right or be happy?

The more you want to be right, the less happy you'll be. You'll become more and more defensive, stubborn, resentful, bitter, petty, suspicious, vicious, and small. Love is big; pride is small! Welcome to the Coma Period. This is where you look like you're still together, but you're not. The battle to be right appears to have worn you both down. You're tired, closed down, exhausted and numb. One of you will have to put down your weapons of guilt before you can both awaken again to the love that is still beneath the battleground of fear.

The Awakening Period usually begins with an apology or forgiveness. You'll want to apologise if love means more to you than guilt, pain, mistakes, and the past. You'll want to *ask* for forgiveness and *give* forgiveness if love is more valuable to you than fear and resentment. If you're really smart, you will no longer try to be right; you will simply try to be loving.

I promise you this – nowhere on your grave or in your obituary will it be written: 'He was always right!' or 'She never, ever had to say she was sorry!' Hopefully, words like *loving, kind* and *forgiving* will be mentioned over and over. Also, I promise you that some of life's sweetest moments are those that follow an honest, heartfelt apology!

Forgive Fast and Be Happy NOW!

Do you want to be superior or be happy?

I often ask participants in my workshops to be still for a moment and become aware of what holding resentment feels like both physically and emotionally. We then list these feelings to estimate the cost of resentment. The cost includes 'anger like black rain', 'constant fear and an inability to relax', 'feeling like a victim', 'physical pain', 'a heavy heart', 'empty superiority', 'no air and no breath', 'a preoccupation with the past', 'vengeful hate', 'a cold heart', 'no joy and no love', and 'a feeling like you're slowly dying'.

The most chilling and accurate description I've ever read of the unforgiving mind appears in *A Course in Miracles*. It reads:

> The unforgiving mind is full of fear, and offers love no room to be itself; no place where it can spread its wings in peace and soar above the turmoil of the world. The unforgiving mind is sad, without the hope of respite and release from pain. It suffers and abides in misery, peering about in darkness, seeing not, yet certain of the danger lurking there.
>
> The unforgiving mind is torn with doubt, confused about itself and all it sees; afraid and angry, weak and blustering, afraid to go ahead, afraid to stay, afraid to waken or to go to sleep, afraid of every sound, yet more afraid of stillness; terrified of darkness, yet more terrified at the approach of light.

Resentment costs too much. Make no mistake – *you* are the one who has to pay the bill for the resentment you hold on to. It is *your* nervous system, *your* lungs, *your* muscles, *your* heart, *your* perception, and *your* mind that deteriorates and decays during every moment you try to defend yourself with hate.

Resentment is an investment in hate – it believes that hate will give you something that love cannot. Resentment is learned; it isn't natural. It is the ego that believes resentment, hate, punishment and attack will protect you and preserve you. According to what you've learned, you are apparently safe with hate in your heart – safer than if you were to love or forgive.

The problem with resentment is that *you cannot be resentful and happy*. There's an old saying: 'If your heart has room for one enemy, it is not a safe place for a friend.' You cannot hate and be happy. You cannot hate and love. You cannot hate and win. You cannot hate and be free. You cannot hate and be present. You cannot hate and have a future. The bottom line is . . .

> you cannot carry resentment and
> peace of mind at the same time.

As long as you still value resentment, forgiveness will have no appeal. Forgiveness only has appeal for those who are interested in freedom, love, peace of mind and joy.

Your ego and your spirit have two completely different opinions about forgiveness. The ego, convinced of your own smallness and weakness, advises you that you cannot afford to forgive. Guilt, fear, defensiveness and attack are the ego's answer. Forgiveness is, ultimately, the betrayal of the ego and all it stands for. Forgiveness is the choice for wholeness.

True forgiveness is not about condoning, agreeing to forget, or sacrifice. True forgiveness isn't about stuffing your emotions or keeping quiet about your resentments. True forgiveness isn't about doing the right thing. Neither is it about being a doormat or about blaming yourself. No! The truth is . . .

> true forgiveness is the willingness to believe
> (1) that you are whole, and (2) that no one
> can threaten or take away your wholeness.

Forgiveness becomes easier when love means more to you than anything else. Also, it helps when you see the cost of resentment for what it really is. See Table F for the contrast between the forgiving mind of the unconditioned Self and the unforgiving mind of the ego.

Unforgiving Mind	Forgiving Mind
Judges you as weak and un-whole	Loves you without judgment
Sees that you're separate and vulnerable	Understands that love sees no separation
Believes that you're guilty and unworthy	Loves you wholly, unconditionally
Projects fear	Extends love
Encourages you to defend yourself	Encourages you to be loving
Attracts attack with defence	Sees that love attracts love
Uses hate, fear and resentment to keep you safe	Calls upon love to keep you safe
Is preoccupied with the past	Continually lets go into the "now"
Mistrusts happiness	Accepts happiness

Table F

True forgiveness is an act of Self-love and Self-acceptance. When you forgive, you put away toys of guilt and embrace love once more.

Forgiveness heals pain. Pain is a fearful nightmare that leads you to believe that you're weak, small, isolated, vulnerable and alone. Pain feels real. Pain feels like it will last forever. And yet, if when you're in pain you can muster even a little willingness to forgive, you'll begin to see differently. In truth . . .

forgiveness is a decision to see the 'whole truth'.

The willingness to forgive is really the willingness to see . . . 'I am not my pain' 'I am not my mistakes', 'I am not my past.' Forgiveness acknowledges that 'this pain is not who I am'. As you pray to your whole Self, to God, or to any symbol of wholeness, your perceptions will change as you begin to see again that . . .

'I am whole. I am safe. I am not a body. I am free. I am the Presence of Love.'

Forgiveness is a miracle – the greatest of all miracles. Every instance of forgiveness is a vote for greater peace, strength, love, freedom and joy. When you forgive, you are truly changing your mind about yourself. You're giving up your fearful, learned self-image for the loving, powerful, whole and original Self that you are. Forgiveness elects love to rule. Happiness flourishes where there is love. Whenever you feel low, you might like to affirm:

I feel tender, and I pick forgiveness now.
I feel afraid, and I choose love now.
I feel hurt, and I want healing now.
I feel angry, and I affirm peace now.
I feel sad, and I wish for happiness now.

I now let go of my fear of forgiveness.
I declare today a day of amnesty in which
I gratefully volunteer to give up all my
resentments and grievances. One by one,
I give away every fear, scar, guilt, and hatred;
for I will not keep what, in truth, does not
belong to me.

I choose wholeness now. I will no longer teach
myself or anyone else that we are guilty. We are
free. We are free. I pray for peace; and I
will sprinkle kindness, radiate love, and
scatter joy wherever I go. And may
God help me to handle well all of
the happiness that must inevitably
follow! So be it.

❖ ❖ ❖

CHAPTER EIGHT

Travelling Light

*O Travelling Light, wrapped up in darkness,
still clinging to fear, convinced of your guilt,
still dreaming of death. Wake up! Wake
up to happiness 'now'!*

Take your mind back to the first thing this morning. Would you describe the way you woke up today as a beautiful performance, or, more simply, a performance? Was it peaceful, or were you in pieces? Did you rise and shine, or rise and whine? Did you wake up fresh, or on auto? Do you ever find that the effort of waking up actually exhausts you for the rest of the day?

How did you greet this new day? Are you, for instance, the sort of person who wakes up in the morning and says, 'Good morning, God', or swears, 'Good God, morning!'? Maybe you like to start the day with a smile, to get it over with. How do you prepare for each new day?

Try to recall specific decisions you made during the very first hour of today. Your first decision may have been to hit the 'snooze' button on your alarm clock. What then? A quick coffee, maybe? Hit the shower? A cigarette? A search for socks? New underwear? Yesterday's underwear? Hurry the children along? Put on makeup? Breakfast on the run? Catch the latest headlines? Hunt for your wallet? Play the 'find the keys' game? Walk the dog? A quick jog?

Most early-morning decisions are about showers, makeup, clothes, children, food, time and transportation. They're 'doing decisions', as opposed to 'being decisions'. What I'm most interested in is not your 'to do' list, but your 'to be' list. In other words, did you make any conscious decisions about how you wanted 'to be' today? To put it another way . . .

what sort of a day did you decide to have today?

Percentage-wise, how much time did you spend preparing your body for today, that is, washing, feeding, and clothing, as opposed to preparing your *mind* for today? What was the split? Body 95 percent; mind 5 percent, perhaps? Body 25 percent; mind 75 percent, perhaps? Generally speaking, how do you like to prepare yourself mentally and spiritually for each new day of your life?

Your first hour upon waking is like the rudder of a ship, in that it serves to steer a course for the rest of your day. More specifically, it is during this time that you make up your mind exactly what sort of a day you'll have. In other words, you set your intention for the day, unconsciously and consciously. So, once again, think back to the first thing this morning and ask yourself, *How did I decide to be today? What sort of a day did I already decide that I'd have?*

Decision is power! Decision, above circumstance, is the key to happiness *now*. Know, therefore, that your decision counts. You really can decide what sort of a day to have today. In fact, you already have. Nothing, absolutely nothing, can happen without your decision.

*Happiness cannot happen without your
decision to be happy.
Love cannot grow without your
decision to be loving.
Peace cannot blossom without your
decision to be peaceful.
Freedom cannot bloom without your
decision to be free.
Miracles cannot flower without your
decision to be open.
Bliss cannot flourish without your
decision to be guiltless.
Heaven cannot bear its fruits without
your decision to receive.*

Everything ultimately rests on your decision, including pain, fear, suffering and death. Your mind is like a TV set with a hundred different channels, and it is *you* who decides which channel you tune in to. You can choose, for instance, the Victim Channel or the Freedom Channel; the Resentment Channel or the Forgiveness Channel; the X-rated Guilt Channel or the Happiness Channel; the Yesterday Repeat Channel or the Now Channel; the Ego Channel or the Spirit Channel. You can flick onto whichever show you want to see today. Intention is your remote control.

Sometimes you may find that you've consciously decided to have a happy day, but still your experience is one of misery. This is a common experience. What has happened here is that, consciously, you've decided for happiness, but unconsciously you've still decided for misery. Often, unconscious conditioning has the casting vote. What really helps is forgiveness, the choice for wholeness, and the decision to let go of all of your guilt and unworthiness. Whatever happens, keep deciding for joy.

Meditation, prayer, silence, stillness, mantras, yoga and reading inspirational texts, for instance, can all be helpful in aiding you to set your intention for the day. There's no strict formula, technique, dogma or ritual that must be followed. Ultimately, intention is a single thought which, when valued above all else, can illuminate your entire day.

The key to happiness *now* is to see that intention creates outcomes. In other words . . .

your intention determines everything.
It is a great 'power'!

Every morning I sit upon my 'flying carpet' – a beautiful silk carpet I bought on my travels through India. While sitting, I set my intention for the day through prayer and meditation. Sometimes I recite set prayers and sometimes I pray spontaneous prayers. I follow whatever feels natural. One of my favourite personal prayers is my 'Peace Prayer'. It reads:

Peace be to my mind.
Peace be to my thinking.
Peace be to my body.
Peace be to my senses.
Peace be to me now.
Peace be to me always.
Peace be to me here.
Peace be to me everywhere.
Peace be to me with you.
Peace be to me with everyone.
Peace be to One and All.

This prayer quite clearly sets an intention for peace. Other times I might pray, *'Dear God, what would You have my intention be today?'* Again, there's no set formula. At all times, what I'm aiming for is to take guidance from my unconditioned Self. Now is new. Today is new. Above all, then, I want to be open and spontaneously available to all that is and all that I am. This is my intention.

Be Wholehearted!

> *A monk asked Chao-chou,*
> *'If a poor man comes, what should one give him?'*
> *'He lacks nothing,' answered the master.*
> – Zen mondo

When my friends and I first arrived in India, we each felt that we'd somehow been flung from Earth's orbit during our flight and had landed on another planet. Everything was completely different from what we'd ever known – everything!

The entire trip was a mixed bag of shock, surprise, wonder, awe, Delhi belly, poverty, peace, ashrams, hotels, adventure, despair, and also magnificent beauty. The geography and landscape of India is truly beautiful, but nothing was more lovely to us than the moments when we were greeted by the local people.

Greeting is a sacred art in India. For many Indians, greeting the day and greeting one another are both cherished events that are performed mindfully with great care and positive intent. When Indians greet you, therefore, they actually *stop to be with you.* They clasp their hands together, smile, stare deeply into your eyes, and sing, 'Namaste!' which means, 'I bow to the Light in You'. This is somewhat of a contrast to, 'Hey, man!' 'Yo, dude!' 'Hello darling', and 'How the hell are you?'

Since our trip to India, I've collected greetings like 'Namaste!' from all over the world. In central Africa, for instance, there's a greeting where one person says to another, 'I am here to be seen', the reply to which is, 'I see you'. In the Far East, there's an old Gnostic greeting that still survives which, translated, means 'I am the Light in You'. These greetings are really blessings. They are blessings of love, and they help set a definite intention and purpose for time spent together.

The beauty of these sacred greetings is that they bless both the receiver and the giver. They're also wonderful affirmations and teachings of our innate wholeness and oneness with each other. This is helpful because I believe that *the true function of friendship is to remind each other of our wholeness.* In this way, the function of friendship and the function of therapy and medicine are the same.

These sacred greetings celebrate the gift of friendship. They also remind you that *every* person who stands before you is a teacher. If there's one certainty in life you really can rely upon, it is that . . .

**if a person is in your life, it is because
you have a gift for each other.**

Yes! The people you know – not *hope* to know – are the ones who have a gift for you, a gift waiting to be received right now. With each person you are close to, ask yourself, 'What is their gift to me?' and also, 'What is my gift to them?' Don't just ask these questions of the people you find easy to love; ask them of the people who are more challenging!

Make it your intention today, all day, to be present and willing to learn, receive, and give fully to the people you meet. It's impossible to overestimate the value of the person standing before you. Look carefully. All too often we have, in the past, overlooked the person in front of us because we were too busy searching for a 'more' suitable person, over 'there', coming 'next'.

Above all, the real reason why greetings are so important is that you never meet just *any-body;* you always meet your Self. In *A Course in Miracles* it is written:

When you meet anyone, remember it is a holy encounter.
As you see him you will see yourself.
As you treat him you will treat yourself.
As you think of him you will think of yourself.
Never forget this, for in him you will find yourself or
lose yourself.[1]

So much of our pain stems from our persistent attempts to cheat what many ancient philosophers have called The Golden Rule, which is: 'Do unto others as you would have them do unto you.' Another version is: 'Do unto others as though you *were* the others', and another: 'Be careful what you do unto others because you *are* the others!'

The point is . . .

you cannot be happy and cheat The Golden Rule!

What you throw at another person hits *you!* Therefore, you cannot throw hate at someone and feel peace. You cannot throw guilt at someone and experience freedom. You cannot throw anger at someone and enjoy love. You cannot throw any attack at someone and be safe.

The Golden Rule also works the other way. For instance, as long as you judge yourself to be 'not good enough', you will invariably end up judging those people most familiar to you as being 'not good enough'. *This is the ego's blessing.* Nothing astounds the ego more than when a friend you know does something wonderful, wise, and world class. 'They can't be great because I know them', says our ego! Whenever you greet someone, therefore, be clear where you're coming from – ego or spirit.

Your greeting is both an affirmation and a teaching of 'who I am'. What you teach yourself, you teach others, also. So what are you today? Are you guilty, unworthy and a victim, or will you be your loving, free and wholly joyous unconditioned Self? Where are you coming from? You decide. A fine way to begin each day is to ask yourself:

What would I have my teaching be today?

Whatever your decision, let your greetings be a demonstration of your teaching. By the way, the power of your greeting isn't necessarily in the words you use, but in the consciousness with which you *speak* the words. In this way, a simple greeting can become a wonderful tool of teaching, inspiration, and healing. Indeed, a simple 'Hello!' is often enough to shift a perception of fear to love, lack to wholeness, and isolation to unity.

Recent social research tells us that 70 per cent of people don't know the names of their own next-door neighbours. That's right –

70 per cent! We live on top of each other, yet we feel increasingly isolated.[2] I remember as a young child, when times were very hard, my family lived in a high-rise block of flats along with 80 other families. We literally *did* live on top of each other. I remember, in particular, how we got to know the footsteps that belonged to 14a, 14b, 14c, but never the faces and the names. We were all so close . . . yet so separate.

I believe that it's time you and I resurrected the art of greeting. Remember today that you're in great company wherever you go. Look for it and you will see it!

Be What You Want!

> *You will never become happy – you can only be happy.*

There's an old Sufi story of a conversation that once took place between Mulla Nasrudin and a good friend of his:

> 'I'm getting married on the morrow, Mulla,' pronounced his friend, smiling wide from ear to ear. Mulla Nasrudin was quiet and thoughtful. 'Isn't marriage wonderful, Mulla! It is quite the best! Have you ever considered getting married, Mulla?'
>
> Mulla Nasrudin sighed. 'In my youth I thought of nothing else. In fact, I so wanted to find the perfect wife that I travelled the world searching for her. In Damascus, I met a woman who was beautiful, spiritual and loving, but, alas, she had no worldly knowledge. In Isphahan, I met a woman who was beautiful, loving and worldly, but, alas, she wasn't interested in the spiritual life.'
>
> 'Where did you travel to next, Mulla?' asked his friend.
>
> 'I forget where, but I met a woman who was truly spiritual, loving and worldly, but, alas, she wasn't beautiful. Finally, I went to Cairo, and there, after much searching, I found the perfect wife. She was everything I had wanted her to be. She was perfect,' sighed Mulla Nasrudin.

'If she was so perfect, why did you not marry her, Mulla?' asked his friend.

'Alas,' said Mulla Nasrudin, shaking his head, 'she was, unfortunately, looking for the perfect husband!'

Often, what we demand of others we are not willing to be ourselves. In particular, we spend too much time *looking* for the right person instead of *being* the right person. The story of Mulla Nasrudin and his friend illustrates very well how you have to *be* what you *want*. Indeed, one of the most hopeful and helpful teachings of my work through The Happiness Project is:

You can be what you want!

Did anyone tell you when you were growing up that you could be what you want? Hopefully, if you were fortunate, there was at least one person in your life who encouraged you to dream, to dare, and to be. The words *You can be what you want* sound so positive, hopeful and affirming. They are also a statement of truth, for they illustrate a very important principle of being, which is outlined in a poem of affirmation I wrote called 'You Can Be What You Want!' It reads:

If you would want love, be loving.
If you would want care, be caring.
You can be what you want.

If you would want joy, be joyful.
If you would want peace, be peaceful.
You can be what you want.

If you would want happiness, be happy.
If you would want kindness, be kindly.
You can be what you want.

If you would want forgiveness, be forgiving.
If you would want acceptance, be accepting.
You can be what you want.

Being is proactive. It is literally being what you want. It is also about being first. For example, if you want honesty, be honest first; if you want loyalty, be loyal first; if you want trust, be trusting first; if you want enthusiasm, be enthusiastic first; if you want courage, be courageous first; if you want inspiration, be a Light first! Be what you want and stick to it! Your courage will be rewarded.[3]

If you are not *being,* you are either waiting or searching. Many times I've said through my work at The Happiness Project that . . .

**there's a world of difference between searching
for happiness and choosing to be happy.**

Between searching and choosing, two worlds are born. Searching for happiness gives birth to an experience of fear, lack and guilt. You only search for that which you fear you do not have, or for that which you are not yet willing to accept you have already. Searching is Self-denial. With Self-acceptance, searching is over. Now you can *choose to be what you want to be.* Now you discover the *power of Being.*

In life there are, broadly speaking, three routes marked 'Happiness', but only one of these routes can take you all the way. The three routes are: (1) the 'Doing Route', (2) the 'Having Route', and (3) the 'Being Route'.

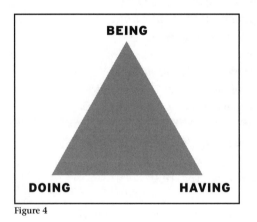

Figure 4

The 'Doing Route' is based on the great hope that enough accomplishment, production and good deeds will make you happy. The key word is *achievement*. The 'Having Route' is based on the great hope that what you buy, collect and own will make you happy. The key word is *accumulation*. In truth, neither of these routes can make you happy, but both can *encourage* you to be happy. The secret is – you cannot 'do happy', and you cannot 'have happy', but you can 'be happy'!

Being is the key to lasting happiness. The 'Being Route' is all about the courage to be what you want. The key word is *acceptance*. Inspirational psychologist Carl Rogers made a study of both *acceptance* and *being* for much of his life. He understood that the power of 'being' is real – more real than any amount of 'doing' and 'having'. He once wrote:

> The individual moves towards 'being', knowingly and acceptingly, the process he inwardly and actually is. He moves away from being what he is not, from being a facade. He is not trying to be more than he is, with the attendant feelings of guilt or self-depreciation. He is increasingly listening to the deepest recesses of his physiological and emotional being, and finds himself increasingly willing to be, with greater accuracy and depth, that Self which he most truly is.[4]

Your ego, born of lack, has a 'do or die' mentality. It would encourage you first 'to do' and then 'to have' so as 'to be'. For example: *do* a good job, *have* a big income, so as to *be* happy. Your unconditioned Self would have you first *be* and then you can *do* what you like and you can *have* what you like. Be first!

It was the great Russian novelist Leo Tolstoy who wrote: 'If you want to be happy, be.'[5] To be is to accept and live from your original wholeness. To be is wisdom.

Give What You Want!

> *Giving is a gain, not a loss.*
> *Give generously!*

One of the healing processes I most enjoy using during my workshops is called 'Complimentary Medicine Therapy'. This process acknowledges the enormous healing potential of kind, loving and encouraging words of compliment.

There are three stages to 'Complimentary Medicine Therapy'. You might want to try each stage for yourself. The first stage is to write down five compliments you would most like to receive from anybody. These compliments may highlight a particular quality, talent, skill or value that is dear to you. Once written, I ask participants to repeat these compliments out loud to themselves. Why? Because . . .

often what you want to hear from others is
what you are currently not saying to yourself.

Other people can compliment you a thousand times over, but you will only truly hear (that is, receive) as many compliments from others as you're willing to give yourself. Thus, giving to yourself can help you receive from others. Keep your list of compliments on hand. Read them not just once, but three times a day, for a minimum of seven days.

The second stage of 'Complimentary Medicine Therapy' is to think of someone in your life who is perhaps overdue a sincere compliment from *you*. The name or face of this person will appear almost instantly. Think carefully now what it is you would most like to compliment this person for. Why do this? First, because being loving is fulfilling your purpose; second, it's great fun; and third . . .

whatever you compliment in another person,
you are strengthening in yourself, also.

Compliments are affirmations. Like sacred greetings, they bless both the receiver and the giver. A good way to strengthen any joyful quality in yourself is to first spot it in others. What you spot in others, you give life to in yourself. The Buddhists refer to this practice as 'sympathetic joy'. The ego, born of lack, cannot afford to be this generous, but *you* can! Remember, giving is a gain, not a loss.

The third stage is to think of a person you feel is overdue in giving *you* a loving compliment. Once again, the name or face of this person will appear almost instantly. Think for a moment . . . what would you most like this person to say to you? Next, make contact with this individual and pay the compliment you would most like to receive. *Give* what *you* want. Why? Because . . .

**often what you're not getting may be
what you're withholding.**

Other people are *you*. They are your mirrors. And just as it would be entirely unreasonable to stand before a mirror and demand to see something you're not presenting, so too is it unreasonable to expect from someone something that you're not willing to give. Many people have experienced great breakthroughs in their relationships (with both the living and dead) during this third stage.

Loving is easy when we perceive that we're being loved. It can be very tempting, however, to withdraw our love whenever we feel mistreated, attacked, or let down in some way. Similarly, even though we may want to be loving, it can be difficult – when someone we know is being dishonest, disloyal, or petty – not to fall into playing the same game. We protest – we offer an attack for an attack. And yet . . .

**the moment you withdraw love from any one person,
you also withdraw yourself from the experience of love.**

The moment you withdraw love, it is *you* who suffers. You are, in truth, the Presence of Love, and it's impossible for you to be authentic and free and not loving. You must be very clear on the consequences of withholding. For instance, withhold love and fear takes hold; withhold kindness and love goes cold; withhold forgiveness and resentment chokes you; withhold acceptance and peace eludes you; withhold trust and betrayal is certain; withhold yourself . . . and you will end up by yourself.

To put it another way:

Withhold love from your brother, and you deprive
yourself of the feeling of Love's Presence.
Withhold kindness from another, and you will no
longer fully enjoy Kindness's sweet essence.
Withhold acceptance from someone, and your
rampant judgment will deny you any peace.
Withhold forgiveness from anyone, and you will die
of the resentments you refuse to release.
Withhold your smile from me, and you will feel
my tears upon your own face.
Withhold your gentle gaze from me, and you
will overlook your own good grace.

Only your ego can be attacked. Indeed, it must be attacked because it's always attacking. The ego is always 'on the take', continually making up for its perceived lack. The ego cannot be generous in giving, for it believes *giving equals loss*. There is, however, a place in you that is whole, safe and beyond any threat. This is your unconditioned Self.

Your unconditioned Self understands that giving is a multiplication and not a subtraction. What you give, multiplies. Also, it doesn't think in terms of 'giving and receiving', but instead, that 'giving is receiving'. Giving, from your wholeness, is the key to abundance. When you give unconditionally, the only cost of giving is receiving. Therefore, look around today, and give what you want!

Today is your gift to the world.
Give what appears to be missing.
Give what you appear not to be
getting.
Give what you think you have
been searching for.
Give what you believe you are
waiting for.
Give generously, without thought
of loss and sacrifice.
Give openly, that you may receive
what you want.
Give freely, that you may find
what you are after.
Give fully, that your waiting may
be over.
Above all, give what you want.

Remember What's Important!

> *Real goals aren't about the future; they're*
> *about your life right here and now!*

'I know who you are! You're the happiness doctor,' said the taxi driver.

I smiled politely. 'I've been called a few things in my time,' I said, 'but that is one of the better ones. Thank you.' I was on my way to a TV studio, and Simon, the taxi driver, had come to pick me up from the train station. The conversation we were about to have proved most illuminating.

'Come sit in the front with me, mate,' said Simon in his strong cockney accent. No sooner had I put my seatbelt on when Simon said, 'I've discovered the secret to happiness, you know.'

'Really?' I said, trying not to sound too surprised.

'Yeah, I've got the secret,' he said.

Call me psychic, but I somehow knew I wouldn't have to ask Simon for his secret!

'I'll tell you my secret if you like,' said Simon.

'Yes, please.' I nodded.

Simon paused a moment, and then he said, 'Triple-bypass surgery!'

'What?' I asked.

'The secret to happiness is triple-bypass surgery!'

'That's a new one on me, Simon,' I said.

'Let me tell you mate, my life was a bloody mess before my triple-bypass surgery. Can you believe I owned this car, 15 others, two Rolls Royce motors, and loads more before my heart attack. There I was, on the operating table, when I rang up my business partner and I sold the whole bloody lot to him. I said "Good riddance". Now I own nothing. But thanks to triple-bypass surgery, I'm a happy man!

'Ever since triple-bypass surgery,' continued Simon, 'I've seen more blue sky, more sunshine, more beauty, more green fields, more friends, more West Ham . . . more everything.'

Now I was really excited. 'Are you a West Ham fan?' I asked.

'All my life,' he said.

'Me, too,' I said. Now we were real friends!

'Anyway,' Simon continued, 'I see everything differently now.'

Just as he said those words, a driver from behind gave a prolonged blast on his horn at us. Without missing a beat, Simon said, 'Take that bloke behind us. Before triple-bypass surgery I would have thought this geezer was giving me grief, but now, I realise he's actually honking his horn to applaud my beautiful driving skills through the busy streets of London!' I tightened my seatbelt.

Simon continued, 'You can put this in your next book if you like, but before triple-bypass surgery, all I ever thought about was the future. I worked so hard that I lost my way. I was away from home 18 hours a day. I used to have to remind my wife who I was. I've got two beautiful daughters, grown up now, and they've both got two children. I'm a granddad! But I never saw my children grow up. I was too busy. I lost my way. I really lost my way.'

'So what's the real secret to happiness?' I asked.

'One thing,' said Simon. 'Wake up every day and ask yourself, 'What's important?' Never ever forget what's important. My only goal every day is to know what's important and then take care of it. Life's too short otherwise.'

Simon paused a moment, and I took my chance. 'So, what's important, Simon?'

Simon smiled. He then went very quiet and began to look quite shy. He leaned over towards me and said in a softer, more hushed voice, 'Don't think me funny for saying this, will you?'

'No,' I said.

'Well, it's love, isn't it? Love's what's important.'

For me, conversations don't get much better than the one Simon and I had. I did most of the listening, and I was happy to do so. Simon was a wise man. He reminded me that . . .

**the key to happiness is to
remember what's important to you.**

During my days with my Stress Busters Clinic, I noticed that people get ill and unhappy because (1) they forget what's important; or (2) they know what's important, but they put their time, energy and attention elsewhere. We mean to take care of the important business of our life, but all too often the small details crowd in and cover the big picture. We get busy, preoccupied, waylaid and forgetful. Like a traveller without stars or compass, we eventually lose our way.

The Happiness Project focuses a lot on goal-setting with a difference. The difference is that we attend to what I call Present-

Time Goals. Most goals are all about your tomorrows, your future, and how great you hope your life will one day be. For me, real goal-setting is all about the present moment. It is about the here and now. Your most powerful goals, therefore, aren't about future happiness; they're about happiness *now!*

Happiness *now!* is about *Present-Time Goals.*

It was the Swiss psychologist Carl Jung who wrote: 'Most of the people I see suffer not from physical illness, but from spiritual aimlessness. They have lost their aim. They have lost sight of who they really are and what is really valuable.'[6] One key to happiness, then, is not to wait until you need triple-bypass surgery before you remember what's important. Let joy be your learning curve . . . not just pain.

Happiness and healing are about remembering what's important and discarding the rest. One simple exercise I use you may want to try. First, write down ten things you love to do. Some people have so lost their way that they can't even think of ten. Now, write down next to these ten things the date you last did each one. After that, write down the names of the ten most important people in your life, and then place next to each name a date when you last spent 'real time' together. Look carefully and see if you're attending to what is really important and valuable to you – *now!*

Today is your whole life, and your only real goal is to live well today. Remember, therefore, what is important. The formula for Present-Time Goals goes like this:

If health is important to you, ask yourself,
how can I be truly healthy today?
If balance is important to you, ask yourself,
what are my real priorities today?
If love is important to you, ask yourself,
how will I show my love today?
If service is important to you, ask yourself,
what can I contribute to today?
If truth is important to you, ask yourself,

how can I make way for wisdom today?
If success is important to you, ask yourself,
what is success today?
If peace is important to you, ask yourself,
what struggle can I let go of today?
If life is important to you, ask yourself,
how can I live well today?

Be Wise

A few years ago, I gave a keynote presentation to the Annual Mental Health Conference for Wales. At this conference I talked on 'Healing, Listening, and Wisdom'. I suggested that the experience of being listened to wholeheartedly by another person is one of life's richest gifts. I said that listening is like love in that it unites us; and that where there is genuine listening, separation is over, fear fades, and wisdom begins.

As I began to talk more specifically about the importance of silence in everyday life, I became aware of how silent the room was. Everyone was silent – deeply, deeply silent.

Why are they so quiet? I wondered. *What's with this silence? They're not impressed,* I feared. Other fearful thoughts came rushing in – *Change the subject! There's no value here! Tell a joke. You're going to die. Make a run for it. Leave Wales now!* And so on.

For some reason I decided to trust that everything was okay. One part of my mind was trusting; the other part was terrified. Never had I encountered an audience so quiet. I was tempted at one point to walk among the participants and check for pulses! I refrained. Somehow, I could see that what was really happening was that I was coming face to face with my own fear and uncertainty about silence, listening, and wisdom.

I decided to go the whole way. Later, when I played back the tape of the conference, I listened to the conclusion of my talk on 'Healing, Listening, and Wisdom', which ended with these words:

Our greatest fear is that if we were to stop still and listen to our Self, there would be nothing but silence. Be not afraid. For there is a silence in you – an eternal silence that is both empty and full. It is empty of the fear, criticism, and judgment that has plagued you; and it is full of the Love that can save you. Trust this silence! This silence is not cold, but warm. Listen to this silence speak to you of your Self that Is, and always will be, wholly free, wholly worthy, and wholly well. Fear not the silence – for it is wise and it brings great peace.

I then said, 'Thank you for listening,' and sat down, feeling very unsure of myself. One person began to clap, and then, to my great surprise, the entire audience rose to its feet to give me a most generous ovation. I stood up twice to accept the applause, and still it went on. Looking back now, it was as if the applause was like a reward for me to dare to speak my truth even though I was afraid to do so. The applause also felt like a collective affirmation of fresh intent to listen to our inner-tuition, to follow the heart more often, and to stand by what is most important.

Immediately after my talk, a man came up to me with a newsletter on mental health, which contained the following poem, called 'Listening'. It was written by a user of the local mental-health services. His name is Mike, and his poem reads:

When God gave out brains
I thought He said trains
– so I missed mine.

When God gave out looks
I thought He said books
– so I didn't want any.

When God gave out noses
I thought He said roses
– so I ordered a big red
one.

When God gave out chins
I thought He said gins
– so I ordered a large
double one.

When God gave out legs
I thought He said kegs
– so I asked for large fat
ones.

When God gave out heads
I thought He said beds
– so I asked for a big soft
one.

Gosh, am I in a mess!

Life is an act of listening. The quality of your life depends on the quality of your listening.[7] In any given moment, you're either listening to the voice of fear (your ego), or the voice of love (your unconditioned Self). Fear always leads to more fear. Love always leads to more love. Learning to switch off the voice of fear is an art. What is unhelpful is to attack fear, resist fear, or defend against fear. One answer is simply to focus on love, and to value love more than fear. The more you value love, the less fear you'll hear.

One of the reasons why we long to be listened to by others is that we don't always listen to our Self. We've stopped listening to our Self because we've learned to believe that there's nothing worth listening to. Just as we refuse to believe that happiness is within, love is within, and peace is within, so too do we refuse to believe that any wisdom is also within. Often in my workshops I will ask, 'Where is wisdom?' My audiences know to say, 'Wisdom is within.' But when I then invite people to stand up and proclaim, 'I am a wise person!' very few people do so. Most often whoever dares to stand up gets a round of applause for their courage and their example.

Like the thirsty fish in water, you're surrounded by, immersed in, and created with wisdom. However, wisdom is, to your ego, blasphemy. And so too is love, peace and happiness. To be wise, therefore, you must first change your mind about yourself. In other words . . .

> **to accept wisdom and guidance, first you must**
> **be willing to give up your belief in guilt.**

You are not guilty. You are not unworthy. You must be willing to give up what you've learned about yourself. Next, you must also be willing to give up your fearful, limiting beliefs about wisdom and guidance. For instance, wisdom isn't special; it's natural. Similarly, guidance isn't rare; it is everywhere. Both wisdom and guidance are never deserved; they are merely accepted. If you can possibly accept that your Self is whole, worthy and well, then you'll find it easy to accept wisdom for yourself. Even a little willingness can bring untold amounts of wisdom.

Wisdom is unconditional. Wisdom is constant. You are never not wise. Wisdom is everywhere. And all that is ever really going on is that *either you're listening to your wisdom or you're ignoring it.* Wisdom is free. It requires no special techniques, no special learning, and no special 'good behaviour'. Wisdom requires no effort, no sacrifice and no suffering. Those who believe in wisdom find wisdom, for . . .

> **wisdom is available to those who make**
> **themselves available to wisdom.**

How often have you let yourself down because you refused to listen to your own innate wisdom and 'inner-tuition'? Many times you've known, with hindsight, that you had the answer all along to the challenges you were faced with. Wisdom wasn't missing. All that was missing was the belief that you can be wise, you can be free and you can be happy.

When you make time to listen to the wisdom of your unconditioned Self, you begin to hear a familiar melody. *A Course in*

Miracles refers to this melody in an inspired passage of poetry called 'The Forgotten Song'. Here are a few of the lines:

> *Listen – perhaps you catch a hint of an ancient*
> *state not quite forgotten; dim, perhaps, and yet*
> *not altogether unfamiliar, like a song whose*
> *name is long forgotten, and the circumstances*
> *in which you heard completely unremembered.*
> *Not the whole song has stayed with you, but*
> *just a little wisp of melody, attached not to*
> *a person or a place or anything particular.*
> *But you remember, from just this little part,*
> *how lovely was the song, how wonderful the*
> *setting where you heard it, and how you loved*
> *those who were there and listened with you.*

Believe and know! This is the key to wisdom. If you listen and have difficulty finding an answer, it's because you're playing out the belief that wisdom is difficult. If you listen and you hear no answer, it's because you're playing out a belief that you have no wisdom. If you listen and are afraid to follow the answer, it's because you're playing out the belief that your wisdom may not be correct. Give up your guilt, take back your projections, and let wisdom be natural to you once more.

People invariably ask me, 'How do I know my guidance is right?'

Because the ego so firmly believes that you are unworthy, it obsesses over 'what is right' and 'what is wrong'. In the past, I would always pray, 'What's the right thing to do here?' Today, I leave 'right' and 'wrong' alone, and, instead, I pray, 'What is the most loving thing I can do here?' or 'How can I be the Presence of Love right now?' When in difficulty, I always call for love, because love is wisdom.

Walk with love today.

Leap!

> There once was a man who went walking along a cliff edge. He strayed from the path, lost his footing, and fell over the edge. As he fell toward the deep blue sea, he grabbed at a branch of thorns.
>
> Hanging there, daring not let go, the man began to pray, 'Is there anybody there?'
>
> 'Yes,' came the reply.
>
> 'Who is it?' asked the man.
>
> 'God.'
>
> 'Help me, God,' prayed the man.
>
> 'Let go and leap,' said God.
>
> The man thought for a moment, and then he prayed, 'Is there anybody else there?'

The man in this story wants it both ways – he wants to cling to pain *and* be free! You can't do both.

All too often we refuse to let go of our fears until we can see love, but we can't see love until we're first willing to let go of our fears. Similarly, we won't give up our defences until we're safe; but we can't be safe until we're first willing to let go our defences. Again, we cling to our painful past until we're sure of a bright future, but there can be no bright future until we surrender our past. We're so reluctant to give up our suffering before we're happy again, but happiness can't happen until we let go of our suffering.

It is only once you're willing to let go of your illusions that truth can unfold; it is only once you're willing to let go of your pain that joy can take hold. It is only once you're willing to let go of your grievances that peace will reign; it is only once you're willing to let go of your limitations that you will be free again. Healing is a letting go.

Happiness is a great big letting go!

Let ego or let go! To the ego, love, truth and happiness look like an awfully big risk, but that's because it cannot see straight. Remember, you can't be in control of your healing, and you can't be in control and be happy. You have to let go of control and fear. Letting go feels like a risk, but, in truth, the only thing you risk losing when you let go is your ego.

Love is not a risk, not if you're willing to give up guilt. Peace is not a gamble, not if you're willing to give away all thoughts of conflict. Happiness is not unstable, not if you stand firm. Trust is not dangerous, not if you give it unconditionally. Freedom is never broken, not if you accept it wholeheartedly.

It all comes down to where you decide to place your trust. Your unconditioned Self is unreasonably joyful because it trusts unconditionally. *Trust is proactive.* Whatever you trust in fully – and that means both consciously and unconsciously – it must come to pass. If, therefore, you trust fully in joy, it must happen; if you trust fully in love, it must happen; if you trust fully in peace, it must happen.

True joy is trust. It is a trust that you are, in spirit, already free and already happy. It is a trust that you are, at heart, wholly innocent and loving. It is a trust that you are, in truth, completely safe and well. It is also a trust that you are, always, blessed with strength, inspiration and power greater than any challenge you meet.

I remember sitting down one afternoon on a crowded beach on a small Greek Island. I was angry and was nursing my wounds. I had just survived a near-fatal car crash only a few hours earlier – having been driven off the road by a drunk driver in a large truck. I was lucky to be alive. I sat down to pray, and the following dialogue just happened:

> *'What is wisdom?' I asked.*
> *'Wisdom is joy,' came The Answer.*
>
> *'And what is joy?' I asked.*
> *'Joy is the knowledge that nothing*
> *that ever happens, in this universe*

*or any other, can take away your
freedom,' answered The Answer.*

'Nothing?' I questioned.
'Nothing,' said The Answer.

'And what is peace?' I asked.
*'Peace is giving up all resistance
to joy,' answered The Answer.*

Walk Free!

Be big! You've played small too long.

The following story perfectly illustrates the only 'real key' you
need to walk free:

Harry Houdini liked nothing better than digging a
hole for himself and then looking for a way out. His ability
to free himself from shackles, locked boxes, straitjackets,
handcuffs, and all kinds of sealed containers brought the
Hungarian escape artist worldwide fame. There was nothing he could not escape from. Well, almost nothing.

At the height of his fame, Houdini issued a challenge
to the world to build a jail that could hold him. Houdini
would escape from jail after jail after jail within moments.
There's a story of one jail, however, where something went
very wrong. This jail was like all the rest – concrete floors
and walls, a set of bars, no furniture. Harry entered, and
the door was shut behind him. The stopwatch started tick-
ing, and Houdini got to work on the lock with a piece of
metal he had concealed in his clothes.

Harry soon realised that this lock was unusual. An
hour passed by and no luck. Another hour passed by, and
still he was imprisoned. Beads of sweat formed upon his
brow. Effort upon effort upon effort got the great Houdini

nowhere. Cuffed by tiredness, choked with frustration, he eventually fell against the door in despair, and . . . the door swung open. The prison door had never been locked.

We've so accustomed ourselves to struggle, suffering, and sacrifice that we often overlook the easy option. So frantic is our search for peace that we often miss what's already freely available. When unhappy, we feel hemmed in, trapped, and imprisoned mentally and emotionally. The prison bars of pain, fear, guilt and grief feel so real that we dare not believe we can simply walk free.

I was once told by a man who'd served a ten-year prison sentence that 'the most fearful day of prison for any prisoner is the day before you get your freedom back'. I also remember him telling me, 'My prison bars had become so familiar to me that I didn't know if I could live without them.' What feels familiar, feels real. What feels unfamiliar can feel frightening.

If you've felt trapped and imprisoned for a long time, freedom can feel unfamiliar and frightening. If you've been depressed and in pain for any period, joy can be scary. If you've been lonely for too long, love and intimacy can be terrifying. If you've been in sacrifice all your life, then the idea of receiving feels like hell. And if you've played small too often, then the thought of living big will feel exciting, frightening, and impossible.

You desire freedom and you're afraid of freedom. Happiness now! is all about feeling the fear of freedom and walking free anyway.

Your unconditioned Self was born free.

You were born free. Despite what you may think and what you may have learned, you are still free. If you could only believe this, you would see that it is so. Like happiness and love, freedom waits on welcome, not on time. Freedom awaits your decision. If only for a moment, now, just let yourself feel free. Feel it. Feel free! Happiness is a decision to be free now. *Be free now.*

Resist yourself no more. Give in to freedom. Accept what is, in truth, already yours, and walk free.

You have suffered enough. Be free now.
You have laboured all your life. Walk free now.
You have searched all over. Be free now.
You have struggled so much. Walk free now.
You have sacrificed too much. Be free now.
You have been guilty too long. Walk free now.
You have waited needlessly. Be free now.

Revel in your freedom. Live wholeheartedly, laugh loud, love much, spread joy, be truthful, and give yourself to everything. You, who are already whole, can lose nothing. Your ego may fall from time to time, but *you* will not. Live big! Think of God, and method-act. Pick a role model like Jesus or Buddha and be brilliant. Choose to be happy, for . . .

the person who is happy has a gift for this world!

You didn't come here to add to the madness of this world. You came to be free. And you didn't come empty, for you're full of gifts to give. Therefore, don't hide your light now – let it shine. Don't hold back on love now – let it flow. Don't temper your joy – let it inspire. Don't deny your truth – let it be. Don't imprison your imagination – set it free. Don't rein in your creativity – let it go. Don't mask your playfulness – let it play. Don't resist your spirit – let it heal.

The call to live and be free is too powerful to resist forever. Be loving now and you will be free of fear; be joyful now and you will be free of pain; be peaceful now and you will free yourself from conflict; be forgiving now and you will be free of suffering; be present now and you will walk free.

The 'real key' to happiness, then, is that *there is no key!* This might seem like bad news, but fear not! The good news is that there is no prison, no door, and no lock. Happiness is open all hours, and if you're willing to be open to happiness, then you can enjoy happiness *now!*

❖ ❖ ❖

Epilogue

There Is No Future!

What sort of an epilogue begins with the title 'There Is No Future!' – especially one in a book on happiness?

Well, it's official. The news is out – 'There is no future!' Please understand that this isn't a message of despair; it is simply a statement of truth. I repeat: 'There is no future!' Therefore, don't save your best for the future. Don't wait to give your best to the next job, the next time, the next person, or the next opportunity. Give your best *now!*

Some things never change. Your greatest opportunity for happiness has been, will be, and still is . . . *now.* Unfortunately, you're often too busy 'past-urising' and 'futurising' to see that everything is here already. Give up the past, give up the future, and give in to happiness *now!* It really is all here. It must be, because *you* are here.

The one piece of good news that is true forever is . . .

the present is here, *now!*

When in search of wisdom, linguists often refer to roots and connections of words from prehistoric civilisations. They explore ancient languages such as Sanskrit, Aramaic and Latin in order to unearth forgotten gems of wisdom. Well, much closer to home and to the present time, it's helpful to note that in the English language the word *present* has three distinct meanings – 'here', 'now', and 'a gift'.

Is this only a coincidence, or could it be that *the greatest gifts of life are always available to you here and now?!* The word *present* also links to 'presence', 'being', and 'being present'. Here is another clue. Give yourself to *now!* The future isn't your answer – it has no true power. *Now,* right here, is good enough for you. All you need to remember is that *nothing is missing within you and nothing is missing here, now.*

Today is brand new. Today is not yet finished. Give today another chance, then. The world has finished with yesterday if *you* have. And the world can't tarnish your future if *you* do not. Be grateful for today. Say 'Thank you' to the present moment. Remember, the gift is . . .

the more you give to *now*,
the more you get from *now*.

Gratitude is a gift in itself. It inspires you to be open, to be present and to receive. Gratitude is good medicine. One single serving of gratitude is often enough to open the heart, energise the body, warm the bones, make your hair curl, put a spring in your step, start you humming and make you smile like a baby! Also, it's impossible to be grateful and lonely, grateful and depressed, or grateful and unhappy.

Let your gratitude be unconditional, and allow yourself to witness its miraculous powers. Decide to be grateful for *everything,* even the stuff that feels 'bad' and 'wrong'. Just be grateful. And let your gratitude reveal the hidden gifts in every situation. Before you practice gratitude, you're in the dark and there appears to be very little to be grateful for; once you begin, a new light dawns, sometimes a brilliant light, a light as bright as heaven itself.[1]

If it appears that you have nothing to be grateful for, it's probably because you're not allowing yourself to receive. Just because you *don't* receive doesn't mean there *is* nothing to receive. On the contrary, there's always something wonderful to receive. No matter how you feel, just be grateful anyway, and let yourself be open and present to 'other possibilities'. Never close yourself off.

It's so unfair, isn't it, that *the people who practise gratitude always have something to be happy about!* True gratitude arises spontaneously in us all; however, when we realise that the true gifts come not from the world but from our own heart. In truth . . .

> **happiness isn't something you can get
> your hands on; it's something you carry in your heart.**

Wouldn't it be wonderful if you could just be happy! Imagine, just for today, giving up the struggle, slowing down a little, cancelling your plans, throwing away your 'to do' list, and simply deciding to be happy. Imagine telling yourself, 'Just for today, I will not struggle'; and 'Just for today, I will not suffer'; and 'Just for today, I will not be in sacrifice'; and 'Just for today, I will stop searching.'

Imagine if you stopped everything and simply allowed yourself to be happy. What a crazy thought! Imagine letting yourself *be happy* for no reason. For a whole 60 seconds, right now, just picture yourself allowing your happiness to bubble up all by itself. You're not meditating on happiness, praying for it, affirming it, visualising it or asking for it – you're simply *being happy*.

My challenge to you is: 'Do not seek love today; merely be loving. Do not seek peace today; merely be peaceful. Do not seek joy today; merely be joyful.' I know it sounds too simple, too silly, too crazy – but, it might just work! Maybe you really can just *be happy*.

> *Ask not for love today; better still, pray that
> you might be the Presence of Love today.
> Ask not for rest today; better still, pray that
> you might be the Presence of Rest today.
> Ask not for kindness today; better still, pray that*

you might be the Presence of Kindness today.
Ask not for victory today; better still, pray that
you might be the Presence of Victory today.
Ask not for laughter today; better still, pray that
you might be the Presence of Laughter today.
Ask not for peace today, better still, pray that
you might be the Presence of Peace today.

❖ ❖ ❖

Acknowledgments

Gratitude inspires joy. It is with great joy, therefore, that I make the following acknowledgments. First, to Miranda, acting midwife for the birth of this book! Next, to The Happiness Project team: Thank you, David Holden, for your 'Mr. Big' love and skill; thank you, Ben Renshaw, for your vision and support; thank you, Alison Atwell, for your joy and creativity; and thank you, Candy Constable, for stepping into the spirit of this project so gracefully.

Thank you to Tom and Linda Carpenter. This book is so thoroughly inspired by our friendship. Thank you to Diane Berke and Tony Zito, for you are truly The Presence of Love. Thank you to Avanti Kumar for the wake-up call! Thank you to Helen Schucman, the author of *A Course in Miracles*. Thank you also to the other teachers of love and joy who have so enriched my life. They include Marika Borg, Deirdre Ahern, Graham Taylor-Chilton, Nick and Anne Davis, Mark Reynolds, Brian Little, Eddie and Debbie Shapiro, Nick Williams, Robert and Anne Redfern, Bob and Cathy Colman, Stephanie Bennett, Ian Patrick, and Jacqueline Heron.

For this book in particular, thank you to Robert Norton whose inspirational album, 'Painting the Ocean', played continually while I wrote. Thank you again to Candy Constable for your help with research. Thank you to my editor, Rowena Webb, for your enthusiasm, support and patience. Thank you also to Laura Brockbank and Rachel Connolly for the same.

Thank you to the Hodder team of Rowena Webb, Laura Brockbank and Rachel Connolly for your work on the original edition of *Happiness NOW!* And thank you also to the Hay House UK team of Michelle Pilley, Jo Lal, Jo Burgess, Duncan Carson and Kim Bishop for your work on this edition.

Thank you to my mother; my father; my family; my friends; my clients; my two cats, Great and Wonderful; and to everyone else who has taught me about happiness and love!

❖ ❖ ❖

Further
Information
and Notes

Further Information

For further information on The Happiness Project and Success Intelligence – and for more details on (1) 'Be Happy – the 8 Week Programme' (made famous by the BBC-TV documentary *How to be Happy*) and (2) 'Coaching Happiness' – the certified training programme – please contact The Happiness Project, Two Birches, The Harris Estate, Laleham Reach, Chertsey, Surrey, KT16 8RP Tel : +44 (0)845 430 9236 Website: **www.happiness.co.uk** and **www.robertholden.org**
E-mail: **info@happiness.co.uk**

Notes

Chapter 1: Happy Already!

1   Sociologist James Gleick has written a great book called *FASTER – The Acceleration of Just about Everything,* Little Brown (1999). This book catalogues in great detail the many ingenious and insane attempts to speed up life.

2   For a beautiful treatise on the principle of Attention, see *Wherever You Go, There You Are* by Jon Kabat-Zinn, Hyperion (1994).

3   The words *joy waits on welcome, not on time,* are inspired by a passage in *A Course in Miracles* (Arkana, 1997), which reads: 'Love waits on welcome, not on time, and the real world is but your welcome of what always was.' (Text, p. 255).

4   The British press has featured a handful of articles in recent years on: (1) happiness is a dysfunctional response to the world; and (2) happiness leads to ineffectiveness at work. Although the media has tried to make much of this, there is very little real support for these ideas.

5   Herbert Spencer, the 19th-century English philosopher and author of *The Principles of Psychology* (1855), introduced two terms: 'objective psychology', i.e., that which can be observed; and 'subjective psychology', i.e., that which cannot be observed. His work inspired Behaviourism and the study of externals. Also, for research on measuring happiness and subjective wellbeing, see *Social Indicators of Well-Being: Americans' Perceptions of Life Quality* by F. Andrews and S. Withey, New York: Plenium (1976), and the QED 'How to Be Happy' booklet, BBC (1997).

6   'Upanishads' are spiritual teachings from India, the oldest of which were composed between 800 and 400 B.C. The Sanskrit word *Upanishads* means 'sitting at the feet of a Master'. In all, there are over 100 ancient Upanishads that are still in print. The *Mandaya Upanishad* is one of the most popular. There are many excellent translations of these 'sittings', one of which is *The Upanishads,* translated and selected by Juan Mascaro for Penguin Classics.

7   Read *The Uses of Enchantment – the Meaning and Importance of Fairy Tales* by Bruno Bettleheim, Penguin Books (1975).

8   For a great anthology of sacred poetry, read *The Enlightened Heart,* edited by Stephen Mitchell, Harper Perennial (1989).

9   See *The Complete Works of Robert Browning,* edited by J. C. Berkey & Dooley, Ohio University Press (1996).

10   See *Stress Busters* by Robert Holden, Thorsons (1998).

11   Many books have been written on the works of Sri Ramakrishna. I would recommend *The Gospel of Sri Ramakrishna,* translated by Swami Nikhilananda, edited by Joseph Campbell (1988); and *Sayings of Sri Ramakrishna,* Amra Press, Madras. Also look up 'Sri Ramakrishna' on the Internet.

12   For a good overview of sacred scriptures and world religions, I recommend *The Illustrated Book of Sacred Scriptures,* edited by Timothy Freke, Thorsons, (1998); *The Complete Book of World Mysticism,* Timothy Freke, Piatkus (1977); and *The World's Religions,* Huston Smith, Harper San Francisco (1991).

13   A spiritual faith can certainly encourage great happiness. See *The Psychology of Happiness* by Michael Argyle, Methuen (1986); 'Religious Involvement and Subjective Well-Being' by C. Ellison; *Journal Of Health And Social Behaviour,* 32, pp. 80–99 (1991); *Man's Search for Meaning* by Viktor Frankl, Beacon Press (1962); and 'Is There a Religious Factor in Health?' by J. Levin and P. Schiller, *Journal of Religion And Health,* 26, pp. 9–36 (1987). For further information about spiritual faith and perceptions of God, see A *History of God* by Karen Armstrong, Harper Collins (1993).

14 *A Course in Miracles* is published by Penguin Arkana. First published in 1976, the *Course* was scribed, somewhat reluctantly, by Helen Schucman, a psychologist at Columbia University, New York, who one day heard an inner voice that said, 'This is a course in miracles. Please take note.' At first she resisted, but with the help of her colleague, Bill Thetford, she listened to the words dictated to her.

A *Course in Miracles* is a remarkable self-study system that combines perennial wisdom and spiritual psychology principles. The book consists of three parts – a text, a manual for teachers, and a workbook with 365 lessons, one for each day of the year. It emphasises the daily practice of its principles, which include letting go of fear, removing the blocks to the awareness of love's presence, practicing miracle-mindedness, participating in holy relationships, and experiencing forgiveness.

For further information on *A Course in Miracles,* i.e., newsletters, workshops, and mail order, contact The Miracle Network, 12a Barness Court, 6/8 Westbourne Terrace, London W2 3UW, tel/fax: 0171 262 0209; Foundation for A Course in Miracles, 1275 Tennanah Lake Road, Roscoe, New York, 12776-5905, (607) 498 4116; and, Miracle Distribution Center, 1141 East Ash Avenue, Fullerton, California 92831, tel: (714) 738 8380.

15 See *Wordsworth, Complete Poetical Works,* edited by Thomas Hutchinson, University Press (1996).

16 See *A Return to Love* by Marianne Williamson, Thorsons, revised edition (1996).

17 See *The Dhammapada,* translated by Juan Mascaro, Penguin Classics (1987).

18 See *Seasons of Your Heart: Prayers and Reflections* by Macrina Wiederkehr, HarperCollins, New York (1991).

19 See 10 above.

20 See *Pythagoras and Early Pythagoreanism,* by J. Philip, University of Toronto (1967).

Chapter 2: Giving Up the Search

1 Eddie and Debbie Shapiro are inspirational teachers of healing, spirituality, and joy. They are the authors of several books, including *Meditation for Inner Peace: Discovering the Joy of Relaxation and True Happiness,* Piatkus (1997); and *Out of Your Mind, the Only Place to Be,* Element (1992). For further information on their workshops, contact 3 Norton Park Cottages, Dartmouth, Devon TQ6 ONH, U.K.

2 In more modern times, the 'pursuit of happiness' was formerly advocated in the American Declaration of Independence, where it is written: *'We hold these truths to be self-evident, that all men are created equal, that they are endowed by their Creator with certain unalienable rights, that among these are life, liberty, and the pursuit of happiness.'* This Declaration did not cause the 'pursuit of happiness'; it merely reflected 'out loud' what most of the world was already thinking, and is still thinking.

3   When people are asked what they need to be happier, the most common answer is: 'More money.' There is now overwhelming research that shows that more money does not guarantee more happiness. See *The Sense of Well-being in America* by Angus Campbell, McGraw-Hill, New York (1981); 'Happiness of the Very Wealthy' by Ed Diener *et al, Social Indicators,* 16, pp. 263–74 (1985); and 'Does Money Buy Happiness?' by R. Easterlin, *Public Interest,* 30, pp. 3–10 (1973).

4   See *The Pursuit of Happiness – Discovering The Pathway To Fulfillment, Well-being, and Enduring Personal Joy* by David G. Myers, Ph.D., Avon Books, New York (1993).

5   There is a large body of evidence that shows that exercise can encourage mental fitness, harmony and wellbeing. See 'Personality Correlates of Physical Fitness' by J. Hogan, *Journal of Personality and Social Psychology,* 56, pp. 284–288 (1989); 'The Role of Aerobic Exercise in the Treatment of Depression' by E. Martinsen; *Stress Medicine,* 3, pp. 93–100 (1987); and 'Physical Activity and Mental Health in USA and Canada' by T. Stephens, *Preventive Medicine,* 17, pp. 35–47 (1988).

6   See *Mental Health & Illness – The Nutrition Connection* by Patrick Holford & Carl Pfeiffer, ION Press (1996). For further information, contact the Institute of Optimum Nutrition, Blades Court, Deodar Road, London SW15 2NU.

7   See 'The Effects of 72 Hours of Sleep Loss on Psychological Variables' by M. Mikulincer *et al, British Journal of Psychology,* 80, pp. 145–162 (1989).

8   See *Living Wonderfully: A Joyful Guide to Conscious Creative Living – for Today!* by Robert Holden, Thorsons (1994).

9   For an excellent overview of psychotherapy and psychology today, I recommend the *Handbook of Individual Therapy,* edited by Windy Dryden, Sage Publications (1996); *Innovative Therapy in Britain,* edited by John Rowan and Windy Dryden, Open University Press (1988); and *The Theory and Practice of Counseling Psychology,* by Richard Nelson-Jones, Cassell (1990).

10   For an excellent introduction to Rumi's work, I recommend *The Essential Rumi,* translations by Coleman Barks with John Moyne, Harper San Francisco (1995).

11   See *How to Be Happy* by John Pepper, Gateway Books (1992).

12   For more information on the development of the Laughter Clinic, read *Laughter, the Best Medicine* by Robert Holden, Thorsons (1998).

13   For more information on workshops, professional training, books, and other products, contact The Happiness Project.

14   Copies of the *QED How to Be Happy* DVD and programme booklet are available from The Happiness Project.

Chapter 3: Being Good Enough

1   The relationship between happiness and high self-esteem is well documented in psychology research, as is the relationship between depression and low self-esteem. Happiness and self-perception go hand in hand. See *The Psychology of*

Happiness by Michael Argyle, Methuen (1986); 'Depression and Components of Self-Punitiveness: High Self-Standards, Self-Criticisms and Overgeneralization' by C. S. Carver *et al*, Journal of Consulting and Clinical Psychology, 92, pp. 330–337 (1983); 'Increasing Rates of Depression' by G. L. Klerman *et al, JAMA*, 261, pp. 229–35 (1989); 'The Changing Rate of Major Depression' by G. L. Klerman, *JAMA*, 268, pp. 3098–3105 (1992); 'Living Conditions in the Twentieth Century' by D. J. Smith in *Psychological Disorders in Young People* by M. Rutter *et al*, Jon Wiley, London (1995); and Social Trends by D. J. Smith, HMSO (1997).

2   For more on the relationship between happiness and achievement, see *Happy People* by Jonathan Freedman, New York: Harcourt Brace Jovanovich (1978); *The Sense of Well-being in America* by Angus Campbell, McGraw-Hill, New York (1981); and *Happiness Is an Inside Job* by John Powell, Tabor Press (1989).

3   For more on the relationship between happiness, circumstance, and attitude, see 'Environmental and Dispositional Influences on Well Being' by Costa *et al, British Journal of Psychology,* 78, pp. 299–306 (1987); 'Personality Correlates of Subjective Well-Being' by R. Emmons and E. Diener; Personality and Social Psychology Bulletin, 11, pp. 89–97 (1985); 'Dispositional Optimism and Physical Well-Being' by M. Scheier and C. Carver, *Journal of Personality,* 55, pp. 169–210 (1987); *The Social Psychology of Subjective Well-Being,* edited by Fritz Strack *et al*, Pergamon Press (1990); *15 Principles for Achieving Happiness* by A. D. Hart, Dallas: Word (1988); and 'Happiness Is a Decision' by Marianne Williamson, Simon and Schuster Audio Cassette Series (1990).

4   See *Paradise Lost* by John Milton, Longman (1971).

5   For more on the connection between happiness and loving relationships, see relevant chapters in *Britain on the Couch – Why We're Unhappier Than We Were in the 1950s – Despite Being Richer* by Oliver James, Century Books (1997); *Happy People* by Jonathan Freedman, Harcourt Brace Jovanavich, New York (1978); *The Psychology of Happiness* by Michael Argyle, Methuen (1986); 'The Changing Relationship of Marital Status to Reported Happiness' by N. Glenn and C. Weaver, *Journal of Marriage and the Family,* 50, pp. 317–324 (1988); and 'The Effect of Marriage on the Well-Being of Adults' by W. Gove *et al, Journal of Family Issues,* 11, pp. 4–35 (1990).

6   Social Comparison Theory was developed by many psychologists, including Leonard Festinger, in the 1950s. In the last few decades a large body of psychology and sociology research has shown quite conclusively that, unless you are happy with yourself, you will not be happy with what you do, where you are, what you have, and who you are with. For the relationship between happiness, wealth, and social comparison, see 'Happiness of the Very Wealthy' by E. Diener *et al, Social Indicators,* 16, pp. 263–274 (1985); 'Will Raising the Incomes of All Increase the Happiness of All?' by R. A. Easterlin, *Journal Of Economic Behavior and Organization,* 27, pp. 35–47, (1995), 'A Theory of Social Comparison Processes' by L. Festiger, *Human Relations,* 7, pp. 117–40 (1954); 'Social Comparison and Depression' by F. Gibbons, *Journal of Personality and Social Psychology,* 51,

pp. 140–148 (1986); 'Depression and Anxiety in Relation to Social Status' by J. M. Murphy *et al*, *Archives of General Psychiatry*, 48, pp. 223–229 (1991); 'Physical Attractiveness, Need for Approval, Social Self-Esteem and Maladjustment' by K. E. O'Grady, *Journal of Social and Clinical Psychology*, 8, pp. 62–69 (1989); 'Social Comparison and Negative Self-Evaluation: An Application to Depression' by S. R. Swallow *et al*, *Clinical Psychology Review*, 8, pp. 55–76 (1987).

7   See *The Bible*, Matthew 16:26.

8   See *Aldous Huxley, A Biography*, by Sybille Bedford, Papermac (1993).

9   The work of American psychiatrist Gerald Jampolsky offers a clear, concise introduction to forgiveness as a tool for self-healing and a choice for wholeness. His Attitudinal Healing programme is inspired in particular by *A Course in Miracles*. See *Goodbye to Guilt: Releasing Fear Through Forgiveness*, by G. Jampolsky, Bantam Books (1985).

Chapter 4: Practising Acceptance

1   Contact The Happiness Project for relevant publications.

2   See *Laughter, a Theological Reflection* by Karl-Josef Kuschel, SCM Press (1994). Also, for excellent reports on the relationship between health, happiness, guilt, and simple pleasures, contact ARISE – Associates for Research into the Science of Enjoyment, P.O. Box 11446, London SW18 5ZH.

3   See *Guilt Is the Teacher, Love Is the Lesson* by Joan Borysenko, Ph.D., Warner Books (1990).

4   For a good introduction to world mythology, see *Gods and Goddesses – 130 Deities and Tales from World Mythology*, general editor Elizabeth Hallam, Blandford Press (1996).

5   The work of Matthew Fox and Creation Centered Spirituality focuses on the concept of original blessing. See *Creation Spirituality – Liberating Gifts for the Peoples of Earth* by Matthew Fox, HarperCollins (1991).

6   See *The Bible*, John 15:11.

7   See *The Bible*, Matthew 5:14.

8   See *The Bible*, John 10:34.

9   See 'The Protestant Work Ethic As a Cultural Phenomenon' by L. Giorgi *et al*, *European Journal of Social Psychology*, 20, pp. 499–517(1990).

10   See *Present Moment, Wonderful Moment* by Thich Nhat Hanh, Rider Books (1993). This is one of an excellent series of books published by Rider Books.

11   British Telecom and the 'BT Forum' has collated excellent research on the changing face of work and society in Europe in the 1980s and 1990s. For further information, contact BT Forum, Telephone House, 2-4 Temple Avenue, London EC4Y OHL.

12   Listen to 'Relaxation for Happiness' by Ben Renshaw (1997), available through The Happiness Project.

13   See *End the Struggle and Dance with Life* by Susan Jeffers Ph.D., Hodder & Stoughton (1996).

14   See *Psychological and Biological Approaches to Emotion,* edited by N. Stein *et al,* Erlbaum Publishers (1990), which includes a chapter on 'The Influence of Positive and Negative Affect on Cognitive Organization' by A. Isen; *Emotional And Social Judgments,* edited by J. Forgas, Pergamon Press (1991), and 'Happiness and Helpfulness' by D. Myers, in *Social Psychology,* second edition, McGraw-Hill (1987).

Chapter 5: Living Unconditionally

1   For an interesting read on being, flow, and happiness, read *Flow – the Psychology of Happiness* by Mihaly Csikszentmihalyi, Rider Books (1992).

2   See *Cognitive Therapy and the Emotional Disorders* by A.T. Beck, International Universities Press, New York (1976); *The Cognitive Therapy of Depression* by A.T. Beck *et al,* Guildford Press, New York (1979); *The Psychology of Personal Constructs – Vols. I and II,* Norton, New York (1955); *Feel Good: The New Mood Therapy* by David Burns, Avon (1980); *Learned Optimism* by Martin Seligman, Alfred A. Knopf Publishers (1991).

3   See *A Guide to Personal Happiness* by Dr Albert Ellis & Dr Irving Becker, Wilshire Book Company (1982).

4   See 'Joy Is Not a Carrot' by Linda Carpenter, *Miracle Worker,* 19 (Nov/ Dec 1997). *Miracle Worker is* published by The Miracle Network, 12a Barness Court, 6/8 Westbourne Terrace, London W2 3UW, tel/fax: 0171262 0209.

5   See *Britain on the Couch – Why We're Unhappier Than We Were in the 1950s – Despite Being Richer,* Oliver James, Century Books (1997).

6   See *How to Have What You Want* by Timothy Miller, Ph.D., Henry Holt and Company (1995).

7   See *Happiness Is an Inside Job* by John Powell, Tabor Press (1989); *Britain on the Couch – Why We're Unhappier Than We Were in the 1950s – Despite Being Richer,* Oliver James, Century Books (1997); *The Pursuit of Happiness – Discovering the Pathway to Fulfillment, Well-being, and Enduring Personal Joy* by David G. Myers, Ph.D., Avon Books, New York (1993); and *15 Principles for Achieving Happiness* by A. D. Hart, Word, Dallas (1988).

8   For studies on the relationship between age and happiness, see *Happy People* by Jonathan Freedman, Harcourt Brace Jovanovich, New York (1978); 'Age and Subjective Wellbeing' by W. Stock *et al, Evaluation Studies: Review Annual,* 8 (1983); 'Life-Course and Satisfaction, Equal for Everyone?' by J. J. Latten, *Social Indicators Research,* 21, pp. 599–610 (1989); and *The Sense of Well-being in America* by Angus Campbell, McGraw-Hill, New York (1981).

9   See *Wordsworth, Complete Poetical Works,* edited by Thomas Hutchinson, University Press (1996).

10   See *How Proust Can Change Your Life* by Alain De Botton, Picador (1997).

11   See *The Joyful Christ: The Healing Power of Humor* by Cal Samra, Harper San Francisco (1985).

12   See *Quotations to Cheer You Up When the World Is Getting You Down* by Allen Klein, Wings Books (1991).

13   See *Lessons of St. Francis of Assisi* by John Talbot, NAL – Dutton (1995).

14   See *Dialogue on Awakening* by Tom Carpenter, Carpenter Press (1992). For further information on workshops, books, and cassettes by Tom and Linda Carpenter, contact The Carpenters' Press, P.O. Box 3437, Princeville, Hawaii 96722.

15   Many of the conversations between Robert and Tom and Linda Carpenter are available on CD, including *My Brother; My Self, Freedom from Projection, Happiness,* and *Returning to Awareness*. Contact The Happiness Project.

16   See *Laughter, the Best Medicine* by Robert Holden, Thorsons (1998).

Chapter 6: Healing Unhappiness

1   See *Weight Loss for the Mind* by Stuart Wilde, Hay House (1995).

2   See 'Social Comparison and Depression' by F. Gibbons, *Journal of Personality and Social Psychology,* 51, pp. 140–148 (1986); and 'Effects of Upward and Downward Social Comparison on Mood States' by F. Gibbons and M. Gerard, *Journal of Social and Clinical Psychology,* 8, pp. 14–31 (1989).

3   See *Tao Te Ching* by Lao Tzu, translated by D. C. Lau, Penguin Classics (1963).

4   See 'Exploring the Limits of Self-Reports and Reasoned Action' by D. Hessing *et al, Journal of Personality and Social Psychology,* 54, pp. 405–413 (1988); and 'The Construct Validity of Subjective Well-Being Measures' by M. Okun and W. Stock, *Journal of Community Psychology,* 15, pp. 481–92 (1987).

5   From *Solitude* by Ella Wheeler Wilcox (1855–1919).

6   For more on the question of 'drugs or therapy', see *Britain on the Couch – Why We're Unhappier Than We Were in the 1950s – Despite Being Richer* by Oliver James, Century Books (1997), 'Combined Pharmacotherapy and Psychotherapy for Depression' by D. W. Manning *et al, American Psychiatric Press* (1990); *Evolutionary Psychiatry* by A. Stevens *et al,* Routledge, London (1996); and 'The Treatment of Depression: Prescribing Patterns of Antidepressant Medications' by J. M. Donoghue *et al, British Journal of Psychiatry,* 168, pp. 164–168 (1996).

7   See *Hermann Hesse: Pilgrim of Crisis – A Biography* by Ralph Freedman, Cape Publishers (1979).

8   See *The Bible,* John 16:24.

9   See *Feel the Fear and Do It Anyway* by Susan Jeffers, Ph.D., Rider (1997).

10   See *Love Always Answers* by Diane Berke, Crossroad (1994).

Chapter 7: Lots of Love!

1   See *If It Hurts, It Isn't Love* by Chuck Spezzano, Arthur James Publishers, revised edition (1996).

2   For a beautiful collection of inspirational sayings on love and relationships, see *A Lively Flame* by Eileen Campbell, Thorsons (1992).

3   For more on individualism and well-being, see 'Individualism and Collectivism' by H. Triandis *et al, Journal of Personality and Social Psychology,* 54, pp.

323–328 (1988); *Reaching Out: The Three Movements Of the Spiritual Life* by Henri Nouwen, Doubleday Books (1975); *Habits of the Heart: Individualism and Commitment in American Life* by R. Bellah *et al*, University of California Press (1996); *Loneliness: A Sourcebook of Current Theory, Research, and Therapy,* edited by L. Peplau and Daniel Perlman, Wiley, New York (1982); 'Psychological Individualism and Romantic Love' by Karen Dion and Kenneth Dion, *Journal of Social Behavior and Personality,* 6, pp. 17–33 (1991); 'Pressures of Modern Life Bring Increased Importance to Friendship' by L. DiStefano, *Gallup Poll Monthly* No. 294 (March 1990); *Individualism and Collectivism* by U. Kim, Sage Publishers (1994); *The Origins of English Individualism* by A. Macfarlane, Blackwell, Oxford (1978); *Social Trends* by D. J. Smith, HMSO (1997).

4   See *John Donne: Complete Poetry & Selected Prose,* Century Hutchinson (1994).

5   See *The Gentle Smile: Practicing Oneness in Daily Life* by Diane Berke, Crossroad (1995).

6   See *William Blake: Complete Poetry & Prose,* University of California (1992).

Chapter 8: Travelling Light

1   For an excellent introduction to *A Course in Miracles,* see *Gifts from A Course in Miracles,* edited by Frances Vaughan and Roger Walsh, Tarcher/Putnam Books (1995).

2   See 'The Need to Belong: Desire for Interpersonal Attachments as a Fundamental Human Motivation' by R. F. Baumeister *et al, Psychological Bulletin,* 117, pp. 497–529 (1995); 'Loneliness and Social Contact' by W. H. Jones, *Journal of Social Psychology,* 113, pp. 295–296 (1981); and 'Responses to Social Exclusion: Social Anxiety, Jealousy, Loneliness, Depression, and Low Self-Esteem' by M. R. Leary, *Journal of Social and Clinical Psychology,* 9, pp. 221–229 (1990).

3   See *Being Peace* by Thich Nhat Hanh, Rider Books (1990).

4   See *The Carl Rogers Reader,* edited by Howard Kirshenbaum and Valerie Land Henderson, Constable (1990).

5   See *Good Advice for a Happy Life,* edited by Armand Eisen, Ariel Books (1995).

6   See *Carl Jung: Selected Writings,* introduced by Anthony Storr, Fontana (1983).

7   An excellent collection of inspirational sayings on silence and solitude can be found in *A Fabulous Gift* by Eileen Campbell, Thorsons (1994).

Epilogue: There Is No Future!

1   See *14,000 Things to Be Happy About* by Barbara Ann Kipfer, Workman Publishing (1990).

❖ ❖ ❖

About the Author

Robert Holden, PhD, is the Director of The Happiness Project and Success Intelligence. His innovative work on happiness and success has been featured on *Oprah* and in two major BBC-TV documentaries, *The Happiness Formula* and *How to Be Happy,* shown in 16 countries to more than 30 million television viewers.

Robert is a consultant and coach to leading brands and organisations such as Dove, Virgin, The Body Shop and Comic Relief. He gives public lectures worldwide and has shared the stage with Deepak Chopra, Wayne Dyer, Patch Adams and Paul McKenna. He's the author of ten best-selling books, including *Success Intelligence* and *Shift Happens!*

Website: **www.happiness.co.uk and www.robertholden.org**

❖ ❖ ❖

Notes

Notes

Hay House Titles of Related Interest

ASK AND IT IS GIVEN: Learning to Manifest Your Desires,
by Esther and Jerry Hicks (The Teachings of Abraham™)

CHANGE YOUR THOUGHTS – CHANGE YOUR LIFE:
Living the Wisdom of the Tao, by Dr. Wayne W. Dyer

THE DISAPPEARANCE OF THE UNIVERSE:
Straight Talk about Illusions, Past Lives, Religion, Sex,
Politics, and the Miracles of Forgiveness, by Gary R. Renard

THE PRESENT MOMENT: 365 Daily Affirmations,
by Louise L. Hay

YOU CAN HAVE WHAT YOU WANT:
Proven Strategies for Inner and Outer Success, by Michael Neill

❖ ❖ ❖

The titles above are available at your
local bookstore, or may be ordered by visiting:

Hay House UK: **www.hayhouse.co.uk**
Hay House USA: **www.hayhouse.com**®
Hay House Australia: **www.hayhouse.com.au**
Hay House South Africa: **www.hayhouse.co.za**
Hay House India: **www.hayhouse.co.in**

JOIN THE HAY HOUSE FAMILY

As the leading self-help, mind, body and spirit publisher in the UK, we'd like to welcome you to our family so that you can enjoy all the benefits our website has to offer.

 **EXTRACTS** from a selection of your favourite author titles

 **COMPETITIONS, PRIZES & SPECIAL OFFERS** Win extracts, money off, downloads and so much more

 **LISTEN** to a range of radio interviews and our latest audio publications

 **CELEBRATE YOUR BIRTHDAY** An inspiring gift will be sent your way

 **LATEST NEWS** Keep up with the latest news from and about our authors

 **ATTEND OUR AUTHOR EVENTS** Be the first to hear about our author events

 **iPHONE APPS** Download your favourite app for your iPhone

 **HAY HOUSE INFORMATION** Ask us anything, all enquiries answered

join us online at **www.hayhouse.co.uk**

292B Kensal Road, London W10 5BE
T: 020 8962 1230 E: info@hayhouse.co.uk